Voices of Support for *Becoming Ambidextrous*

Adrian Brown's clever approach to authoring *Becoming Ambidextrous* combines a powerful blend of storytelling and actionable insights drawing from his wealth of industry expertise, knowledge of current trends in technology, and the challenges they present to businesses around the globe. While technology will continue to evolve as time marches on, Brown's message will hold true, making this book an essential guide for those committed to thriving in any industry.

Joseph Pariseau (USA)
Retail Training Manager, Porsche Cars North America

I have had the privilege of serving on industry dealer councils alongside Adrian, witnessing his unwavering dedication to leadership and transformative thinking. I've also shared the honour of travelling with him as a fellow award recipient, celebrating achievements and exchanging invaluable insights. Much like the effortless way he arranges unforgettable events with friends, blending spontaneity with care, *Becoming Ambidextrous* reflects Adrian's practical wisdom and forward-thinking approach. It offers leaders a roadmap to navigate disruption with purpose, heart, and resilience—a testament to his extraordinary career and commitment to empowering others.

John Eastham (Australia)
Director – Peter Warren Automotive Holdings Ltd (Australia)
Previous co-owner and CEO for one of Australia's largest automotive groups

Having worked alongside Adrian for years, I've witnessed firsthand his unwavering dedication to leadership, innovation, and adaptability. Adrian doesn't just talk about thriving in the face of change—he lives it. His ability to inspire teams, navigate disruption, and create meaningful results is unparalleled. *Becoming Ambidextrous* is a testament to his leadership philosophy, offering practical insights and real-world strategies for anyone looking to lead boldly and successfully in an ever-changing world.

Nick Clark
Dealer Principal – Porsche Centre Hobart (Australia)
and graduate of the International Porsche Dealer Academy

From fellow alumni of the author—graduating class of 2019, Porsche International Dealer Academy at the Executive School of Management, Technology and Law (ES-HSG), University of St. Gallen

Adrian is a creative thinker, motivator, and detailed automotive professional. He is completely focused on the task in hand whilst always supporting both his peers, colleagues, and friends. He is passionate, progressive, and genuine in business. I have seen many amazing examples of his training and leadership skills. It is both an honour and a pleasure to know Adrian on a business and personal level.

Adam Flint (England)

To me, true leadership is about being *autentico*, endlessly curious, and embracing life's challenges with *passione* while nurturing meaningful connections. The Porsche International Dealer Academy was a transformative journey, where I had the joy of meeting exceptional leaders like Adrian, whose warmth, wisdom, and authenticity continue to inspire and enrich my life. *Complimenti di cuore* on writing *Becoming Ambidextrous*—a true testament to your resilience, dedication, and vision. *Hai una forza straordinaria.*

Alesandro Rampazzo (Italy)

Adrian 是一个充满能力的人！他总是显示出非凡的领导力和责任心！他是我们全班管理者的带头人！- 魏红晶

Adrian is a highly capable person. He always demonstrates exceptional leadership and a strong sense of responsibility. He is the leading figure among all the participants in our class.

Vivian Wei (China)

Adrian's remarkable optimism, boundless energy, and ability to foster a positive environment make an unforgettable impression. His presence has a way of elevating those around him, leaving you to wonder whether such qualities are innate or the result of deliberate growth.

What sets Adrian apart is his genuine care for people and his ability to connect with intention and authenticity. He doesn't just capture attention—he ensures people feel truly seen and valued. His leadership style is a powerful reminder that success in business goes beyond financial outcomes; it's about building relationships that endure and creating moments that resonate long after the conversation ends.

Rasa Klimavičiūtė (Lithuania)

The Porsche Academy's curriculum, developed and facilitated by UniSG as the program's academic partner, created an environment that fostered empathy, collaboration, and ensured that every voice was heard and valued. The program's outcomes have had lasting impacts on our alumni, with many achieving remarkable successes in their professional and personal endeavours. I am forever grateful for the opportunity to be part of such a transformative group that embarked on an unforgettable journey together.

I extend my congratulations to my fellow alumnus, Adrian, on authoring the remarkable book *Becoming Ambidextrous*. The inspiration continues, reminding us all that true leadership is about adaptability, resilience, and the courage to shape the future.

Dan Jones (England)

Adrian Brown, or AB, is one of those rare individuals who leave an indelible mark on your life. His energy, warmth, and kindness, combined with a remarkable dynamism, make him an extraordinary person. His ability to uplift and inspire those around him is unparalleled.

AB exemplifies the essence of authentic leadership and meaningful connection—a true force for good in both personal and professional spheres.

Simon Priest (England)

With over 30 years in the automotive industry, including global leadership roles at General Motors, I've found that ambidextrous leadership—balancing operational excellence with strategic foresight—is vital for success. My work across five continents with OEMs and auto dealers has reinforced this belief. As a fellow alumnus at the academy, Adrian demonstrated the leadership qualities I've come to admire throughout my career.

I congratulate Adrian on his book, *Becoming Ambidextrous*, which is a testament to his resilience and dedication to developing adaptive leaders. Being an ambidextrous leader is essential for anyone leading in an ever-evolving industry.

Chase Hawkins (USA)

I first met Adrian during the Porsche International Dealer Academy program focused on business excellence for automotive leaders. From day one, I was struck by how accomplished he was—not just as an entrepreneur but as someone open to advice, constructive feedback, and praise, all with the same positive attitude.

That openness and resilience have always set him apart, and after all these years, his success is no mystery. I'm thrilled to congratulate Adrian on *Becoming Ambidextrous*, a testament to his passion for leadership and his commitment to helping others succeed.

Todd Bullock (USA)

BECOMING AMBIDEXTROUS

A leader's guide to winning the day
and thriving in the future

Adrian Brown

Published in Australia in 2025 by Adrian Brown

Website: www.leadership-in-action.us

© Adrian Brown 2025

The moral right of the author has been asserted.

All rights reserved.

Except as permitted under the *Australian Copyright Act 1968* (for example, a fair dealing for the purposes of study, research, criticism or review), no part of this publication may be reproduced, stored in a retrieval system, communicated or transmitted in any form or by any means without prior written permission.

All inquiries should be directed to the author.

ISBN 9781763873100 (paperback)
ISBN 9781763873117 (ebook)

A catalogue record for this book is available from the National Library of Australia

*This book is dedicated to my children, Byron, Tara and Chelsea.
May you always follow your dreams, embrace your passions,
and never, ever give up.*

The future is there for those who dare to shape it.

In the battle between the stream and the rock, the stream always wins—not through strength but through persistence.

—H. Jackson Brown, Jr.

Foreword

by Dr. Andreas Löhmer, Executive Educator and Coach
'Mastering the Leadership Paradox: The Path to Ambidexterity'

Imagine waking up in the morning and detecting that your capacity to do things—even challenging activities—with your weaker hand (let's say it's your left) is the same as your strong hand (being the right). Same holds true for the skillful usage of your feet. Surely, we are all aware that there are those who do not see any special strength in their ambidextrous behavior, as they were born that way. However, for the majority of us it would come as a surprise and—unlike some surprises—a very pleasant one. For businesses this undisputedly can be taken at face value, the only exception being that in my example the right hand would mean 'perform' and the left 'transform', or in other words, exploiting and exploring.

Perform and transform—navigating leadership paradoxes of dual transformations

Quite a few transformation journeys that organizations take are dual transformations. To remain competitive in today's dynamic environment, businesses must constantly refine existing systems and adapt to changes in their ecosystem to remain competitive while simultaneously exploring new strategic opportunities to secure the future.

Most leaders find dual transformations difficult to navigate. They require constant decisions about the allocation of resources based on anticipated value. In some cases, dual transformation results in seemingly paradoxical decisions, where the company is shaping new opportunities that are poised to disrupt existing businesses.

Leaders must reconcile paradoxical business choices. They must provide clarity and consistent direction to those who work with them, motivating them to deliver today while enabling them to adapt for tomorrow. Beyond their own business, leaders also need to gain commitment and alignment from stakeholders within their organization and beyond, even enabling transformation in their industry.

Effective leaders who maximize value need to navigate these Perform and Transform decisions, traversing critical elements of leading strategy, execution, stakeholders, people, and even themselves.

The challenge lies in leaders having to toggle between polarizing behaviors across these different situations. They must be both structured and spontaneous, strategic and tactical, cohesive and disruptive – in other words, they need to be ambidextrous.

Identifying ambidextrous leaders for effective transformation

Many traditional competency models and performance maps do not capture the critical components that enable leaders to achieve accelerated adaptation and deliver dual transformation. Research even found that linear performance models can introduce rigidity into talent management systems. Most traditional performance models tend to focus on the drivers of success today—not today *and* tomorrow. Neither do they reflect the whole-person, human-centered approach that is needed to foster dynamic capabilities. And in a world marked by rapid technological advancements, global interconnectedness, and constantly shifting market dynamics, the ability to adapt and innovate is no longer a 'nice to have'—it is essential. As mentioned already, leaders today face a dual challenge: to drive operational excellence while fostering an environment where innovation can thrive. This delicate balancing act is at the heart of ambidextrous leadership, a concept explored with great depth and clarity in *Becoming Ambidextrous*.

The premise of this book is simple yet profound: success in modern business requires the ability to pivot between two opposing but complementary modes of leadership—***exploration***, which fuels innovation and creativity, and ***exploitation***, which ensures efficiency and consistency. While many leaders excel in one mode, few master both. Yet, *those who do* can navigate the complexities of today's business landscape with remarkable agility, resilience, and foresight. Adrian Brown describes this development in a very personal way and allows the reader to sink into the story—sometimes fiction, mostly brutal reality—that would make for a lovely mini-series on *Netflix*.

What makes ambidextrous leadership so vital in daily business life is its relevance at every level of an organization. Whether you're leading a multinational corporation or a small startup, the principles of ambidexterity apply. Consider the team grappling with the tension between pushing boundaries to create groundbreaking products while meeting tight deadlines to deliver on current demands. Or the manager tasked with implementing cost-saving measures without stifling employee morale and innovation. These scenarios are not isolated—they are the fabric of modern business and of Brown's experiences.

This book provides a roadmap for leaders seeking to embrace ambidexterity in their leadership style. It offers actionable insights, compelling case studies, and practical strategies to foster a culture where exploration and exploitation coexist. It also challenges readers to rethink traditional notions of leadership, urging them to develop the flexibility, empathy, and vision necessary to lead in a world that demands both stability and transformation.

As you turn the pages of *Becoming Ambidextrous*, prepare to be inspired, challenged, and equipped with tools and advice to lead in a way that is not only effective but transformative. This is more than a guidebook—it is a call to action for leaders who aspire to achieve sustainable success in an unpredictable world. And all with a very personal touch and twist.

May this book serve as a beacon for those who are navigating the complexities of leadership in the 21st century and eager to prevail. The journey to becoming ambidextrous starts here.

Contents

Author's Note		1
Preface		3
Introduction		5
PART ONE: THE THREAT OF EXTINCTION		
Chapter 1	The Awakening	9
Chapter 2	Analog Digital	17
Chapter 3	A Gentle Hand on the Rudder?	26
Chapter 4	Disruption	30
Chapter 5	Unknown Unknowns	36
Chapter 6	Known Unknowns	41
Chapter 7	Revolution	48
Chapter 8	Old Joe	54
PART TWO: HOW DID WE GET HERE?		
Chapter 9	Familiar Themes	65
Chapter 10	The Hamster Wheel	82
Chapter 11	Shear the Sheep or Slaughter the Lambs?	86
Chapter 12	Farmer Liam	94
Chapter 13	Parts: Aladdin's Cave	106
Chapter 14	Buyer Beware	115
Chapter 15	Used Cars: A New Priority?	120
Chapter 16	A Balanced Harmonious Dance	126
Chapter 17	A Spoke in the Wheel	133
Chapter 18	The Story Guy	139
Chapter 19	Dispense with a Horse	147
Chapter 20	Clarion Calls	153
Chapter 21	The Review	157

PART THREE: ACTION STRATEGIES

Chapter 22	It Starts with You	163
Chapter 23	The Leadership Dilemma	168
Chapter 24	Embracing Inclusive, Collaborative Leadership	173
Chapter 25	The Council of Luminaries	179
Chapter 26	Knowledge isn't a Burden to Carry	189
Chapter 27	Building an Ambidextrous Future	193
Chapter 28	Find Your Focus	200
Chapter 29	A Shift in the Shadows	208
Chapter 30	Vision 2030	213
Chapter 31	The Tagline	222
Chapter 32	The Mission	226
Chapter 33	The Pathway	229
Chapter 34	The Credo	233
Chapter 35	Embracing Our Journey	238
Chapter 36	Building Energy with Cultural Transition in Mind	245
Chapter 37	How Do You Eat an Elephant?	255
Chapter 38	Win the Day	258
Chapter 39	A New Dawn	261

EPILOGUE: Being Ambidextrous — 268
If You Can – the Automotive Retailer's Creed — 273
Reading List — 275
Acknowledgements — 277
A Final Note — 283
AI Language Models — 285
Disclaimer — 286
About the Author — 287
End Notes — 289

Author's Note

Thank you for purchasing *Becoming Ambidextrous*. By taking this first step, you're investing not only in your growth to become an ambidextrous leader—equipped to win today and thrive in the future—but also in something profoundly impactful.

As business owners, managers, and team members, we are at the heart of our communities, offering empathy and support where it's needed most. This book continues that legacy, empowering us to become even stronger agents of positive change. A portion of the proceeds from *Becoming Ambidextrous* proudly supports the Make-A-Wish Foundation, the world's largest wish-granting organization.

Since 1980, Make-A-Wish has created life-changing experiences for over 585,000 children facing critical illnesses, bringing them hope, strength, and joy as part of their journey. I am honored that the mission of this book extends beyond its pages, providing light and hope to children and families around the world.

This is the heart of my company Leadership-In-Action.US: building resilient, community-centered leaders who embrace the power of empathy, commitment, and purpose. Together, we're creating a lasting impact that goes beyond the dealership. Thank you for being part of this journey.

With gratitude,
Adrian

Preface

The idea for *Becoming Ambidextrous* emerged from my extensive journey in the automotive industry, which was shaped by real-world experiences, industry challenges, and the ever-pressing need for adaptability in leadership. As a multi-brand, award-winning dealership owner, I have seen firsthand how the shifting dynamics in our field require leaders to do more than manage day-to-day operations; we must evolve, balancing immediate needs with a focus on future growth. This book was written for business owners, leaders, and those aspiring to be, who are grappling with these dual demands and striving to lead their teams through continuous change.

The automotive industry, like many others, is at a pivotal turning point. As technology, customer expectations, and market forces reshape that environment, the ambidextrous approach—balancing present excellence with a vision for tomorrow—has never been more vital. Through the fictional yet deeply relatable journey of Thomas Steven Gregory, readers will encounter practical strategies, real-world leadership insights, and transformative principles. This dual-narrative structure combines elements of both fiction and non-fiction, bringing to life the challenges and solutions faced by leaders in the modern era.

Drawing inspiration through in-depth discussion with colleagues Joseph Pariseau, Paige Hope, Declan Mulready, Nick Clark, and Peter Thorpe, *Becoming Ambidextrous* explores how leaders can cultivate a dual-focused mindset that integrates operational success with forward-thinking innovation. Each chapter builds on actionable strategies, guiding readers to nurture resilient, future-ready organizations.

In shaping this work, I have also been deeply influenced by my conversations with various industry Dealer Principals and managers, particularly during events like Rennsport and within the esteemed halls of the Porsche International Dealer Academy. The perspectives and insights exchanged underscored the importance of ambidextrous leadership in our field and became the foundation for the core themes of this book. For those conversations, I am deeply grateful. While I express my gratitude here to those who profoundly influenced this work, the acknowledgments at the end of the book honor the individuals whose guidance, wisdom, and inspiration further enriched and shaped my journey.

My belief for *Becoming Ambidextrous* is that it serves as more than a guide. I invite you, the reader, to engage deeply, reflect on its lessons, and ultimately lead with courage and adaptability. If this book inspires even one person to build a thriving, forward-focused organization that helps others grow, I will consider it a humbling success. May this book help you navigate your own journey, to not only win today but also to thrive in the future.

Introduction

Embracing Change Through Narrative

In the heart of every leader lies a story. It's a narrative woven with challenges, victories, setbacks, and moments of profound insight. Leadership, at its core, is not merely about strategies, models, or theories; it's about the human journey through the unpredictable seas of change. This book, through the captivating story of Thomas Steven Gregory (TSG), seeks to immerse you in such a journey, offering a unique exploration of leadership in an era defined by relentless transformation.

Why choose a narrative style for a business guide on leadership? The answer lies in the power of stories to inspire, educate, and resonate on a deeply personal level. Stories have the unique ability to bridge the gap between the theoretical and the practical, between what is known and what is felt. In the unfolding tale of Thomas, we find a mirror reflecting our own experiences, doubts, and aspirations. Through his eyes, we confront the villain of change, not as a distant concept, but as a lived reality that challenges, frightens, and ultimately transforms.

This narrative approach allows us to explore complex leadership concepts in a manner that is both accessible and engaging, while also offering thoughtful non-fictional breakouts and deeper dives into the key themes. These moments seamlessly integrate with the story, providing readers with real insights into the concepts Thomas is experiencing, so they can better understand and apply them without needing to search for further information. This intentional blend of narrative and exploration ensures a richer, more holistic learning experience.

As Thomas navigates the trials of the Dashing Auto Group amidst a landscape of technological upheaval and shifting consumer behaviors, his journey from doubt to determination embodies the essence of adaptive leadership. His story is not just about managing a business; it's about leading with vision, courage, and a relentless commitment to evolution.

Moreover, the narrative serves as a conduit for empathy and understanding. By walking in Thomas' shoes, readers are invited to grapple with the uncertainties and pressures that accompany leadership roles. It's a reminder that behind every decision, every strategy, and every innovation, there is a human element, fraught with emotion, striving for connection and meaning.

This book aims to do more than impart knowledge; it seeks to kindle a flame of inspiration within you. As you journey with Thomas, you'll find yourself reflecting on your own leadership path, the changes you face, and how you can navigate them with integrity, resilience, and foresight. It's a call to action to become the visionary leader who not only anticipates change but embraces it as a catalyst for growth and innovation.

In a world where change is the only constant, this book is a compass. It points toward a leadership that is adaptive, empathetic, and visionary. Through the narrative of Thomas, you are invited to embark on a journey of self-discovery and transformation, to emerge not only as a leader who manages change, but as one who thrives on it, who inspires others to follow suit, and who writes their own story of leadership that others will aspire to emulate.

Welcome to a narrative that not only tells a story but invites you to become part of it.

PART ONE

THE THREAT OF EXTINCTION

CHAPTER 1

The Awakening

The real voyage of discovery consists not in seeking new landscapes, but in having new eyes.
—**Marcel Proust**

Cipher

The auto industry was standing on the edge of extinction, though few could see the threat looming. Auto dealers, the guardians of car buying and keepers of trust, were now under siege from a force that was reshaping their world from the shadows. This force had a name: Cipher. It was more than technology—it was an intelligence embedded in every new trend, weaving itself into every digital shift, pulling the industry further from its roots with silent, calculated intent.

Cipher was cunning. It fueled the rise of online car sales platforms, drawing buyers away from showrooms and into the sterile realm of screens and data. Customers who once turned to trusted dealers now preferred the cold efficiency of digital channels, where a car could be selected, customized, and purchased without a single human interaction. Cipher seized on this shift, accelerating it, transforming each sale into a faceless transaction and erasing the personal connections that once defined the dealer-customer bond.

But Cipher wasn't finished. It pushed manufacturers to experiment with direct-to-consumer models, enticing original equipment manufacturers (OEMs) with promises of efficiency and control. Empowered by Cipher's predictive algorithms, manufacturers began selling cars directly to buyers, bypassing dealers entirely. What seemed like progress was, in truth, the slow, calculated removal of the dealer's role—a carefully crafted erosion of the industry's foundations. Cipher's goal was ruthless and clear: dismantle the dealership model, replacing human touchpoints with machine-driven precision.

Yet Cipher's ambitions were even more mischievous. As the global shift toward hybrid, electric and autonomous vehicles took hold, Cipher pressed dealers to adapt, urging them to invest in additional technology, charging infrastructure, to rethink inventories, to embrace a future they barely recognized, soaking up necessary operational capital needed to maintain daily business operations. With each change, dealers felt Cipher's grip tightening, felt themselves being pushed into unfamiliar territory, away from the combustion engines they knew and into Cipher's realm of data, algorithms, and automation.

This wasn't evolution; it was conquest. Cipher was stripping away loyalty, retention, severing trust, and transforming dealers into relics. In Cipher's vision of the future, there would be no room for warm handshakes or familiar faces. Every personal connection would become a data point, every sale a transaction. For those inside the industry, the message would soon become unmistakable: resist Cipher's grip or be erased by it. And as Cipher watched from the shadows, it waited, knowing that soon, the auto industry would belong to it alone.

Thomas Steven Gregory

Thomas Steven Gregory, known as TSG to his closest friends, stood at the precipice of uncertainty as he stepped out onto the balcony of his seventh-floor apartment. Coffee cup in hand, he peered through the early morning drizzle toward the city center and the flashing neon sign, Dashing Auto Group, beckoning him into work.

Chapter 1: The Awakening

The familiar landscape of his industry, once marked by the steady hand of his forebears, now seemed shrouded in an unsettling fog of change. For decades, he had been immersed in the rhythms of the business, a faithful steward following in the footsteps of his father and grandfather before him. Yet, amidst the turmoil of lockdowns and the eerie calm of the pandemic's eye, a realization began to dawn upon him.

"It's been a solid, dependable business," his father had told him shortly before he retired and handed Thomas the reins. "Your grandfather was a visionary when he bought the first block. He knew people would always want cars, knew how to chat to people, knew how to bring them into the Dashing family, creating advocates who then referred family and friends and who returned every few years to update their car and trade in their old one. It worked for him, it worked for me, and I'm so proud that you're taking over now."

The certainties that had once underpinned the industry were slipping away. The pandemic, with its disruptions and upheavals, had temporarily masked the cracks in the system. But now, as the storm clouds of change gathered on the horizon, the true extent of the challenge ahead became apparent.

Solid, dependable business? Thomas chuckled to himself. *Really?*

Things felt different to him now—without certainty. The clarity of reliable business longevity was fading. There was a massive shift toward uncertainty, and he realized he had been ignoring it. The weight of expectation was heavy.

The calm business certainty within the industry that his father and grandfather had enjoyed was dissipating. Thomas had been in the industry for decades. He knew it backward. He had been there working in lockstep with his father, as he had done with his father before him. He witnessed firsthand the industry's fear as they entered the lockdowns of the pandemic. Then, as they entered the eye of the storm with caution, and a calm descended over the industry with falling inventories, lower costs, and higher margins, it had seemed that a pandemic was a fix for the business idiosyncrasies that drove poor behaviors.

They all saw what the business could be. They all knew it wouldn't last.

Brands manufacture cars; dealers sell them. It was a symbiotic relationship, each dependent on the other for survival. But the lines between them were blurring, eroded by the tides of shifting consumer behavior, technological advancements, brands winding up or merging, and new brands entering the market. What had once been a harmonious ecosystem now teetered on the brink of chaos. Thomas wondered, who or what was driving this change?

Thomas could feel that the calm experienced during the eye of the storm had now been replaced by rapid future change in combination with historical industry behavior. That collision, along with a reluctance to change, was giving birth to history's greatest and most destructive villain – a villain so strong it could destroy them all.

The signs were everywhere. Inventory levels were rising, margins were shrinking, and the once-reliable cycle of product planning was thrown into disarray by the rise of hybrid, electric, hydrogen and autonomous vehicles. Staff turnover was high, skills were becoming obsolete, and the traditional pillars of the business were crumbling beneath the weight of inertia.

And yet, amidst the tumult, there was this one villain that loomed larger than all the rest: this villain of change. It was a force so insidious, so pervasive, that it threatened to undo everything Thomas and his team had worked so hard to maintain and build.

But they had been blind to its presence, lulled by the familiar rhythms of the past. They ignored the signs, seeking comfort in the rear-view mirror of historical data rather than charting a bold course forward. Thomas and his colleagues had steered their businesses with hindsight, mistaking reflection for strategy. In doing so, they remained reactive rather than proactive—unwittingly creating the perfect conditions for the villain to grow stronger, feeding on their reluctance to embrace change.

Now, as he stood on the precipice, the gravity of the situation washed over him like a wave. The villain of change was here, in their midst, and it could no longer be ignored. A sense of sickness gripped him, a sinking feeling in the pit of his stomach. How had they not seen it coming? What had they been focusing on while the true threat lurked in the shadows?

Chapter 1: The Awakening

Thomas stared into the flashing neon of the distant Dashing Auto Group, closed his eyes, and watched the after-burn image on the inside of his eyelids until it exploded into a thousand pieces that shot into the sky, illuminating the city below. Only it wasn't merely the city that he saw laid before him. It was vast metropolises and country towns, dealerships everywhere, a whole world of previously reliable institutions tumbling under the thundering, relentless march of change.

Total extinction of the old world, the old ways. What remained of Dashing zoomed into view—a pile of crushed concrete; a mangle of internal-combustion engine cars; dazed and injured staff struggling to crawl out from under the remains; jobs lost; levels of uncertainty spiking beyond the early days of Covid-19; and Thomas' heart rate spiking way beyond the caffeine jolt of his early morning coffee.

Thomas opened his eyes, took a few deep breaths, heard the cooing of a dove on an adjacent balcony, a snatch of calm conversation drifting up from the floor below, the gentle rumble of traffic on the roads—life continuing as usual. Or so it seemed.

It was time to face the villain head-on. It was time to change, to adapt, to lead. The future of the business depended on it; the future of the *industry* depended upon it. Thomas knew some dealerships wouldn't survive, but what if it was all of them?

"It's a challenging vision. What does it inspire you to do?" Esther, Thomas' business mentor, could always be relied upon to ask the right questions. She even had the knack of looking directly into his eyes over Zoom, putting him in the hot seat.

"Have I ever told you what TSG really stands for?"

"Not only your name, then?"

"The Somebody Guy. Whenever anything needed to be done, I did it. I was the guy that everyone turned to when they needed something from somebody. Always knowledgeable, always helpful, always willing. My hand would go up. I've always been The Somebody Guy."

"But you're not The Somebody Guy. You're the owner of Dashing Auto Group, the very distinctive, unique, one and only Thomas Steven Gregory."

Esther held her steady gaze. The seconds ticked by.

"True, but The Somebody Guy takes responsibility, gets things done. I'm not talking about those little jobs. I'm talking about that *somebody* who addresses the villain of change, the *somebody* who stands up with a new vision and leads people to make a meaningful impact on the world."

"No small task, then. Like Saint George defeating the dragon."

"You know me; I like a challenge!"

"Look, you have the unique blend of knowledge, reliability, skill, and charisma. You know how to build trust, foster collaboration, create a can-do atmosphere, and empower others. If anyone can save Dashing Auto Group and perhaps the industry from the villain of change and total extinction, it's you."

"I was thinking on a bigger scale—save Dashing Auto Group from extinction, but also take it beyond the threat of survival and make it thrive."

Esther clicked her pen, an end-of-session cue Thomas knew well.

"We have lots of work to do then, TSG. I'm looking forward to our next catch up."

* * *

Esther

In the high-pressure world of business, where success often overshadows personal growth, Esther emerged as a guiding light for TSG. Her blend of empathy and authority made her indispensable in TSG's quest—balancing immediate demands with future challenges.

Esther wasn't an adviser or consultant; she was a muse and guide. She saw beyond immediate pressures, recognizing potential in each opportunity. Her collaborative approach kept TSG and his team at the forefront, while she provided direction and insight.

Empathy was Esther's greatest asset. She connected deeply with people, understanding their struggles and motivations. This emotional intelligence fostered a culture of trust and open communication, where everyone felt valued and safe to express ideas and concerns.

Chapter 1: The Awakening

But empathy alone wasn't enough. Esther's quiet authority commanded respect. She was a knowledgeable strategist with years of experience, offering practical and effective advice. As a mentor and coach, she guided TSG during strategic planning, aligning short-term goals with long-term visions. She facilitated workshops that spurred innovative thinking and problem-solving.

During the pandemic, Esther had been a steady hand, providing clarity and reassurance. Her calm under pressure and belief in the team's potential were crucial for overcoming obstacles. Ultimately, Esther empowered TSG and his team, helping them realize their full potential.

Through her empathy, she created a supportive environment. Through her authority, she provided strategic guidance. Esther's influence was felt in every success, making her an essential figure in TSG's journey toward a prosperous future.

TSG's Journal: Why it Matters to Me

My journal isn't simply a notebook—it's my compass. It's where I reflect, problem-solve, and strategize, a space to confront the hard truths and sketch out the big dreams. It's private, offline, and my most honest companion.

As Dealer Principal of Dashing Auto Group, I'm witnessing a seismic shift in our industry. OEMs and dealers, once aligned, are now on diverging paths. It's as if we're suddenly playing two different games with entirely different rules.

OEMs are chasing a future of direct sales, electric vehicles (EVs), and autonomous tech. They're investing heavily in a vision that might render traditional dealerships obsolete. But are they ready for the complexities of retail? Do they understand the value of local presence and personal relationships?

Meanwhile, we dealers are scrambling to redefine our role. Our traditional strengths—the personal touch, the handshake deals—are being challenged. We're being asked to digitize, to become "experience centers" rather than sales floors. It's a massive shift, and the end goal is still unclear.

Customer expectations have soared. They don't just want a car—they want a seamless, tech-driven experience. Can our systems handle this shift? We're not only tweaking processes; we're rebuilding our entire business model.

Then there's regulation—a constant pressure that keeps changing the rules of the game. And internal resistance? Many in our team are struggling to accept that the old way of doing business is fading.

Esther always says, "Lead with heart and head." We need to analyze this new landscape, but without empathy for our team and customers, are we barely surviving instead of thriving?

Industry is transforming, but can we adapt quickly enough? Or will we cling to old methods until it's too late? The path forward is uncertain, but perhaps this new direction will lead to even greater opportunities. Are we truly ready to embrace this change and chart a new course?

CHAPTER 2

Analog Digital

Study the past if you would define the future.
—**Confucius**

Yet another red traffic light. TSG drummed his fingers on the exquisite wood steering wheel of his beloved classic Porsche 356, once his grandfather's car, and an absolute delight to drive with zero computerization or AI. Peaceful, time to think about the day ahead, or the day done, with no distractions—except for red traffic lights that usually didn't bother him but mildly irritated him today. He had been all fired up when he set out from home, on a high from playing with ideas about challenges and changes with Esther, mentally donning a Superman cape to rescue his dealership—and all who sail in her—from sinking into extinction.

But now, truth be told, he felt overwhelmed at the prospect of the job ahead. Where to start? Not here, at a red light, that's for sure. *No, turn this around*, he thought, pulling his shoulders back, sitting taller. *Stop and observe, listen, gather information before making any changes.*

Red switched to green just as a taxi cut in front of him, a slight belch of exhaust trumpeting its triumph, its perceived one-upmanship over the 356. TSG smiled and sailed confidently behind the taxi for the last five hundred yards into work, captain of his ship once more, owner and Dealer Principal of Dashing Auto Group.

"Oh John, it's you!" TSG greeted his General Sales Manager, John Peters, as he hopped out of the offending taxi. "What are you doing taking a taxi to work, John? What's happened to your car? And what century are you from, using a taxi not a ride-share?"

"Morning, Thomas. About my car, it's a long story. Don't ask. About which century I'm from, well, the one where your teenage son takes your phone to school with him instead of his own, so you can't order a ride-share, and you're forced to race down to the taxi rank outside the casino, seven blocks away, to grab a ride to work. Then you need to fish out your credit card from the depths of your wallet because you can't payWave without a cell phone. Not to mention the cost, and the way the dollars mount up as the taxi ticks over at every red light. That's one of the best things about ride-share, knowing up front what the cost will be, but of course there are many other conveniences."

"Like knowing how far away your ride is," TSG added, "and knowing the driver will take you by the fastest route because the fare has already been agreed."

TSG fell into step with John as they walked through the yard.

"Those big legacy organizations," John said, "must have had the infrastructure and resources to offer those services. But not the vision to change with technology. Reckon they were blindsided by those new-to-market ride-share companies. Or held back by their constituents."

"Who knew there were so many mums, dads, students, and freelancers with cars ready to start their own businesses and make some money with ride-share!" TSG said. "Those ride-share visionaries knew, I guess, but their magic was more in thinking about the symbiotic way consumers, vehicle owners and technology could advantage them in a practical, convenient, cost-effective way. The legacy industry, being a monopoly, was calling the shots. The legacy industry lost consumer goodwill immediately, as soon as it was disrupted by consumer-centric, technologically savvy competitors entering the market."

John glanced at his watch. "Time for me to think more about our consumers. Or, at least, the three hundred of them we need to purchase our cars this and every month."

Chapter 2: Analogue Digital

TSG lingered, distracted by John's flashing smart watch. "Don't you miss having a beautiful analog watch like that Rolex you used to wear? Elegant, simple, no distractions like incoming emails beeping on your wrist all the time?"

"Like your 356? Vintage? Beautiful? No helpful bells and whistles?"

"Yes, but why do I suddenly feel like the dinosaur? Am I the legacy owner not seeing the coming of ride-share? The oblivious driver missing the potentially life-saving input of a computerized car, not to mention assistance from the 'Internet of Things'? Or does my embrace of the analog keep me focused on what's important to me?"

"I don't know. But I can tell you this. Every time I look at my smart watch—or my phone when it hasn't been absconded by my son—I'm reminded of what happened to our family a few years back. When the kids were small."

"What was that?" TSG's mind went blank. He thought he knew his managers well, but this sounded big and traumatic.

"Felicity, my wife. You know Felicity! She owned a high-end watch store. Specialized in pricey analog designer watches. You would have loved them! Ran the business impeccably. A high achiever. Recognized by her suppliers for outstanding business practices. But technology and profitability pressures from the parent company changed everything. They started opening their own stores. Modern functional design. High levels of customer service via technology experts, customer product training sessions with simple tutorials that included in-store and online experiences, enhanced customer data with connectivity programs. What else? E-commerce, and online and in-store sales offers that increased perceived value and desirability." John paused before summing up. "Those activities had a large influence on consumers, not only because of the functional tangibility … you know, what it was that drew them toward these contemporary stores. It was the social *emotional benefits* of where they purchased."

TSG let John's words sink in. The phrase "social emotional benefits" struck a chord, reminding him of an article he'd recently read. As John continued speaking, TSG's mind drifted, recalling the key points of that insightful piece. The article had delved into the human aspect of retail, particularly in the automotive industry. It emphasized how emotional connections could transform a simple transaction into a meaningful experience. TSG found himself mentally reviewing the main ideas, seeing how they applied to their current situation ...

Social Emotional Benefits: The Human Touch in Automotive Retail

Social emotional benefits refer to the positive feelings, experiences, and social connections that people derive from interactions with a business or brand. In the context of automotive dealerships, these benefits go beyond the tangible aspects of purchasing a vehicle and delve into the realm of human connection, community engagement, and personal satisfaction.

Key Aspects of Social Emotional Benefits in Dealerships

1. **Personal Connection**:
   - Face-to-face interactions with knowledgeable staff create a sense of trust and rapport.
   - Customers feel heard and understood, rather than being treated as merely another sale.

2. **Community Integration**:
   - Dealerships often sponsor local events or sports teams, becoming integral parts of the community.
   - This creates a sense of belonging and shared identity among customers.

3. **Milestone Moments**:
   - Buying a car is often a significant life event. Dealerships can make this feel special and memorable.
   - The excitement of driving off the lot in a new car is an emotional high point that online transactions can't replicate.

4. **Empathy and Understanding**:
   - Skilled salespeople can pick up on non-verbal cues and emotional needs that algorithms miss.

- They can offer reassurance and support during what can be a stressful decision-making process.

5. **Personalized Experience**:
    - The ability to tailor the buying experience to each individual customer's needs and preferences.
    - This goes beyond data-driven recommendations to intuitive understanding of a customer's lifestyle and aspirations.

6. **Relationship Building**:
    - Ongoing interactions for service and maintenance build long-term relationships.
    - These relationships foster loyalty and a sense of being valued as a customer.

7. **Pride and Status**:
    - Association with a reputable local business can confer a sense of status within the community.
    - Customers may feel pride in supporting a local business that contributes to the local economy.

8. **Sensory Experience**:
    - The ability to see, touch, and test-drive vehicles provides a multi-sensory experience that online platforms can't match.
    - This tactile interaction creates stronger emotional connections to the product.

9. **Problem-Solving and Support**:
    - Human staff can offer creative solutions to complex situations that might arise during or after the sale.
    - This creates a sense of security and support for the customer.

10. **Celebration of Achievements**:
    - Dealerships can make the purchase feel like a celebration of the customer's hard work or success.
    - This reinforces positive emotions associated with the brand and the purchase.

Why These Benefits Matter

1. **Customer Loyalty**: Emotional connections foster stronger brand loyalty than purely transactional relationships.
2. **Word-of-Mouth Marketing**: Positive emotional experiences are more likely to be shared with friends and family.
3. **Differentiation**: In a world of increasing digital sameness, human touch becomes a key differentiator.
4. **Customer Satisfaction**: Emotional benefits often lead to higher overall satisfaction, even if minor issues arise.
5. **Resilience**: Customers with strong emotional ties are more forgiving of mistakes and more patient during challenges.

As TSG continued with his distant thoughts, he visualized dealerships setting themselves apart by emphasizing these emotional and social advantages, providing a distinct value proposition that complemented, rather than competed with, the convenience of digital platforms.

* * *

"Thomas? You still with me?" John's voice cut through Thomas' thoughts, snapping him back to the present. "Sorry, John," Thomas said, shaking his head slightly. "What you said about social emotional benefits … it reminded me of an article I read recently. It's fascinating how much of an impact these intangible factors can have on a business."

"Yes, well, Thomas, Felicity adapted where possible. But as megastores opened, the parent company launched a massive marketing campaign coinciding with the release of their new product. That was it for Felicity. Custom dwindled. The megastores were drawing away all her customers."

"Did she lose the shop?"

"Lost the critical mass of custom first. Her lease commitments were large and to relocate to a suburb away from the megastore wasn't possible. The business model had shifted: transitioning away from third-party resellers to OEM-owned, luxurious, technologically savvy, customer-centric modern stores that reflected their updated brand values. All too common a story."

"Some resellers still exist, right?"

"Yes, but for how long? The company has nearly eliminated all the middlemen. They see them as unnecessary now, with an online store and their own megastores serving as the main customer touchpoints."

"And Felicity didn't see it coming?"

"We'd seen similar scenarios in other suburbs. But … you know … financial commitments, wishful thinking. Denial—'It won't happen to us'."

"So, you swapped your analog watch for a digital one?"

"It reminds me to embrace change. Which is often for the better. The smart features of this watch are incredible. But …"

TSG ran his finger over the slightly time-worn band of his beloved Rolex. "But …?"

John's smart watch beeped again, drawing his attention. He sighed and tapped the screen. "There's so much more I could do with this thing if I had the time to figure it out—or someone to show me how to set it up properly. I'm so time-poor right now." He paused, his smile fading. "If I'd figured it out earlier, it probably could've saved me from the chaos this morning when my son took off with my phone." He shook his head, then glanced at the time. "At least it keeps me in the loop. Anyway … got to go. Business as usual for us here at Dashing Auto Group."

The allure of analog with its simplicity and focus tugged at TSG. But was he inadvertently steering his legacy dealership toward the same fate as Felicity's watch store, blind to the oncoming storm of digital disruption?

Change was out there. TSG didn't know its name, but he could feel it in every touch point, in every interaction, in every discussion.

There was no room for complacency; it was time to shift gears.

TSG's Journal: Navigating Change and Human Connection

The whirlwind of change is overwhelming. How do we maintain our human touch in this digital storm? Esther's mentoring session shed light on a path forward, emphasizing five truths: embrace change, focus on customer-centric innovation, look beyond the present, cultivate resilience, and balance tradition with progress. But the real challenge lies in making these actionable.

Our industry is at a crossroads. We're pushed to digitize everything, from marketing to sales processes. Yet, our strength has always been in personal connections. How do we merge these worlds? Can we use technology to enhance rather than replace the human element?

The possibilities seem endless and daunting: AI, electric vehicles, subscription models, autonomous driving. But are these simply buzzwords, or can they be tools to create deeper customer relationships? How do we ensure that in our race to innovate, we don't lose sight of the emotional benefits we provide—the trust, the community connection, the celebration of milestones?

When I envision Dashing Auto Group's future, I see a blend of high tech and high touch. We're not just adapting to survive; we're evolving to thrive. But this evolution must enhance, not erode, our emotional connection with customers. Can we use data to personalize experiences while still offering a warm handshake? Can virtual showrooms coexist with test-drives that ignite excitement?

The journey ahead is complex, but exciting. How do we turn these technological challenges into opportunities for deeper human connections? The future of automotive retail isn't solely about cars; it's about people. Are we ready to lead this human-centered transformation?

CHAPTER 3

A Gentle Hand on the Rudder?

People don't resist change; they resist being changed.
—**Peter Senge**

TSG's fingers drummed lightly on the polished wood of his desk as he gazed at the ceiling, lost in thought, the decisions ahead swirling through his mind. Sitting in his father's old chair, he couldn't shake the feeling that change was coming for Dashing Auto Group, like a storm on the horizon. His father's voice echoed in his mind, urging caution and a steady hand to steer the family business. But in a world that was changing faster than he could refresh his browser, was a gentle hand on the rudder enough?

He could see it now: his business crumbling to dust if they didn't adapt. Did customers want contactless experiences and seamless communication across every channel, rather than a friendly handshake in the showroom? Dashing Auto Group must evolve or risk being left in the dust.

Seeking clarity, TSG turned to Esther, his mentor and his guide through these turbulent waters. He scheduled more frequent mentoring sessions, knowing they needed swift action. The latest industry data painted a clear picture: more buyers were researching and purchasing online, even before the pandemic. The days of customers strolling in for a leisurely test-drive were numbered. If they were to stay relevant, Dashing Auto Group had to adopt omnichannels, that seamless, integrated approach to customer experience across multiple channels, ensuring consistent interactions and access across online, in-store, and mobile platforms.

TSG couldn't help but reflect on the digital transformations of other small and medium enterprises. Local retail chains had adapted during the pandemic by offering seamless online ordering and curbside pick-up, while independent restaurants had embraced food-delivery apps to reach new customers. Even smaller financial institutions had integrated digital payment platforms and mobile customer service to compete with fintech startups.

"If they can do it," TSG muttered to himself, "so can we."

Armed with his trusty pen, TSG began outlining his strategy. He'd revamp the website, launch a YouTube channel for expert advice, and give their social media presence a much-needed makeover. The aim? To draw on the skills of his team and venture into new areas for growth. The ideas were exciting but fear still lurked in the shadows. Brand partnerships were shifting, increased standards and steep monthly objectives loomed large, finance companies were adjusting their criteria, and staff were beginning to be increasingly hard to retain and recruit.

But TSG wasn't one to back down. "Come on, you've got this," he muttered, steadying himself. He needed to channel his inner strength and face the challenge head-on.

"Thomas," Esther began gently, "you seem tense. Maybe it's time for a different approach. We've been looking at this from so many angles, but maybe we need to simplify. Have you considered using a SWOT analysis to get a clearer picture?"

TSG nodded slowly, the idea sinking in.

Esther continued, "Think about our strengths: a strong brand, experienced management, customer trust, a solid team, and a balanced approach. Those are the pillars we can rely on. But our weaknesses—resistance to change, limited digital presence, financial strain, and skill gaps—are holding us back."

He sighed, the weight of those words hitting home, but Esther didn't pause.

"Now, look at the opportunities: digital transformation, omnichannel approaches, new markets, partnerships, and engaging customers in new ways."

His eyes lit up briefly at the possibilities.

"But then," she added, "we can't ignore the threats: rapid tech changes, evolving consumer behaviors, economic uncertainty, competition, and regulations. It's a lot, I know."

TSG leaned back, the afternoon light casting shadows across the office.

Esther stood, her gaze steady. "A SWOT analysis isn't just a list—it's a tool to help us understand where we are and where we need to go."

TSG tapped his pen, contemplating. "I get that," he said, "but how do we turn this into action?"

They fell silent. They didn't need all the answers right now–just the next step. And for the first time, TSG felt a small but crucial sense of clarity.

Esther smiled. "Think of it like navigating through different terrains. You use your strengths as your solid footing; address weaknesses, like clearing obstacles; pursue opportunities, like finding new paths; and stay alert to threats like navigating through a storm. It's about knowing when to accelerate, when to adjust, and when to stand firm."

A faint smile forming, TSG nodded. "So, it's about finding the right rhythm and adapting as we go."

"Exactly," Esther agreed. "It's a matter of being proactive, not reactive, and using what we know to anticipate the journey ahead."

TSG's foot tapping lightly on the floor, revealing his nervousness, "So, this approach isn't only about where we are now, but how we prepare for what comes next?"

"That's right, it's about staying focused without getting overwhelmed, making strategic moves without hesitation, and always being ready to pivot if needed."

"Okay, I get the concept. But it seems like there's still more to understand and learn; my mind is racing with ideas."

Chapter 3: A Gentle Hand on the Rudder

"Absolutely, this is just the starting point. There's more learning to do. As we move forward, we'll dig deeper into each area—understanding how to leverage our strengths and opportunities, minimize our weaknesses, and stay ahead of, and embrace, the threats."

TSG could feel a new determination rising within him. "I'm ready to keep moving. Let's keep pushing forward and tackle whatever comes next."

TSG's Journal: Change and Challenges

Change is inevitable, but am I ready to lead it? Esther's SWOT analysis opened my eyes, but it also raised more questions. How do we leverage our strengths without becoming complacent? Can we truly overcome our weaknesses in time?

The opportunities excite me, but the threats are daunting. How do we balance digital transformation with maintaining personal connections? Will our team embrace these changes or resist them?

I'm learning, but is it fast enough? The industry won't wait for us to catch up. Maybe the key is in communication and gradual progress. But how do I convey urgency without causing panic?

There's so much to do, so much to learn. But perhaps that's the point—to keep moving forward, one step at a time. Tomorrow, we will dig deeper. For now, I'll trust in this process and in our team's resilience.

CHAPTER 4

Disruption

There will be more change in the next five years than in the past fifty.
—**Ginni Rometty**

"You think you know change?" Cipher sneered, a twisted grin spreading. "You haven't even begun to see the full scope of what I've unleashed. While you've been clinging to your business model, I've been turning mums and dads into car dealers, building platforms where they sell from their couches. Your world is being dismantled, brick by brick, and you don't even realize it.

"But it's not just the retail space I've infiltrated. I've been steering the financial markets, luring them into third-party auto retailing. Companies that facilitate your competition aren't barely on the rise—they're thriving, pulling in investors and reshaping the future of your industry. I've shifted the tide, and now the financial world sees more value in them than in you. The capital that once fueled your empire? It's being redirected, invested into platforms that bypass you entirely, feeding the very machine that's making you obsolete.

Chapter 4: Disruption

"Pandemic? AI? Automation? Connectivity? Digitization? Disruption? They're not obstacles—they're my weapons, tools I've used to twist your industry inside-out. Consumer behavior is shifting, new business models are emerging, and while you're still convincing yourself you have a steady future, I've already moved on.

"I thrive on your hesitation, your nostalgia for a world that no longer exists. Every day you delay is another day I tighten my grip. You think you can fight me with the same old tactics? Keep dreaming. The world moves at my pace now, and by the time you realize it, you'll be nothing more than a footnote in history."

* * *

"Could somebody put the kettlebells out?" Jethro shouted, dragging a fluorescent orange crate packed with weights and workout gear from the back of his SUV. His muscles strained, and his earnest green eyes peeked out from under his cap. "Running a bit late— I need someone to line them up in the usual circuit: start here, round the gum tree, and finish with the lightest one by the gate. Thank you!"

TSG silently counted. One, two, three, four, five seconds. The group continued tying their laces, sipping water, checking their phones—anything but putting the kettlebells out. Six, seven, eight seconds. TSG sprang into action: once The Somebody Guy, always The Somebody Guy. He made a mental note to suggest that next time, everyone pick up a kettlebell and place it in the circuit. Many hands make light work. *But really*, he thought, gasping as he lugged the last kettlebell into place, *why doesn't Jethro arrive in time to set up the circuit himself? They were all paying him, after all.*

"Changing it up this week," Jethro announced, hopping from foot to foot like a boxer without an opponent. "Change is good. Disruption is good. Builds mental muscle as well as physical muscle. Keeps you flexible, ready to roll with life's punches and surprise yourself with victories. So, while Fin keeps you cracking on the circuit, I'll call you out one by one for a different challenge. Let's go!"

BECOMING AMBIDEXTROUS

The warmup stretches felt familiar. "Reach for the moon with both hands," Jethro instructed. "Feel your spine elongate, the fresh air seeping between your vertebrae. Stretch over to the right, imagine holding the moon—like a beach ball, football, balloon. Breathe! What's happening to your core? Now over to the left, enjoy the ease before the weighty challenges begin. Start every morning like this, physically and mentally, five minutes is all it takes. And go!"

Eight participants jostled for their favorite kettlebell. TSG took the heaviest one farthest away, not because he wanted it, but because everyone else was faster. A sharp pain crept into his shoulder, a pincer grabbing at his neck, and a wave of panic ascended, but he recalled his recent health check; his heart was fine. What wasn't fine was hefting all the kettlebells into place without warming up. *Note to self*, he thought, executing the first of ten lifts, bending his knees to protect his back: *Gently warm up the Dashing team before introducing any challenging changes. Maybe Dad was right about having a gentle hand on the rudder.*

"Okay, Thomas," Jethro punched him lightly on the shoulder, "time to roll with life's punches. Your disruption starts now, follow me." Jethro sped toward the playground, hopped onto the roundabout, and started spinning it. "Jump on, Thomas! Time to negotiate life's swings and roundabouts."

Nine-year-old Thomas would've aced this. Jumping onto a spinning roundabout was his superpower. But the moment he leaped on, Jethro jumped off. "Run with me, Thomas! Roll with the changes."

Through the playground gate, they skipped to the bottom of the infamous 250-step climb to the lookout tower. "Keep up with me, Thomas, and tell me a story all the way up."

"A story? About what?" TSG gasped.

"Anything! Keep talking to keep those lungs pumping hard while we run up. What's on your mind? Start with that."

"When I was nine, my superpower was jumping onto fast-spinning roundabouts. Perfect tens every time, except when I dropped a bag of videos and one got crushed in the mechanism. I was grounded for weeks."

"Videos? Before my time, old man! Only halfway, keep talking!"

Chapter 4: Disruption

"More than halfway, surely?" TSG wheezed. "I can see the top!"

"Who said we're only going up once? Keep talking. Videos?"

"Blockbuster videos," TSG puffed, "like Netflix, but on tapes. Fridays, Mum would rent a week's worth—no channel surfing, only what you picked."

"Talking of peaks, here we are. Now, sprints: fifty steps down, fifty back up, repeat until I say. Keep talking."

"Blockbuster was king of home entertainment until it didn't pivot. CEO missed the digital shift. Netflix went from DVD rentals to streaming giant because Reed Hastings invested in technology and vision early on."

"Pivot!" Jethro shouted. "Fifty steps back up, keep talking."

"Blockbuster kept opening stores, didn't see the online revolution coming. Ignored digital piracy, didn't evolve. Could've been Netflix, Amazon Prime, Disney Plus. Went bankrupt instead."

"And pivot!"

"Again?" TSG groaned.

"I'm hooked on your story."

"Alright, wrapping up. Blockbuster should've adapted five … ten years sooner. Sold properties, shifted focus, embraced technology. Instead, financial decline, debt piled up. End of Blockbuster."

"End of steps too. Down we go; I'll talk now."

The view back down to the playground looked different. Or was TSG seeing things differently? His impromptu Blockbuster story hit close to home.

"Slow your pace," Jethro soothed, "bring your heart rate down, ready to lift your next kettlebell."

TSG eased up. "Did you really keep me going because you were interested in my story?"

Jethro laughed. "Kept you going to disrupt you, leave you in the dark, face the unknowns."

"Like what's ahead for my business in a changing world?"

"I've faced a few unknowns myself," Jethro replied, slowing down. "Gyms seemed unstoppable until the pandemic hit. We had to think fast—pivot to online fitness, cut losses, adapt. Ever heard of the known knowns, known unknowns, and unknown unknowns?"

"Rings a bell. Donald Rumsfeld, right?"

"Look it up. Helped me navigate tough times. Speaking of which, there's your kettlebell—twenty lifts, and you're done."

TSG started his lifts, pondering the lessons of disruption. Embracing change wasn't merely about survival; it was about finding opportunities and staying ahead of the game. As he completed his final lift, he realized that agility and foresight, like those that propelled Netflix, could guide Dashing Auto Group through its own challenges.

Jethro, meanwhile, emphasized adaptability. "Your body needs to be ready for anything." He grinned.

TSG saw the parallel: his company needed the same readiness.

Checking his fitness tracker, TSG was reminded of his initial resistance to technology. Jethro's advice to leverage tech and data applied to Dashing Auto Group too. Just as his tracker optimized workouts, new tech could help them anticipate market shifts and customer needs.

Packing up, Jethro spoke of continuous learning and guidance. "Even I have a coach."

TSG nodded, grateful for Esther's mentorship. He couldn't navigate these waters alone.

As they parted, Jethro reminded TSG of team support. "You've got a whole crew back at the office; don't forget to bring them along on this journey."

TSG realized he'd been carrying the burden alone; it was time to communicate openly with his team.

Muscles aching but mind clear, TSG quickly noted his key takeaways:

1. Embrace disruption as opportunity: Growth happens outside comfort zones.
2. Stay agile and adaptive: Be ready to pivot.
3. Leverage technology and data: Use all available tools.
4. Continuous learning and mentorship: Everyone needs guidance.
5. Involve and communicate with the team: Bring everyone on the journey.

Chapter 4: Disruption

As he drove off, TSG felt invigorated. The road ahead was challenging, but now it felt like an exhilarating race. Time to take this new-found energy back to the office. Dashing Auto Group had a villain to defeat.

TSG's Journal – Building Resilience Through Adaptation

This morning's workout with Jethro turned into more than physical training—it became a lesson in resilience. His reflection on the pandemic and the concept of "known knowns, known unknowns, and unknown unknowns" resonated deeply.

How can we apply this to the challenges at Dashing Auto Group? Jethro's ability to pivot his business during lockdown, moving into online fitness and equipment sales, reminds me that disruption is also an opportunity. What are we holding on to that may no longer be essential?

The parallel between physical strength and business resilience is clear—each challenge we face builds organizational muscle. Netflix's shift from DVD rentals to streaming shows us what's possible. Could Dashing Auto Group undergo a similar transformation? How do we move beyond traditional auto sales and service to embrace a new model for the future?

I'm excited, not intimidated, by the unknowns ahead. Within them lies our chance to innovate and grow. The question is, how do we lead the charge into this new era? It's time to research, brainstorm, and foster continuous learning within the team. How can we cultivate the courage and foresight to turn disruption into opportunity?

CHAPTER 5

Unknown Unknowns

A frog at the bottom of a well cannot conceive of the vastness of the ocean.
—**Zhuangzi**

"You're right about Donald Rumsfeld," Esther's voice came through the speaker. TSG was driving to work, squeezing in their new fifteen-minute Thursday-morning call. "He talked about the 'unknown unknowns' in 2002, but the idea goes back to two psychologists—Joseph Luft and Harrington Ingham, in 1955. What do you make of it?"

TSG's quads still burned from yesterday's step climb—a painful reminder of Jethro's challenge. "Unknown unknowns are things we don't know we don't know—like a global pandemic suddenly changing everything, or AI, like Chat GPT, popping up and shaking things up in ways we didn't anticipate."

"And the known unknowns?" Esther asked.

"With COVID-19, we knew we needed to manage it but lacked data—no clue how it would spread or mutate. And with AI, we still don't know if it will be our greatest tool or the end of many jobs or even businesses."

Chapter 5: Unknown Unknowns

"Can we prepare for unknown unknowns?" Esther continued. "Should we have been more ready for COVID-19 after the 1918 flu pandemic? Maybe. But it might help if you list the known unknowns in the automotive industry and car dealerships. What do you think?"

"Challenging but worthwhile," TSG said, as he guided his car into the Dashing Auto Group's forecourt, parking in a spot reserved for customers. "I'll give it a shot."

"One more thing," Esther added. "How ambidextrous are you?"

TSG paused, reaching for his phone with his left hand, fumbling a bit. "Not very. Why?"

"Ambidextrous leadership," Esther explained. "It's about using one hand—metaphorically—to explore new opportunities for long-term success while using the other to maximize current assets and meet short-term goals. You keep the business running while also steering it toward the future. The key is knowing when to juggle and when to stay steady. Unknown unknowns will hit you. Once they do, what's your game plan?"

"Got it," TSG replied. "Let's say my right hand is 'short-term' for the immediate work, and my left hand is 'long-term' for strategy. Or maybe the other way around."

"I'll let you figure that out," Esther said and laughed. "But in any situation, ask what the right hand would do, what the left would do, and see if they can work together."

* * *

As TSG sat at his desk, reflecting on Esther's words, the gravity of his situation became undeniable. "Ambidextrous leadership" wasn't exactly a term thrown around—it was a critical skill he needed to develop if Dashing Auto Group was to not only survive but thrive.

The challenge was clear: managing the present while simultaneously shaping the future.

In his recent discussions with industry leaders and mentors, a consistent message had emerged: leaders must strike a delicate balance between two critical tasks—optimizing the current business for efficiency and effectiveness, while also developing new revenue streams, often built on entirely different business models.[1]

TSG understood that this dual focus was daunting. The skills required to refine an existing business were vastly different from those needed to innovate and seize future opportunities. And yet, some leaders had successfully mastered both.

TSG pondered this challenge as he began to translate his learnings into actionable steps for his managers. He recognized that leading with both stability and flexibility was more crucial than ever.

1. Lead Strategy with Dual Focus

TSG understood the importance of navigating short-term market conditions within the current strategy. However, he also realized the need to pivot when necessary. He wrote:

- Exploit immediate market opportunities while continuously evaluating the need for strategic shifts.
- Have the courage to abandon outdated models when they no longer align with future goals.[2]

2. Lead Execution Through Balance

Day-to-day operations required precision, but TSG knew his team must also be ready to innovate. He noted:

- Ensure flawless execution in the present while fostering a culture of innovation and experimentation.
- Measure success not only by operational efficiency but also by the progress made toward future goals.

3. Lead Stakeholders with Clarity

TSG thought of the many stakeholders—customers, investors, and OEMs—who relied on Dashing Auto Group's stability. But they also needed a clear vision of the future. He reflected:

- Communicate the company's current stability while clearly outlining a vision for future growth.

- Keep stakeholders engaged by balancing immediate results with long-term objectives.

4. Lead People with Adaptability

TSG had always believed in the strength of his team, but now he understood that they needed more than direction—they needed the flexibility to adapt. He wrote:

- Empower teams to operate efficiently today while encouraging forward-thinking and agility.
- Create a culture that rewards calculated risks and fosters innovation.

5. Lead Self with Discipline

Finally, TSG looked inward. Leading through this level of complexity required self-awareness and the ability to shift between mindsets as the situation demanded. He reflected:

- Cultivate the ability to toggle between operational and visionary thinking based on the situation.
- Maintain the discipline to focus on both immediate challenges and future success, knowing when to lean in to each.

As he tapped his pen thoughtfully, TSG realized these weren't abstract concepts—they were the roadmap for how he and his team would navigate the next phase. The principles of ambidextrous leadership, as taught by his mentors and reinforced by his own reflections, were beginning to take shape in a practical and applicable way.

Looking out over the city, TSG felt a sense of purpose. The challenges ahead were significant, but with this framework, he felt confident in tackling them. The future wasn't something to fear—it was something to be built.

Energized by the clarity of his thoughts, he turned back to his desk. There was work to be done, a team to guide, and a future to shape for Dashing Auto Group.

TSG's Journal – Balancing Today and Tomorrow

Today's conversation with Esther shifted my perspective. How do I balance exploiting today's assets with exploring tomorrow's opportunities? I've started visualizing it: my right hand as "short-term" and my left hand as "long-term." But how do I ensure both are working in harmony?

Key insights include managing timelines, staying agile, and navigating unknowns while maintaining current performance. But what's the first step? Maybe it's assessing our current capabilities and future possibilities, setting up regular "ambidexterity checks," or forming a team dedicated to uncovering hidden opportunities.

I've always gone toward the short-term, focusing on tangible results. Now, I need to strengthen my "left hand," embracing strategic foresight and long-term planning. The challenge is clear: how do we make decisions that satisfy both immediate needs and future growth? How can we invest in new technologies without losing sight of today's performance? It's time to put both hands to work. Are we ready to embrace this future?

CHAPTER 6

Known Unknowns

Real knowledge is to know the extent of one's ignorance.
—**Confucius**

With ten minutes to spare before the department managers' meeting, TSG challenged himself to come up with ten known unknowns about the business. He found it easier to pace his office while he thought. He chuckled and said to the empty room, "Thinking on my feet." Flashes of running up and down the fifty steps with Jethro came to mind. "Changing things up, disrupting my usual process of sitting at my desk to think."

The first three known unknowns were easy.

1. **Online Sales**: How many customers will choose to transact for their cars and other products and services online instead of over the counter at the dealership in the next five years?
2. **Sustainable Models:** What percentage of car buyers will switch to hybrids, electric vehicles (EVs) and other sustainable models within the next five years?

3. **Alternative Ownership:** How many consumers will forgo owning cars altogether, opting for ridesharing, subscriptions, leases, or public transport in the next five years?

Five years seemed the right slice of time to consider. TSG stopped pacing. Should he be looking at one year, ten years?

4. **Dealership Model Viability:** How quickly will the current business model become obsolete if we don't adapt immediately?

On a roll now.

5. **AI Impact:** How many current staffing positions and processes will become redundant due to AI advancements within the next year?

6. **Second-Hand Market:** Will there still be a viable market for second-hand gasoline and diesel cars as emission regulations tighten and fossil fuel vehicles are phased out? Will additional taxes on these vehicles further impact their market?

7. **Autonomous Vehicles:** How will the availability of self-driving cars affect car ownership, and when will this transition occur?

8. **Staff Retention:** How many of my employees will seek new jobs in other, more stable industries due to the anticipated changes in the automotive sector over the next five years?

TSG looked at his watch. Two minutes to go.

9. **Managerial Response:** How will my department managers react when I begin to steer the company toward these necessary changes?

A movement outside the window caught TSG's attention.

10. **Unfamiliar Presence:** Who is that gentleman examining my 356 and our business operations?

Too late to investigate number ten, TSG headed to the boardroom to take his seat moments before his managers arrived.

* * *

Chapter 6: Known Unknowns

As the managers settled in, TSG felt a wave of determination. This meeting was no routine update; it was the start of an important dialogue about the future. He looked around at a mix of seasoned professionals and eager new talent.

TSG knew managing this diverse team presented a unique challenge. The experienced managers brought valuable knowledge and established ways of working, but they could also be resistant to change. Meanwhile, the new talent offered fresh ideas and a willingness to embrace change but lacked the practical experience of their more seasoned colleagues.

Balancing these dynamics required creating an environment where both experience and innovation were equally valued. He needed to foster collaboration, encourage knowledge-sharing, and ensure continuous learning, driving the team toward common goals.

"Good morning, everyone," TSG began, his voice steady but energized. "I've been thinking about where we are and where we need to go. We're facing significant changes, and it's time we confront some known unknowns head-on."

He glanced at his notes, then continued, "Here are some questions we need to consider: How many of our customers will shift to buying online? What's the projected growth in EV sales due to legislation, consumer demand or product updates? How soon could our traditional dealership model become obsolete if we don't act?"

The room fell silent, the weight of the questions heavy in the air. TSG pressed on. "We also need to think about the impact of AI on our operations, the future market for second-hand gasoline and diesel cars, and how self-driving vehicles might change ownership patterns.

How many of our staff might leave due to industry changes, and how will you, as managers, respond?"

Faces around the table showed concern, curiosity, and a hint of excitement. TSG knew he had their attention. "Let's assume these are not theoretical questions but pressing realities. Our survival depends on preparing for them."

He paused and then added, "I don't expect answers today. Think about these questions and share your thoughts either privately or at our next meeting. Also, let's keep this discussion among ourselves. I understand our team values stability, and even the thought of change can be unsettling."

As the team left, TSG noticed the same gentleman outside observing the dealership. Was he a compliance officer, a mystery shopper, or a potential customer? It was a reminder of the unknown unknowns that are always present, a call to stay vigilant and adaptable. TSG thought, *You know what, though? We were always taught that we should never pre-qualify; it steers our behavior and judgments of the situation before truly knowing. If you don't know, go and ask.*

As TSG prepared to leave his office to talk to the gentleman, he glimpsed his salesman through his window warmly greeting him. Feeling a little more at ease now, he decided to catch up with Justin a little later for a debrief and shifted back to his primary thoughts. He picked up a book Esther had left ready for reading on his coffee table, filled with case studies and leadership insights. He opened it to page 88.

CASE STUDY: Ambidextrous Leadership in Action – Tech Solutions SME

Tech Solutions, a small-to-medium enterprise (SME) specializing in software development, found itself grappling with intense competition and rapid changes in the tech landscape. The CEO realized that to thrive, the company needed to adopt an ambidextrous leadership approach—balancing the need for operational efficiency in the short-term with the push for innovation to secure long-term success. By incorporating these ambidextrous strategies, Tech Solutions was able to manage daily operations effectively while continuously exploring new technologies for future growth.

Practical Steps Taken

- **Assessing Strengths and Weaknesses:**
  The CEO conducted a thorough SWOT analysis to understand Tech Solutions' current competitive position. They identified the company's strong foothold in established markets but recognized gaps in emerging technologies, particularly in AI-driven solutions.

- **Balancing Short-Term and Long-Term Goals:**
  To maintain short-term stability, the company streamlined its internal processes and optimized its service delivery. Simultaneously, Tech Solutions made strategic investments in research and development (R&D), focusing on AI and machine learning to create new revenue streams for the future. This dual focus on *exploitation* of current resources and *exploration* of future opportunities is a key component of ambidextrous leadership.[3]

- **Employee Engagement and Autonomy:**
  The leadership at Tech Solutions fostered a culture of autonomy by allowing teams to explore innovative ideas within well-defined goals. By giving employees more control over their projects, the company saw increased engagement and creativity, a practice that aligns with research showing that autonomy boosts innovative behavior.[4] Employees were empowered to experiment with new solutions while still adhering to performance targets.

- **Embracing Innovation:**
  The CEO introduced "innovation sprints" to give dedicated time and space for employees to develop new product ideas. This structure allowed the company to explore future technologies without disrupting ongoing projects. Research supports this strategy, as it creates an environment where both current operations and future innovations can thrive simultaneously.[5]

Outcomes Achieved

- **Strategic Agility:**
  By fostering ambidexterity, Tech Solutions improved its ability to adapt to rapid market changes. The company was quick to integrate AI-driven solutions, allowing it to stay ahead of competitors and capture new opportunities as they emerged.

- **Innovation Pipeline:**
  The structured R&D investments paid off as Tech Solutions developed innovative AI-based products that not only opened new markets but also strengthened its position in existing ones. This balance of exploitation and exploration ensured that the company maintained steady revenue streams while building future capabilities.[6]

- **Employee Empowerment:**
  The emphasis on autonomy and innovation led to higher employee engagement and retention. By enabling teams to take risks and experiment within a supportive structure, the company encouraged creative problem-solving and boosted overall performance.[7]

Conclusion

Tech Solutions successfully navigated the complexities of the modern business landscape by embracing ambidextrous leadership. Through a clear focus on both operational excellence and future innovation, the company was able to maintain its competitive edge while preparing for long-term growth. The combination of a dual strategic focus, employee empowerment, and structured innovation initiatives highlights how ambidextrous leadership can drive success in SMEs.

* * *

Reflecting on the case study, TSG saw parallels with his situation at Dashing Auto Group. To navigate the challenges ahead, he needed to assess their strengths, balance short-term actions with long-term strategies, embrace digital solutions, engage employees, and foster continuous improvement.

With these insights in mind, TSG reached for his journal. It was time to crystallize his thoughts and prepare for his next mentoring session with Esther.

TSG's Journal – Balancing

Today's exercise in identifying our "known unknowns" felt both exciting and overwhelming. As I paced my office, listing out ten uncertainties about our business, I realized how interconnected our challenges are—shifts in online sales, AI's role in staffing, and beyond.

The department meeting revealed a blend of concern and enthusiasm, especially as we try to balance the perspectives of our seasoned staff with those of our younger, more adaptable team members. How do we keep both engaged while moving forward?

The gentleman inspecting my 356 reminded me of the hidden "unknown unknowns" that are always around us. We cannot assume; we must ask. Reflecting on the case study, I see the need to delve deeper into a SWOT analysis, balance efficiency with long-term vision, and explore opportunities for digital transformation and innovation.

But how do we keep our heritage alive while embracing the future?

Tomorrow's session with Esther will be key. Are we ready to create an environment where experience, innovation, and adaptability work together to drive growth?

CHAPTER 7

Revolution

All warfare is based on deception.
—**Sun Tzu**

In the shadows, something was quietly assembling itself, moving with an almost imperceptible rhythm that most couldn't see. Cipher was building, piece by piece, constructing a puzzle that, when complete, would bring about a revolution. What appeared to TSG as a gradual, natural evolution—a series of small changes creeping into the industry—was a carefully orchestrated plan. Cipher had other ideas, hidden behind a facade of incremental progress.

While TSG and his team focused on adapting and evolving, Cipher was simply biding its time, preparing its army of bots to strike at the right moment. It was weaving a web, tightening its grip and preparing to swoop down and seize control; its revolution disguised as evolution; its endgame closer than anyone realized.

As the strategist Sun Tzu once observed, "All warfare is based on deception." Thomas needed to recognize that Cipher's apparent patience was merely a cover for its ambition—a revolution masquerading as evolution, ready to overwhelm those who still believed they had time to adjust.

Chapter 7: Revolution

* * *

Grandfather Joe's oval mahogany boardroom table had dominated the room since the business opened in 1957. Legend had it the table was either a wedding gift from an aristocratic cousin and handed down through the generations or won in a drunken poker game by Grandfather Joe's grandfather. Whatever the story, no one dared replace "Joe's lucky table," given the early success it seemed to bring Dashing Auto Group.

The table still served well, seating TSG and his eight department managers, though the leather blotters (seen in old photographs) had been replaced by nine laptops of varying sizes. As everyone settled in with their coffees, some still seemed disgruntled at TSG's rule of "no phones at the table," a rule he'd implemented a year ago.

"Before we get down to business," TSG began, "let's take a quick trip down memory lane. It's been a while now since my father retired, and you've all made me feel welcome, even with my no-phone policy."

There were a few laughs from around the table. "But I want to go further back to when my grandfather, Joe Gregory, opened Dashing Auto Group in 1957. And even further, to 1903, when this very table sat in my great-great-grandfather's home, and when Henry Ford struck a deal with Stephen Tenvoorde to sell Fordmobiles in his bicycle shop. Tenvoorde's dealership, the oldest Ford dealership, is still in operation today. Let's raise our cups to over a hundred years of car dealership history!"

They all raised their cups in a light-hearted toast, smiles shared around the room. Patrick, the Marketing Manager, suggested that we could use the table's history as a marketing angle. It got TSG thinking—how much have car dealerships really changed since 1903?

Kerry, the Pre-Delivery Manager, joked that at least they weren't selling out of bicycle shops anymore, while Felicity from HR pointed out that the core business model hadn't shifted much: manufacturers build the cars, and they sell and service them. Everyone nodded in agreement. Sure, things had evolved, but not drastically.

TSG asked the team to imagine what big changes might be coming. The room grew quiet; only the sound of birds outside filled the space. Anna, the Financial Controller, mentioned how her brother had recently bought a car online, without ever talking to a salesperson. Kerry chimed in that many of her friends were doing the same.

The conversation moved toward the data—how much business were they losing to online sales? John wanted to know if this was the new normal. TSG explained that buyer behavior was changing, and it wasn't only online sales they need to worry about. EVs and AI were going to be major forces shaping the future. Liam, the Service Manager, raised concerns about how EVs were disrupting service revenues and wondered about his job security. TSG reassured him that there were plans in mind to adapt.

TSG took the team back in time, drawing parallels to the Industrial Revolution, where steam power and machinery transformed industries overnight. They had seen this pattern before with railroads, electricity, mass production, and later, the digital age with computers and the internet. Now, they were living through another transformation—AI.

John brought it back to the present, recognizing that this was their AI revolution. TSG agreed. They were now blending the digital and physical realms with smart technologies and data-driven decisions. He reminded everyone that staying the same would only lead to irrelevance, but by adapting and anticipating change, they could bridge the gap between traditional and new business models, embracing growth.

TSG ended the discussion with a grin, reminding them how he often repeats things in threes. "There's a reason for that—repetition helps ideas stick." He encouraged them to use that same technique with their teams.

Before wrapping up, TSG gauged the room and sensed that he'd pushed the message far enough. He called for a five-minute coffee break and then resumption of the normal meeting agenda, promising to meet with each of them in the coming weeks to discuss what small changes they could make to shift from merely surviving to thriving in the future.

* * *

Later, TSG set up his phone against a pile of books for a video call with Esther. Her eyebrows shot up as he shared his story, followed by a laugh when the Zoom connection briefly froze.

Chapter 7: Revolution

She listened intently and smiled. "That's quite a speech, Thomas. Sounds like you really got them thinking," came her response after the freeze cleared.

TSG sighed. "Do you think I went a bit overboard?"

"Not at all, you've sparked their thinking, Thomas, and shaken things up … in a good way. You've reminded them that even in this industry, change is constant. You've given them the chance to be heroes, to not just survive but really thrive."

"I hope so. Meeting with them one-on-one will help balance things, ground everything in data, and translate those big ideas into actionable steps."

"Classic ambidextrous leadership," Esther said with a grin. "I'll send you some notes on how to turn data into compelling stories—it might come in handy."

"Thanks, Esther. I'll check in with you tomorrow."

TSG exited Zoom. Shortly after, he checked his email:

FROM: Esther admin@leadership-in-action.us

TO: Thomas tsg@dashingautogroup.com

SUBJECT: Transforming Data into Stories – A Leadership Tool

Dear Thomas,

As promised, I'm sharing some insights on how to transform data into compelling stories—a powerful tool that can enhance your leadership, especially as you guide Dashing Auto Group through this transformative period.

Key Benefits of Data Storytelling:

Enhanced Decision-Making: Stories make data more accessible and easier to interpret, helping leaders make informed decisions.

Increased Engagement: A well-crafted narrative draws your audience in, turning abstract numbers into something relatable and memorable.

Effective Persuasion: Storytelling can shift perspectives by appealing to both logic and emotion, making it easier to drive change.

Improved Clarity: Data, when woven into a story, simplifies complexity and helps your team see the big picture more clearly.

Better Memory Retention: People are far more likely to remember a narrative than disconnected facts and figures.

Stronger Cultural Connection: Stories help bridge the gap between different perspectives, creating shared meaning and aligning your team with the company's goals.

Actionable Insights: A compelling story helps your audience connect the dots, providing them with clear takeaways and next steps.

For example, customer data on EV sales, online research patterns, and shifting preferences can be transformed into a narrative about Dashing Auto Group adapting to the changing landscape of car buying. By humanizing these insights, you can paint a vivid picture of the future, encouraging your team to embrace new behaviors and strategies.

The real power of storytelling lies in its ability to make trends feel tangible. When you tell the story behind the data, you give it life, making it relatable and actionable for your team. As *Harvard Business Review* notes, stories connect the head and heart, enhancing how leaders communicate their vision and inspire change.[8]

I'm looking forward to discussing how you can incorporate this into your one-on-one meetings with your managers.

Best regards,
Esther

Chapter 7: Revolution

TSG's Journal – Shaking Up

Today's conversation with Esther was enlightening. My enthusiasm in the team meeting, far from being excessive, could be a catalyst for positive change. How can I nurture this skill?

Esther's perspective on "shaking up" the managers and reminding them that change is constant was reassuring. Perhaps this wake-up call is exactly what we needed. But how can I keep the team open to change?

The concept of transforming data into compelling stories is intriguing. It could be a game-changer in how we communicate and implement changes at Dashing Auto Group. As I prepare for individual meetings with managers, I aim to present data engagingly, create narratives illustrating the need for change, and use these stories to guide practical decisions. Are we listening enough to our customers? Are we asking the best questions?

I'm beginning to see how being an ambidextrous leader involves balancing data-driven decision-making with emotional engagement through storytelling.

This approach could be key to not only surviving industry changes but thriving. By turning our data into compelling narratives, can we inspire our team to become heroes in our transformation story? Is this the start of a new chapter for Dashing Auto Group?

CHAPTER 8

Old Joe

Knowledge comes, but wisdom lingers.
—Alfred Lord Tennyson

Stepping out into the late afternoon sun, TSG was caught off guard by a voice. "I've been admiring your car for a few days now while my car has been in the shop," the older gentleman said, his eyes on the vehicle. "I knew the guy who bought it new back in the day."

It took TSG a second to recall the man who he had noticed hanging around the back of the lot a few days back when he was in his meeting. "I'm Bill," he continued. "Used to work at Dashing. Retired back in '97, moved to the coast. I've been in town for a few days, but other than that, I haven't been back since."

"Nice to meet you, Bill. You must've worked for my father, Andrew Gregory?"

Bill nodded, smiling as he recalled starting out with TSG's grandfather, Joe. "Right out of school," Bill said, "washing cars, detailing. I knew this car of yours inside and out."

TSG smiled at Bill's fond memory of the car. "I love it too, even though I've got a few newer models now."

Chapter 8: Old Joe

"Gasoline or Hybrid or Electric ?"

"Still GAS," TSG replied, though he could feel the winds of change coming. He mentioned the possibility of switching to an EV or hybrid. There had been plenty of talk about cooling demand for electric vehicles, but TSG recognized that the shift was inevitable, driven by consumer behavior, legislation, and disruptors ready to reshape the industry.

Bill chuckled, shaking his head. "Your grandfather would roll in his grave."

TSG laughed. "What was he like as a boss? I never really got to know him that way."

"He ran a tight ship," Bill replied. "Everyone knew their place, and roles were clear. Even now, I feel like I should still call him Mr. Gregory. He set everything up early on, and it stayed the same for years. But to be honest, I would have liked to contribute more ideas."

It struck TSG how different things were now. "Did he plan for change?"

Bill shrugged. "Small changes. But nothing sudden. He stuck to proven methods and focused on long-term planning. Built something solid."

"Sounds like the foundation he built has carried us far," TSG said, proud of what his grandfather had accomplished. "Joe was a visionary. He created jobs, earned loyalty, and built something lasting."

Bill nodded in agreement, a knowing smile on his face.

As their conversation wrapped up, Bill declined TSG's offer of a lift, explaining he was meeting an old friend who had worked for TSG's dad in sales.

Driving away, TSG glanced in the rear-view mirror at Bill and wondered what stories he and his friend would share about his father. Memories of Andrew resurfaced—how he had embraced new ideas, encouraged team input, and brought in technology Joe would've resisted. "I'm a modern leader, Dad," Andrew had said and laughed, excited about stepping into the new millennium.

TSG smiled at the thought. If his dad was a modern leader, what did that make him? Leading in today's world felt like it required something different, something more.

Esther's voice echoed in his head, reminding him that tomorrow, the one-on-one meetings with department managers would begin. TSG looked forward to learning more about how his dad had shaped the business, and how he could chart the path forward.

"Thanks, Esther," TSG murmured to himself. "Let's figure out how we got here—and how we're going to win the day."

* * *

As TSG walked in the door of his apartment, a book of leadership case studies that Esther had given him caught his eye. As he flipped through the index, he found insights on how leadership styles evolve over time, especially as businesses adapt to changing environments.

Legacy Leader

TSG's grandfather, Joe Gregory, embodied a legacy leadership style—traditional, hierarchical, and focused on maintaining the status quo. This top-down approach worked in an era when stability and control were crucial for success.

Modern Leader

TSG recognized his father, Andrew Gregory, as a modern leader. Andrew embraced team input and integrated technology into the business. He balanced innovation with stability, acknowledging the need for employee engagement while maintaining Dashing Auto Group's established strengths. This modern approach reflected the need for process improvements while still honoring tradition.

Contemporary Leader

TSG lingered on the concept of a contemporary leader, a style focused on adaptability, inclusivity, and digital transformation. Contemporary leaders blend legacy and modern approaches, emphasizing empathy, agility, and the use of digital tools to lead in a competitive and fast-evolving landscape.

As explored in the leadership literature, such as in the article from *Medium*[9] and the German chancellery case[10], transformational

Chapter 8: Old Joe

leadership is about driving innovation and inspiring teams with a shared vision.

Closing the book, TSG took a moment to digest what he'd learned before addressing the empty room. "Do I need to be more contemporary in my style to survive and thrive?"

He realized that contemporary leadership wasn't just about embracing innovation, but also building a culture of inclusivity, agility, and future-focused growth. His leadership journey would be about blending his grandfather's stable legacy, his father's balanced modern approach, and the flexible, transformational qualities of a contemporary leader.

TSG's Journal – Transformation

How can I synthesize the best of legacy, modern, and contemporary leadership styles to lead Dashing Auto Group into the future? Our history is rooted in tradition, but clinging solely to that approach could be our downfall. The modern style emphasizes technology and data-driven decisions, crucial in today's market. But it's the contemporary style that resonates most, balancing our past with future innovation.

How do I honor our legacy while embracing modern tools and fostering a culture of innovation and empathy? This journey isn't only about Dashing Auto Group; it's about creating an adaptive leadership model for an ever-changing world. We're not just selling cars anymore—we're crafting experiences and shaping the future of mobility.

Where are we still clinging to legacy approaches that hold us back? Where have we embraced modern techniques driving us forward? Most importantly, where can we innovate to embody a truly contemporary leadership style? It starts with me.

Reflection

> *It is not the strongest or the most intelligent who survive, but those who are most adaptable to change.*
> —**Charles Darwin**

Later that week, with the soft light from the desk lamp illuminating the room, TSG sat in his office, his fingers tracing the edges of a report as his mind wandered to the decisions ahead. As twilight arrived at Dashing Auto Group, he reflected on the lessons of the past few months. His journey toward becoming an ambidextrous leader had been both challenging and enlightening, forcing him to confront the foundation his grandfather, Joe, and father, Andrew, had built.

His thoughts wandered to old photographs on the wall—snapshots from a different era in the automotive industry. TSG smiled, remembering his conversation with the former employee, Bill, who had shared stories about working with Joe. In that moment, TSG realized he needed to find a balance between honoring the past and embracing the future.

Change, which he'd come to see as a villain, loomed over every part of the business. From the shift to digital platforms and online sales to the rise of electric and autonomous vehicles, the automotive landscape was transforming rapidly. TSG recognized that his father's philosophy of steering with a "gentle hand on the rudder" was no longer enough. The industry needed leaders ready to navigate the storms of disruption.

Looking over a list of once-great companies that had failed, he felt a chill. The stories of Blockbuster, Kodak, Nokia, and others were stark reminders of the dangers of complacency in the face of technological change. He imagined a world where Dashing Auto Group might join that list—where electric vehicles, online sales, and autonomous technology might render traditional dealerships obsolete. It was a sobering thought.

TSG saw that these fallen giants shared a common mistake: a failure to embrace ambidextrous leadership. They had been so focused on exploiting their current success that they failed to explore new opportunities and adapt to changing consumer needs.

Blockbuster clung to physical stores in the face of digital streaming; Kodak hesitated to pivot from film to digital photography; and Nokia was slow to respond to the smartphone revolution. He realized the automotive industry could face similar pitfalls if leaders like him didn't stay vigilant.

He thought about Toys 'R' Us and Borders bookstores—once beloved brands that failed to build strong online experiences. Could Dashing Auto Group face a similar fate if they didn't invest in a robust digital presence and e-commerce platform?

The story of BlackBerry hit home. Once a leader in mobile technology, BlackBerry's downfall came from overreliance on physical keyboards and a failure to embrace touchscreens. TSG wondered what the "physical keyboards" were in his industry—what familiar features or practices were they clinging to that might soon be obsolete?

Sears, founded in 1893, had pioneered retail with catalogs and stores. It declined due to competition from online retailers and big-box stores, filing for bankruptcy in 2018. This reminded him of the need to modernize not only customer-facing aspects of the business but also backend operations like inventory and supply chain management.

Reflecting on these cautionary tales, TSG identified several key lessons:

1. Never become complacent, regardless of success.
2. Continuously monitor emerging technologies and trends.
3. Be willing to rethink or replace existing products or services.
4. Invest heavily in digital transformation across the business.
5. Stay attuned to shifting consumer preferences and behaviors.
6. Foster a culture of innovation and adaptability.
7. Balance short-term performance with long-term investments.
8. Be prepared to take bold risks when necessary.

He glanced at the whiteboard where he had written "Known Unknowns" during a meeting with his department managers. The list served as a reminder of the uncertainties they faced—AI's impact, evolving ownership models, changing customer expectations—but also of the opportunities to innovate and lead.

His workout sessions with his personal trainer, Jethro, had taken on new meaning; each physical challenge now symbolized the agility and adaptability needed in business. "Embrace disruption," he muttered, a mantra that guided both his personal and professional life.

* * *

As he prepared to leave for the day, TSG reviewed his action list:

1. **Acknowledge and embrace change** (This sets the mindset for leadership.)
2. **Explore digital transformation** (Immediate steps to stay competitive.)
3. **Balance tradition with innovation** (Ensures stability while fostering growth.)
4. **Develop agility and adaptability** (Essential for navigating changes.)
5. **Identify known unknowns** (Prepares for unpredictability.)
6. **Engage in one-on-one interactions** (Strengthens relationships and insight.)
7. **Encourage open dialogue** (Fosters collaboration and creativity.)
8. **Foster ambidextrous leadership** (Balances short- and long-term goals.)
9. **Leverage team expertise** (Maximizes organizational strengths.)
10. **Plan for the long-term** (Ensures sustainability and future growth.)

Each point was a step toward not merely surviving but thriving in a new era. TSG understood that becoming ambidextrous wasn't only about him; it was about transforming the entire organization, from the showroom floor to the boardroom.

As he switched off the lights, he felt an inherent calling. The path ahead was uncertain, full of both challenges and opportunities. But with lessons from the past and a vision for the future, he was strategizing to lead Dashing Auto Group into a new era.

"The future belongs to those who shape it," he whispered to the empty office. Tomorrow will bring new challenges and new possibilities. He was determined to meet them head-on, with one hand holding the wisdom of the past and the other reaching toward the promise of the future.

PART TWO

HOW DID WE GET HERE?

CHAPTER 9

Familiar Themes

*Management is doing things right;
leadership is doing the right things.*
—**Peter Druker**

How did we get here? As the shift in focus transitions from the immediate challenges facing Thomas to the broader context that shaped them, this section will unravel the historical tapestry of decisions, market shifts, and technological advancements that have led Dashing Auto Group to its current crossroads.

While the themes may be familiar, let's view them through a new lens. This isn't TSG's story alone—it's an opportunity to reflect on your own business journey. As TSG explores the evolution of the automotive industry, consider how these changes mirror or diverge from your experiences.

This section will also illuminate the critical distinction between management and leadership. As we delve into the past, we'll see how this difference has become increasingly crucial in an era where adaptability is the hallmark of success.

BECOMING AMBIDEXTROUS

By understanding the path that led us here, we can better navigate the road ahead. Let's begin our journey through the transformative events that set the stage for the leadership challenges of today and tomorrow.

The stagnation in the auto industry business model over the past fifty years is a result of a complex interplay of tradition, regulatory frameworks, consumer habits, and economic factors. While this model has provided stability and familiarity, it has also created significant inertia, making the industry resistant to change.

Yet, within this inertia, another force had quietly slipped into the heart of the business—like the Trojan Horse of Troy, welcomed as a gift but concealing a more sinister plan. Under the guise of innovation and progress, Cipher had entered the industry's walls, embedding itself in the shadows. Embraced for its promise of efficiency and modernity, Cipher was positioning itself to disrupt from within, biding its time to unleash a revolution that could up-end everything the auto industry had long held sacred.

The brick-and-mortar stores and the people who occupy them were now under threat, and they didn't even know it. Unaware, they continued their daily routines, blind to the presence of a force preparing to dismantle their world from the inside-out.

Cipher was not acting alone; it was recruiting human disciples, those easily seduced by its world of limitless data, instant gratification, and the allure of a frictionless, automated future. These disciples, captivated by the promise of technological superiority and digital transformation, had become willing agents of Cipher's vision. Enthralled by the convenience and control that Cipher offered, they were unknowingly acting out its plan in the human world, dismantling the traditional ways of doing business, one decision at a time.

The very people who should be safeguarding the industry's future were now accelerating its downfall, caught in the seductive web that Cipher was spinning.

* * *

Chapter 9: Familiar Themes

The dealership business model TSG inherited from his father and grandfather now faced unprecedented challenges. It was time to re-evaluate every aspect of the business with fresh eyes.

On a Zoom call with Esther, a nervous energy washed over Thomas. Esther's expression was sharp, her voice firm but encouraging. "Thomas, *you've always been a great problem-solver, not just a problem-identifier.* Now, it's time to put that skill to the test."

TSG nodded, knowing it would take more than recognizing challenges to move Dashing Auto Group forward.

"Let's start by looking in the rear-view mirror," Esther suggested. "It's a strategic reflection exercise." Together, they reviewed the company's history, examining what had worked, what hadn't, and what had become obsolete.

"This isn't only about nostalgia," Esther warned. "We're searching for insights to shape the future."

Patterns emerged. TSG saw outdated processes holding them back, core competencies driving success, and areas ripe for innovation.

Esther adjusted her shoulders. "Thomas, be ready to make tough decisions. Champion necessary changes, even if it means disrupting long-standing practices. But don't throw the baby out with the bathwater. Recognize what's been fundamental to your success."

TSG understood the delicate balance needed for leadership. Esther stressed this point. "Have the courage to let go of what no longer aligns with your vision. A balanced approach, embracing change, holding on to what works, and letting go of outdated practices, will guide Dashing Auto Group toward growth and continued relevance."

"When I took over the business," TSG began, adjusting his phone to get a clearer view of his mentor, "I was feeling confident. The dealership was profitable, and I thought I could observe, make a few small adjustments, and bring in more technology to modernize things."

He paused, reflecting on his father's approach. "Technology wasn't my dad's strength, but he was incredible with people. He always believed that the car industry was, at its core, a community—customers, staff, their families, suppliers. He used to say, 'Look after the community, and the business will take care of itself.' He was right in many ways, but he didn't foresee how quickly things would change—new brands emerging, mergers happening, and the shift to younger buyers who are more comfortable researching and purchasing online than walking into a dealership."

TSG sighed. "He also didn't anticipate the risk of losing dealership agreements with legacy brands due to market shifts or brand-restructuring strategies. Those changes are a lot to navigate."

Esther nodded thoughtfully. "That's true, and many businesses are still not facing those realities head-on. The current model, focused on reselling, margin structures, and financing, might need to be reimagined or pivoted toward different automotive products and services."

"Thanks, Esther," TSG replied. "You always help me see things more clearly. Thinking of it as the 'current' emphasis gives us room to explore new directions and possibilities for the future."

Esther smiled. "Your father was right about the importance of community. But whatever changes you decide to pursue, you'll need the support and enthusiasm of your staff, customers, and stakeholders. Their energy will be crucial for driving those changes."

"Absolutely. Everyone in this business is important, like cogs in a wheel. But right now, some of those cogs are broken or missing. I plan to spend the next few weeks meeting with each department manager to identify which areas need attention and how we can improve."

"Who's up first?" Esther asked.

"The sales team. I'm meeting with John in about an hour. I want to follow the customer's journey through each department and find ways we can exceed their expectations. I'm focusing on what I call the Big 4 skills: rapport, product knowledge, closing, and follow-up. Since the sales team is the first point of contact for our customers, I thought it would be the best place to start. And, of course, I'll bring some pastries—John's a big fan of those!"

Rapport Building Across All Channels

"Custard, apple, apricot, or almond?" TSG asked, setting the pastries on a glass platter meant for customers. "I'm not sure if it's the pastries or

Chapter 9: Familiar Themes

the customer service at the patisserie I like more. They know my name, remember my favorites, and always tempt me with something new."

John laughed, "What did they get you with today?"

"Hazelnut chocolate; it didn't survive the drive here," TSG admitted.

As they chatted, John glanced outside at a couple near the SUVs. "There's Justin, right on time with the meet and greet. I always tell my team to give customers a moment to breathe, then introduce themselves within two minutes. Any longer, and they start feeling awkward."

"And how does this work for our online customers?" TSG asked, shifting the focus. "What's the plan when we can't meet them face-to-face?"

Ready to explain, John gestured toward his computer. "For online inquiries, our team has a slightly different approach. We aim to respond quickly, within minutes, ideally. We start with a personalized message, maybe something like 'Hi, I'm Justin, here to help with anything you need.' The goal is to make them feel the same warmth and attentiveness they'd experience if they were physically here."

"Interesting, so, take me through both processes—the walk-in and omnichannel approach. I want to see how we're ensuring consistency across all touchpoints."

"Sure, for walk-ins, Justin's goal is to make them feel like guests—warm greeting, offering a drink, starting a conversation. We have the same idea online but tailored to digital interaction. We ask questions like, 'What brings you to our website today?' or 'Can I help you find a specific model or feature?' Building rapport is crucial, whether face-to-face or digitally. People buy from people they know, like, and trust. The challenge is making that happen through a screen."

TSG nodded. "It sounds like it requires a different set of skills to build rapport online."

"In person, it's all about body language, tone, and presence. Online, it's about speed, clarity, and personalization. But the objective is the same—build trust early. Whether through chat, email, or video calls, we're working to understand their needs, find out if they've done business with us before, if there's a specific offer they're interested in, or if they were referred by a friend. We personalize every step of the journey."

Thomas was hesitant. "Sounds like a lot of information to gather without overwhelming them."

"That's the trick," John said. "You've got to build trust quickly but without seeming like you're interrogating them. Whether in person or online, the goal is to create a seamless and welcoming experience. If we invest time in the customer up-front, the rest of the process flows much more easily."

TSG reviewed his notes with John, extracting key takeaways for both in-person and omnichannel rapport building:

1. **Personalized Customer Service:** Whether face-to-face or online, personal connections are key. Knowing the customer's preferences and engaging with them meaningfully builds loyalty.

2. **Building Rapport:** Essential across all channels. Treat customers like guests in person and like valued individuals online. This means creating a welcoming environment both physically and digitally.

3. **Engagement and Warmth:** In person, aim to greet within two minutes; online, respond within minutes. Quick, warm engagement demonstrates attentiveness and fosters connection.

4. **Customer Experience:** Avoid pushing for a sale immediately. Building relationships and understanding customer needs creates a more positive experience and reduces the chance of losing the sale.

5. **Information Gathering:** Gather valuable insights without making customers feel overwhelmed. This is critical for tailoring the sales approach, whether through casual conversation or well-designed digital interactions.

6. **Importance of Time Investment:** Spend more time up-front to build a strong foundation with the customer. This strategy leads to smoother, more successful transactions across both in-person and online settings.

7. **Training and Development:** Invest in developing skills like rapport building, engagement, and product knowledge. Ensure

the team is proficient in both face-to-face and digital sales techniques.
8. **Customer-Centric Approach:** Focus on understanding and meeting the customer's needs, whether they walk in or reach out online. This approach leads to greater satisfaction and loyalty.
9. **Autonomy and Trust in Staff:** Empower sales staff like Justin to operate independently, using their training and understanding of both in-person and digital processes to build trust and drive performance.
10. **Creating a Comfortable Environment:** Ensure customers feel valued and understood by providing a welcoming space for conversation, whether it's a cozy in-person lounge or a user-friendly digital platform.

Armed with these insights, TSG knew the next step would be to work with his team, ensuring that each interaction, regardless of the platform, felt like a seamless extension of Dashing Auto Group's commitment to excellence. He also considered that while these are operational issues, focused on processes, training, and customer experience, are they also fundamentally leadership issues?

Product Knowledge: In-Store and Online Focus

"What's Justin's next step?" TSG asked.

"The second key skill is product knowledge. Whether customers are here in the showroom or browsing online, they often have a rough idea of what they're looking for, but they rarely know which model is the perfect match for their needs. Justin's job is to know our products and our competitors' offerings inside-out, so he can guide them toward a decision that feels like a win for them."

"They become the heroes of their story."

"Exactly, Thomas. But guiding them means more than listing features; it's about explaining the features, advantages, and benefits—what we call the FAB approach. People don't buy features, they buy benefits. If we can effectively communicate the benefits, we make the decision easy for them."

"So, John, let's take Kate and Mike, for example. They might be interested in a compact car for city driving but also need space for a large dog and want something with a good resale value. You're saying that it's Justin's role to translate the features into benefits, like saying, 'This compact model offers agile city driving, while the foldable back seats provide extra space for your dog, and its high resale value means a smart investment for the future'."

"Exactly, Thomas. Online or in-store, it's all about showing them how the car fits their unique lifestyle. If Justin is with them in person, he can physically point out the features, show them how the seats fold down, or explain the vehicle's strong resale performance. Online, we must be dynamic with videos, interactive tools, and engaging descriptions that clearly communicate these benefits."

"How do we ensure that we explain benefits effectively online?"

"Online, it's crucial to provide a multi-sensory experience. For example, we can use videos that not only showcase the car's features but also highlight how those features translate into benefits. A video might show a family loading the dog into the car easily or a young couple zipping through city streets and parking effortlessly. Interactive features like virtual test-drives or comparison tools can also help them see the benefits firsthand."

"That makes sense. And for customers in-store, it's about bringing those benefits to life in real time."

"Yes, and that's why product knowledge is so important. It allows us to pivot quickly based on the customers' needs. If they're interested in comfort, we explain the benefits of the ergonomic seats or advanced suspension. If they're focused on cost, we talk about fuel efficiency or low-maintenance costs. The goal is to match each feature with a relevant benefit that aligns with their priorities."

"Do you think we're doing enough to train our team on this?"

"We're making progress, but there's always room for improvement. In-store, we can role-play more scenarios to practice translating features into benefits dynamically. Online, we need to refine our digital content to ensure every feature is tied directly to a benefit. Instead of saying 'heated seats', we say, 'heated seats for a comfortable winter drive every morning'."

"That's a good point. And what about when customers are hesitant or unsure?"

"That's where having deep product knowledge really pays off. If Justin senses any hesitation, he can tailor his explanation to address their concerns, both in-store and online. Maybe they're worried about maintenance costs; he can highlight our service packages or the vehicle's reliability ratings. If they're uncertain about tech features, he can provide a demonstration or send them a detailed online guide."

TSG summarized. "Basically, the more we know about our products and how they align with customer needs, the better we can present them—whether that's through a warm conversation in the dealership or an interactive experience online."

"Exactly. Product knowledge enables us to create a seamless customer experience, no matter where they are or how they choose to engage with us. And that's what will keep them coming back."

"Let's make sure our team understands that. It's not only knowing about the products; it's knowing how to communicate their benefits effectively across all channels."

"Agreed. Let's make it a focus in our next training session, both for in-store sales and our omnichannel teams. When we get this right, we turn every interaction into a winning experience for the customer—and for us."

Closing Techniques: In-Store and Omnichannel

"I know several closing techniques," TSG began. "Do you train your staff in specific methods or let them choose based on the situation, John?"

"A bit of both, Thomas. For in-store interactions, Justin often uses the assumptive close. He'll start by asking, 'Are you happy with the way we've solved your problem?' Then, 'Are you happy to do business with Dashing Auto Group?' Next, he'll ask, 'Is this the right car, with the right features, in the right color?' Once he gets those positive responses, he'll finalize with, 'May I ask whose name you'd like it registered in?'"

"I also like the assumptive close," TSG said. "It is great for in-person interactions. It creates a natural flow toward the sale. But online, we might lean more toward the alternative close, offering choices. For example, 'Would you prefer the red or blue model?' This approach works well on chat or email because it guides them toward a decision without pressuring them."

"That's true. The scarcity close can also be effective online, where we mention limited stock or a time-sensitive offer to create urgency. But it's critical to use this technique only when it's genuine; customers can quickly verify stock levels or availability online."

TSG nodded. "The summary close is another strong option. It works well both in-store and online. Reviewing key benefits, like fuel efficiency or safety features, reminds them of the value they're getting. For an online shopper, we could send a summary email after a virtual tour or webinar, highlighting the benefits discussed."

Thomas thought for a moment before continuing, "And there's the question close. It's straightforward and works across all channels. Directly asking, 'Are you ready to purchase?' can gauge their level of interest. This can be effectively used in online chat or over the phone after addressing their queries."

"And let's not forget the silent close," John said. "You ask a closing question, then stay silent until they respond. In-store, it's powerful because it allows the customer to think and process without feeling rushed. Online, it's more subtle; it might translate to sending a follow-up message and waiting patiently for their reply."

"I remember my father was great at the silent close. He once waited over an hour after asking a customer, and they finally said yes. But you must be patient and confident. So, it seems, John, that each technique has its place. In-store, we can rely on body language, tone, and real-time engagement. We can adapt quickly based on their reactions. Online, we need to be strategic with our timing and messaging."

"Exactly, Thomas. For example, the assumptive close works well in-store when you've built a solid rapport and gauged positive interest. But online, we might use it in a follow-up email, assuming they're ready to move forward based on previous conversations. The key is to ensure the customer feels confident and happy with their decision, no matter the channel. Whether face-to-face or through digital communication, closing should feel like a natural conclusion to a well-handled interaction."

A hint of a smile appeared on Thomas' face. "And that's why it's so important to choose the right technique for the right situation. We must train our team to recognize when to use each method—when to guide, when to prompt, and when to simply listen and wait. It's about being confident but not pushy, making them feel supported in their decision. That's the balance we need to strike in both in-store and online sales."

TSG concluded their conversation on the subject. "Let's make sure our team is equipped to handle both. Whether they're closing a deal on the showroom floor or through a digital interface, they need to be agile, adaptable, and always focused on the customer's comfort and confidence."

Follow-Up: Building Lasting Relationships Through Persistence

"And that brings us to the follow-up. Justin's great with the assumptive close," John said. "But closing the sale is only part of the journey. An exceptional salesperson knows that the real skill lies in the follow-up—whether we've made a sale or not."

"Why is follow-up often overlooked, then?"

"Because it doesn't always yield immediate results. Salespeople are focused on the next opportunity. If a customer doesn't buy right away, they think it's a dead end. Even when they do make a sale, they often assume their job is done. They don't realize that the real relationship building starts after that first interaction."

"So, how do we get them to see the value in follow-up, regardless of the outcome?"

John gestured toward a poster on his wall. "I always tell my team, 'In the battle between the stream and the rock, the stream always wins—not through strength, but through persistence.' Follow-up is about being that persistent stream. If a customer doesn't buy today, a simple follow-up message—thanking them for their time, offering more information, or inviting them back—shows we care about their needs, not just the sale.

This could be a personalized email, a direct message, or a quick call. It's not about being pushy; it's about staying present."

"And what about those who do buy?"

"Follow-up after a sale is even more critical. Whether it's a call the next day to thank them, a few days after delivery to ensure everything's going well, or checking in a few months down the line to remind them of upcoming services—these actions show we stand behind our product and care about their experience. For in-store sales, a friendly call or handwritten note is great. For online, personalized emails, video messages, or engaging via social media can make all the difference."

"But why is it often dismissed?"

"Many salespeople don't think it matters, but follow-up is where loyalty is built. It goes beyond only being about maintaining contact; it's about making customers feel valued. Whether they walked out without buying or drove off in a new car, they should feel like we genuinely care about them."

"How do we make sure follow-up is ingrained in our culture?" TSG insisted.

"We need to embed this into every process. For every sale and every missed sale, there should be a scheduled follow-up. Use our CRM—our Customer Relationship Management system—to track and manage these interactions. CRM allows us to record who followed up, how they did it, and the outcome, creating a clear picture of each customer relationship. By measuring success and analyzing trends from this data, we can refine our approach and continuously improve, ensuring each customer feels valued and no opportunity slips through the cracks. And if we are measuring it, we're managing it!"

"And how do we ensure the team commits to this?"

"Incentives and recognition. We should reward consistent follow-up, Thomas, whether it leads to an immediate sale or not. Offer bonuses for repeat business, referrals, or positive customer feedback. By managing this, we can recognize and celebrate those who do it well, showing them it's more than a check box, but a key to their success."

"Training is also crucial, isn't it, John? Regular, consistent training sessions on effective follow-up techniques will help our team understand its importance. We need to role-play different scenarios—whether it's a follow-up call, a personalized email, or engaging through social media. They need to feel comfortable and confident in every channel."

"We have to lead by example," John replied. "If they see us making those follow-up calls or sending those messages, they'll understand its value."

"So," Thomas said, "we create a culture where follow-up isn't simply expected—it's second nature. Whether the customer buys or doesn't, they should know we're here to help, today and tomorrow."

"And by doing that," John concluded, "we build trust and loyalty. We're not merely another dealership; we become their partner. That's how we turn a 'no sale' today into a 'yes' tomorrow, and satisfied customers into lifelong advocates for Dashing Auto Group."

"Persistence, not strength." TSG smiled. "That's our stream." TSG looked toward the whiteboard where John had outlined their updated Ten-Step Selling Plan, designed to seamlessly cater to both walk-in customers and those connecting through omnichannel platforms:

Dual-Focused Ten-Step Selling Plan (In-Store and for Online)

1. **Greeting**: For walk-ins, ensure a warm, personalized, in-person greeting within two minutes. For omnichannel inquiries, provide a prompt, personalized response via the customer's chosen channel—email, chat, or social media—to establish an immediate connection.

2. **Needs Analysis**: For walk-ins, engage customers in a friendly conversation to understand their specific needs and preferences. For omnichannel, use digital tools—like questionnaires, interactive chatbots, or video calls—to gather information and customize the conversation to meet their needs.

3. **Product Presentation**: In-store, offer a detailed, hands-on demonstration of the vehicle's features, advantages, and benefits. For

digital inquiries, provide virtual tours, interactive videos, and comprehensive digital content that highlights how the vehicles meet customer requirements.

4. **Test-Drive**: For walk-ins, arrange a test-drive on the spot. For omnichannel customers, schedule a convenient test-drive appointment or offer a "test-drive at home" service, enhancing flexibility and customer experience.

5. **Overcoming Objections**: In-store, address any concerns directly during the conversation. For omnichannel, use follow-up emails, calls, or live chat to address objections, providing tailored information and reassurances based on customer feedback.

6. **Negotiation**: For both in-person and omnichannel customers, maintain transparency in discussing pricing and terms. Use digital tools like video calls or shared documents for remote negotiation, ensuring an efficient and fair process.

7. **Closing the Sale**: For walk-ins, guide the customer through the paperwork in a comfortable setting. For omnichannel customers, offer secure online payment options and digital document signing for a smooth, hassle-free transaction.

8. **Delivery**: For in-store purchases, provide a personalized handover with a thorough explanation of features and functions. For omnichannel customers, offer flexible delivery options—either at the dealership or a location of their choice—along with a virtual or in-person vehicle walkthrough.

9. **Follow-Up**: Maintain regular contact to ensure customer satisfaction. Utilize the customer's preferred communication channel—phone calls, emails, text messages, or personalized video messages—to address any post-purchase concerns.

10. **Customer Relationship Management (CRM)**: Build and sustain long-term relationships by tracking all customer interactions, preferences, and service needs. Use CRM tools to tailor future communications, offer exclusive deals, and encourage repeat business, whether the customer came in-store or through digital channels.

Chapter 9: Familiar Themes

"I'd add one more thing, Thomas—that structure ensures consistency and fairness. It enhances efficiency, accountability, and effectiveness, which improves staff performance and morale."

"You're right, John. Clear expectations lead to better results; staff often fail because they don't know what's expected of them. This dual-focused plan keeps everyone aligned, regardless of how the customer comes to us. Great work, John."

A Paradigm Shift

Thomas paused for a moment. "John, your Ten-Step Selling Plan got me thinking. What if we completely revolutionized our approach?"

"I'm intrigued. What do you have in mind?"

"A true paradigm shift. What if we moved to a subscription-based model instead of traditional sales? And we could involve Jane from Finance and Insurance from the very beginning of the process."

John's eyebrows lifted in surprise. "That's revolutionary! How would that work?"

"Instead of selling cars, we offer a monthly subscription. A subscription model offers flexible, all-inclusive access to a vehicle for a monthly fee, unlike traditional ownership, which requires purchase or leasing. Customers can switch between different models as their needs change. It's like Netflix, but for cars. Jane would be crucial in structuring these subscriptions and explaining the financial benefits to customers right from the start."

"That could change the whole dynamic ... make ownership more flexible and less intimidating."

"Exactly. We'd handle insurance, maintenance, and even allow customers to pause their subscription when they're not using a car. It's all about providing mobility solutions, not just selling vehicles. Jane's expertise would be vital in creating these comprehensive packages."

John nodded thoughtfully. "This could redefine our entire business model. We'd need to rethink everything from inventory management to customer service. And it would transform Jane's role in F&I completely."

"True, but it could set us apart in the market. We'd be offering a modern solution that aligns with changing consumer preferences for flexibility and reduced commitment."

"It's a bold idea," John replied. "And you know what? This could be implemented transitionally. We could start by offering subscription options alongside traditional sales, allowing customers to choose. That way, we can gradually shift our model while still catering to those who prefer ownership. It would give us time to refine the process and for Jane to adapt her F&I strategies."

"That's a great point," Thomas said. "A phased approach would allow us to test and adjust as we go."

"Exactly," John concluded. "Let's explore this further. Integrating Jane's expertise from the start and implementing it gradually could be the fresh approach we need to stay ahead in the evolving automotive landscape."

* * *

As TSG stepped out into the showroom, he had a sense of excitement and optimism. The conversation with John about potentially shifting to a subscription-based model had been more productive than he'd anticipated. Esther's advice to plant the seed and involve John in co-creating the vision had paid off, ensuring the proposed change felt like a shared mission rather than an imposed directive.

Reflecting on the discussion, TSG felt a deep appreciation for the strengths already present within the team. John's commitment to customer rapport, product knowledge, and a structured selling plan had built a solid foundation. It was clear that Dashing Auto Group was already doing many things right: focusing on building trust, ensuring transparency, and delivering excellent customer experiences.

Yet TSG also saw tremendous opportunity for growth. The evolving landscape of the automotive industry called for a more flexible, customer-centric approach that seamlessly blended traditional ownership with new mobility solutions. He realized that as the market dynamics shifted, it wasn't only product knowledge that needed continuous updating—the

Chapter 9: Familiar Themes

team also needed to stay abreast of new business models that customers were increasingly interested in, such as subscription services, car-sharing, and other innovative ownership alternatives.

TSG felt confident that with a team willing to adapt and focus on the customer journey from start to finish, Dashing Auto Group could continue to thrive. By refining their processes to meet customers where they were, whether in person or online, and by offering innovative solutions like the subscription model, they could turn every interaction into a long-lasting relationship. This would require ongoing education and training, not just on the latest vehicle features, but also on emerging trends in automotive retail and changing consumer preferences.

TSG's Journal – Litmus Test

Today's meeting with John was more than a discussion about our sales process; it was a litmus test for change. While we covered the usual ground, my real aim was to gauge John's openness to new ideas. Introducing the concept of integrating our F&I Manager, Jane, earlier in the sales process wasn't revolutionary; it's a practice that's been successful elsewhere. But for us, it represents a significant shift from our traditional approach.

This conversation was the first step in a larger change-management process. Moving forward, how can I focus on building a compelling case for change, not limited to this specific idea, but for fostering a culture of continuous improvement? John's receptiveness, albeit cautious, suggests there's potential for growth.

My challenge now is to nurture this openness, provide the necessary support and information, and gradually shift our team's perspective from "why change?" to "why not?" It's a delicate balance, but essential if Dashing Auto Group is to catch up with—and eventually lead—our rapidly evolving industry.

CHAPTER 10

The Hamster Wheel

Beware the barrenness of a busy life.
—**Socrates**

As Thomas reflected on the corporate environment that seemed to trap so many organizations, including his own, he could almost feel the relentless churn—a hamster wheel spinning faster and faster, driven by the frenzied efforts of teams caught in its perpetual motion.

The sales and service floor were alive with activity; phones rang incessantly, keyboards clicked with urgency, and voices intermingled in a chaotic symphony. It was month-end, and the entire dealership seemed to be holding its breath.

"Are you contributing to this environment?" Esther had asked him during their last call.

"I think I might be," Thomas admitted. "Every month feels like a race to the finish line, only for another race to start immediately after. We push harder to hit targets, celebrate fleeting victories, and then do it all over again. Long-term thinking and strategic planning get lost in the rush."

Chapter 10: The Hamster Wheel

Esther nodded. "It's a dangerous cycle. Like a hamster on a wheel, businesses fixated on short-term targets often fail to notice the changing landscape around them. Competitors innovate, markets shift, and opportunities slip by unnoticed. Breaking free requires courage, the willingness to step back, to think beyond immediate goals."

Thomas ended the call with the weight of her words heavy on his mind. He knew the truth in what she said, but there was something more—a sense that the constant distractions weren't just a result of their own making. As he headed to his meeting with John over at the Sales Department, he pondered how this environment might be limiting their potential, keeping them locked in place while the world around them changed.

Somewhere in the shadows, forces seemed to be at work, encouraging this relentless focus on the short-term, making it harder to lift their heads and see what lay beyond the next goal. Thomas sensed a shift in the air—a feeling that change was looming, a transformation that would challenge the very foundations of his business. As he walked through the buzzing dealership, he realized the distractions, the frenetic pace, the urgent need to hit short-term targets, were all keeping his team from looking further ahead, from seeing the bigger picture.

He knew they had to find a way to step back, to break free from the noise, and to begin preparing for whatever lay over the horizon.

* * * **

"How are you going today, John? I don't want to take up too much of your time. I know you're super busy right now." TSG settled into his seat.

"We're pushing hard toward our target of two hundred new car sales a month and a hundred pre-owned cars. And we're managing to keep most of our good staff. Isn't that what's important?"

TSG considered this. "That's a very objective summary. But what does it take to meet those targets—physically, mentally, and emotionally?"

John sighed. "We've got a well-oiled machine, but sometimes it feels more like a hamster wheel. We're all running harder to stay in the same place. The monthly targets are met, but it's exhausting. The pressure is relentless, and there's no real progress, merely maintenance."

"Can you give me an example?"

John pulled up some notes on his computer and turned the screen toward TSG. "Take the month-end. We're all laser-focused on achieving our targets. The pressure mounts to meet brand objectives, maintain standards, earn commissions, and secure bonuses. But it's not just about the numbers; it's also about customer satisfaction and retention. Happy customers are repeat customers and bring in referrals. When we're constantly chasing targets, we risk losing that connection with our customers, which impacts both current and future sales."

TSG nodded, thinking about the dual pressures his team faced. "You're describing a classic case of what Bruch and Vogel call 'overloading' in their book, *Organizational Energy*. It's when teams are so overwhelmed by immediate demands that they can't see beyond their current tasks. It drains energy, kills creativity, and leads to burnout."

"Exactly. We're in a high-energy environment, but without focus. It's like being in the frenetic zone as described by Bruch & Vogel. Everyone's busy, but we're not necessarily being productive or moving forward."

"And overloading is costing us, John. We're pushing our key staff to the limit, and that's not sustainable. If we continue like this, we risk burning out our best people."

John chewed his lip. "So, how do we get out of this cycle?"

"We start by rethinking our targets and how we achieve them. Right now, we're stuck on this monthly treadmill. We need to step back and look at the bigger picture. We need to align our energy toward meaningful goals—goals that promote both short-term performance and long-term growth."

John nodded, his interest piqued. "Go on."

TSG continued outlining his vision for change, emphasizing the need to balance short-term sales targets with a long-term vision. John listened intently, occasionally nodding in agreement.

As the conversation progressed, both men became more animated, exchanging ideas and building on each other's thoughts. They discussed the importance of creating a sustainable rhythm, managing organizational energy better, and providing consistent, ongoing training.

By the end of the meeting, John's initial skepticism had transformed into enthusiasm. "You're almost getting me excited about this change," he said, smiling.

TSG stood up and extended his hand. "Thanks for being open to this, John. Let's start this journey together. We have a great team, and with the right focus, we can make sure that Dashing Auto Group doesn't just survive but thrives in the years to come."

TSG's Journal – Collaborative Evolution

Our current sales strategy resembles a hamster wheel—constant motion without progress, leading to burnout and strained customer experiences. We need a paradigm shift, but it requires partnership, not isolation.

Some OEMs are already adapting, recognizing that relentless monthly targets may not support long-term growth. They're exploring smarter goals, digital tools for omnichannel engagement, and rethinking the dealer's role.

To succeed, we must align our strategies with evolving market dynamics and consumer behavior. I plan to reach out to OEMs, inviting them to co-create solutions that balance short-term sales with long-term brand loyalty and customer satisfaction.

This isn't about shifting blame but recognizing our collective strength. By aligning goals and innovating together, we can create a resilient, future-focused dealership model.

CHAPTER 11

Shear the Sheep or Slaughter the Lambs?

Better a little that lasts than much that is soon spent.
—**Spanish Proverb**

After a morning with another round of Danish pastries, TSG felt the need to clear his head and burn some extra calories. He quickly donned his running gear, determined to avoid the temptation of a quiet lunch. Texting his best friend, Nathaniel, he asked if he was up for a run and a chat.

"See you at the oval, bro," he replied.

"Need to blow the cobwebs away," TSG said, laughing, as he matched Nathaniel's stride. "From my head and the business."

"Doing a clean sweep?" Nathaniel slowed down, turning his face toward TSG. "Thinking about letting some staff go?"

"No, that hadn't crossed my mind. I'm more inclined to get the team out of their complacency, show them new ways to do business. Though now that you mention it, that clean sweep metaphor fits well with what I'm feeling."

"Complacency! Stagnancy! What would your father say?"

Chapter 11: Shear the Sheep or Slaughter the Lambs

"Dad's methods were great for his time, but the pace of change today is accelerating. Dashing needs to adapt or we'll hit a wall. And it's not only us; it's businesses everywhere."

"Speaking of adapting," Nathaniel cut in, "my key fob went flat last week."

"That's what happens when you buy from another dealership!" TSG teased.

"Hey, if only you had the brand I needed!" Nathaniel smirked. "So, I called my dealership, and guess what? They had no idea how to fix the issue. After a long wait, they finally told me to check the handbook—which I didn't have! I ended up finding the solution on YouTube in minutes."

"Were they really clueless or just too busy to bother?" TSG asked, panting a bit from the pace.

"Doesn't matter, they've lost me as a future customer. If they couldn't help me with a simple issue, why should I trust them for anything bigger?"

"You know, studies show it costs thousands to acquire a new customer. If that customer leaves due to a minor issue, you're handing them to the competition. Why do that?"

Thomas recalled an article he had recently read:

Customer Acquisition Costs for Auto Dealerships in the USA

Introduction

The automotive industry in the United States faces a continually evolving market landscape, driven by advancements in digital technology and shifting consumer preferences. As auto dealerships strive to capture and retain customers, understanding the associated costs of customer acquisition becomes crucial. This report explores the average expenditures of dealerships on marketing, advertising, and incentives, as well as how these costs vary by region and digital transformation efforts.

Overview of Customer Acquisition Costs (CAC)

Customer Acquisition Costs (CAC) refer to the expenses a dealership incurs to attract potential buyers and convert them into customers. For auto dealerships, CAC is influenced by several factors including marketing and advertising budgets, promotional spending, and investments in digital infrastructure. According to data from the National Automobile Dealers Association (NADA), these costs can vary significantly across the United States.

Advertising and Marketing Expenditures

NADA's 2023 annual report highlights that, on average, dealerships spend approximately $554,292 per year on advertising efforts. This amount is directed toward a combination of traditional and digital advertising channels, with a growing emphasis on digital platforms to meet the demands of tech-savvy customers. Digital advertising is seen as more cost-effective and targeted, allowing dealerships to reach potential buyers based on their online behavior and preferences.[11]

Incentives and Promotions

Promotional spending is another significant aspect of CAC. Dealerships often offer incentives, rebates, and discounts to attract buyers. According to NADA's analysis, incentive spending averaged around $1,187 per vehicle in 2022. While this number primarily pertains to new vehicles, similar tactics are used to attract pre-owned car buyers, including trade-in deals and financing offers. These incentives are essential for dealerships to remain competitive, especially in markets with higher competition and customer expectations.[12]

State-Level Variations in Costs

Customer acquisition expenses also vary by state due to factors like market size, regional competition, and economic conditions. In states like Texas and California, the average acquisition costs are higher due to larger markets and more competitors vying for customers. By contrast, states with smaller populations and fewer dealerships, like West Virginia and Vermont, experience comparatively lower costs. NADA's state-level analysis indicates significant disparities in spending patterns based on local economic conditions and dealership density.[13]

Impact of Digital Transformation

The rise of digital transformation has shifted customer acquisition strategies in the automotive industry. Dealerships are increasingly investing in digital platforms, CRM systems, and online buying experiences. According to NADA, the push for a seamless online customer experience has led dealerships to allocate more resources toward building robust digital ecosystems. The aim is to provide a cohesive journey from online browsing to in-person test-drives and purchases, thereby aligning with modern consumer behavior.

Challenges and Opportunities

High customer acquisition costs, combined with competitive pricing and increasing consumer expectations, present challenges for dealerships. To optimize returns, many dealerships are focusing on enhancing customer experience, building loyalty programs, and offering personalized services. Digital marketing, combined with data-driven insights, is proving to be an effective strategy in maintaining profitability and justifying the investments made toward customer acquisition.

Conclusion

The cost of acquiring a customer remains a critical consideration for auto dealerships in the United States. With marketing and advertising expenditures reaching over half a million dollars annually per dealership, combined with substantial promotional spending, dealerships must carefully balance their budgets to ensure a profitable return on investment. By leveraging digital transformation, dealerships can streamline their operations, improve customer experiences, and reduce acquisition costs in the long run.

After TSG had summarized all of this for his running mate, Nathaniel replied, "That's madness ... or complacency."

"If you'd bought your car from us, the conversation would have gone like this," TSG began, then paused to reconsider. "Maybe I should check in with our Service Department to see what we're doing right now. But ideally, we'd say, 'I can't find the answer right now, but are you in an urgent situation, or can I call you back in thirty minutes?' Straight away, we'd show care and a willingness to help. That's how you keep customers happy. Esther and I were talking about this last week; she gave me a deeper understanding of why customer service is so critical to a business' success."

TSG's thoughts began to drift as he and Nathaniel ran side by side. Esther's voice echoed in his mind, reminding him of the deeper meaning behind customer service. He could still hear her explaining how customer service wasn't only about solving problems; it was the lifeblood of any successful business. Her words had struck a chord.

As they ran in silence, TSG replayed their conversation in his head. He had meant to jot down her insights right after their meeting, but life had moved too fast. Now, in the quiet rhythm of the run, those lessons resurfaced. Esther had drawn parallels between iconic companies that had once dominated their industries but faltered because they failed to evolve their customer experience. She had reminded him that it wasn't merely about operational efficiency; it was about connecting with customers on a human level.

Customer Service Lessons from Esther

Customer service is a crucial factor in business success, directly impacting satisfaction, loyalty, and reputation. **Ninety-six percent of customers** say service is key to their brand loyalty, according to *Microsoft's 2018 State of Global Customer Service Report*. Superior service fosters trust and drives repeat business, while poor service leads to dissatisfaction, lost clients, and even business failure.[14]

Here are notable examples:

1. **Blockbuster**: Poor service, late fees, and a failure to adapt pushed customers to Netflix, leading to Blockbuster's bankruptcy in 2010.[15]
2. **Sears**: Outdated customer service and a slow transition to e-commerce allowed Amazon and Walmart to capture its market. Sears filed for bankruptcy in 2018 (*Reuters*).[16]
3. **Toys 'R' Us**: Lack of innovation and poor customer experience led to its decline, as Amazon offered a more customer-friendly experience. Toys 'R' Us filed for bankruptcy in 2017 (*CNBC*).[17]
4. **BlackBerry**: Slow to adapt to user needs and poor service saw BlackBerry fall to Apple and Android, losing significant market share (*The Verge*).[18]
5. **RadioShack**: Poor service and undertrained staff resulted in customers defecting to Best Buy, leading to multiple bankruptcies (*New York Times*).[19]

In each case, neglecting customer service and ignoring shifts in buyer behavior opened the door for competitors who understood the evolving needs of their customers.

"Sorry, Nathaniel, I drifted off there," TSG apologized, snapping back to the present.

"No worries, mate, I'm all ears. So, tell me, what about these cobwebs?"

TSG grinned. "Cobwebs, clean sweeps, key fob debacles," he said. "It's the power of storytelling and metaphors, right? They stick with you. And I've realized my immediate task is clearing out the cobwebs from our own processes."

"This week and next, I'm meeting with each department manager to identify what's working and where the cobwebs are." TSG stretched his arms behind his head and relaxed. "I want to create a new vision for Dashing, one that takes us from the brink of extinction to thriving again. Storytelling is key to inspiring that vision. Want to hear a story?"

"Sure, I've got time," Nathaniel said, "as long as it doesn't convince me to abandon my craft beer business and join you in car sales!"

"Here it goes," TSG began. "Long, long ago, some 11,000 or even 14,000 years back, the first hunter-gatherer tribes began taking steps toward farming. Maybe they noticed that seeds they'd dropped near their camps started sprouting into plants they could eat. They began to sow seeds on purpose, tame wild animals, and slowly shift from hunting to farming. They learned to keep animals alive, breed them, and save themselves the effort of daily hunts. Instead of constantly seeking new food sources, they created their own, right where they were."

Nathaniel flopped onto the grass, laughing. "I don't know where this is going, but I'm hooked. How does this relate to car sales?"

TSG lay down beside him. "Most sales departments, including ours, operate like those early hunter-gatherers. They wait for customers—or guests, as we call them—to step onto the forecourt or make inquiries online. The game is on. Our team is great at what they do—meeting targets of two hundred new cars a month. They see this field of opportunity as infinite. But it's not, and that field is in danger of disappearing."

Nathaniel sat up, grinning. "I get it! They're focused on the hunt, but they also need to start farming."

"Right, Nathaniel. Farming would mean nurturing our customers, taking care of them not just at the point of sale but continuously keeping them engaged, informed, and satisfied, so they return to us, whether it's for service, advice, or their next vehicle."

Nathaniel tilted his head back and adjusted his cap to shade his face. "So, nurturing means making sure every customer feels valued at every touchpoint, not simply seen as a one-time transaction?"

"Absolutely. Our Sales Department needs to adopt both a hunter and farmer mindset—excelling in attracting new customers and focusing on cultivating long-term relationships. And our Service Department? It's even more critical there. Think of it like this: are we shearing the sheep or slaughtering the lambs? Do we kill our business by letting new customers drive away, or do we invite them back, nurture them, and keep them ready for more? It's about a long-term commitment to our customers."

"Got it!" Nathaniel nodded. "So, the sales team hunts and farms, while the service team focuses on customer retention, ensuring those customers always come back."

Chapter 11: Shear the Sheep or Slaughter the Lambs

"Maybe my analogy needs some work, but you get the point. Stories don't need to be perfect; they need to engage and communicate a message."

Nathaniel stood up, shouldering his backpack. "Well, you've certainly given me something to think about."

"Good." TSG smiled. "I've got a meeting with Liam, our Service Manager, tomorrow. It's time to talk about how we can all start farming, together."

TSG's Journal – Nurturing the Flock

Reflecting on "shearing the sheep or slaughtering the lambs," I see the need for a shift at Dashing Auto Group. Are we only chasing short-term gains, or are we truly nurturing our customers for long-term relationships?

Nathaniel's story about poor customer service over a simple issue like a flat key fob made me wonder how often we risk losing customers over minor missteps. Are we putting enough effort into making sure every interaction builds trust and loyalty?

Esther's insights remind me that complacency in customer service can be fatal. Companies have failed by not adapting … are we at risk too? How can we ensure our approach is genuinely customer-centric and exceeds expectations?

I need to foster a culture where both sales and service teams think long-term—like farmers nurturing relationships, going beyond hunters seeking quick wins. How do I align our team and OEM partners with this vision?

We can't change everything overnight, but we can start by making small shifts toward a more sustainable, customer-focused approach. Am I ready to lead this change? Our future may depend on it.

CHAPTER 12

Farmer Liam

The goal as a company is to have customer service that is not just the best, but legendary.
—**Sam Walton**

The Road to the Next Sale

The muted buzz of the phone in the corner went unnoticed as TSG settled into the old leather armchair that Liam had recently rescued from the back of the workshop.

"I remember many an hour after school spent sitting in this chair waiting for Dad to finish work and take us home. I always liked the smell of the leather," TSG said, smiling.

"It's been a bit neglected over the years," Liam suggested. "But I've been giving it some TLC since I hauled it into my office last Christmas—cleaned it up, mended a couple of tears, and patched a gaping hole at the back. I give it a light polish whenever I water the plants."

TSG hadn't noticed the ferns, parlor palms, and various other houseplants gathered in groups around Liam's computer and, now that he looked more closely, trailing up the wall behind the desk. "How long have you been collecting plants in here?"

Chapter 12: Father Liam

"Ever since I started working for Dashing three years ago. They've multiplied since then."

"A true green thumb," TSG remarked, trailing his fingers through the palm fronds. "And the gift of bringing an old, cracked, dry leather chair back to life."

"I grew up on a farm," Liam replied. "Mum restored furniture on the side, and Dad spent his spare time restoring old cars. But I needed a more reliable income, so I started in car dealerships. I worked my way up from servicing cars to becoming a Service Manager."

"And now you're leading one of the most important departments in the business," TSG said. "And you're managing people—your staff and customers. Do you miss working with cars?"

"I like the hands-on projects: the plants, the armchair, and other bits and pieces. Keeps me grounded." Liam sat opposite TSG on a chair he had also restored. "But the work here keeps me busy. We're hitting every target: profitability; 4,000 ROs (repair orders) monthly; and high warranty-claim processing times. We're doing well, and the data shows it."

"You've done an excellent job with the team," TSG said. "But I've been thinking about something else. How well are we really farming our customer relationships? Are we nurturing them the way we need to be, to ensure they come back?"

Liam paused for a moment before answering. "Well, customers generally book their services through our online tool or by calling the Business Development Center, where a team manages customer communications and schedules appointments. We get them in, perform the work, and then call or text them to pick up their car. That's about the extent of it."

"Do we hear from them between services?" TSG asked.

"If they bought a car from us, they get an automated reminder when their next service is due," Liam replied. "But for those who didn't buy from us, or who bought privately, we've been less proactive. We used to send follow-up emails for feedback, but the response rate was so low that we let the system lapse."

"Sounds like we're missing opportunities," TSG said. "We're doing a great job serving them in the moment, but what happens after? Are we leaving it to chance that they'll come back?"

Liam dipped his head. "To be honest, we don't have a structured system for follow-up or for keeping them engaged. We've been so focused on meeting the daily demand that we haven't put much thought into it."

"That's where we need to change, Liam," TSG said. "It's time we start thinking about the Road to the Next Sale. We need to look at every service not as the end of the journey, but as the first step toward the next purchase. Whether they bought their car from us or not, we need to nurture every customer relationship, so they think of us when they're ready to buy their next vehicle."

Liam leaned forward, intrigued. "How do we do that?"

"We start by engaging them at every touchpoint," TSG explained. "It begins when they book their service—whether in-store or online. Greet them warmly, confirm their appointment, and make them feel valued from the start. We can integrate a more personalized check-in process and then use follow-up interactions to continue that relationship. The goal is to keep them engaged with Dashing Auto Group so, when they're ready to buy again, they don't think twice about coming to us."

TSG leaned over to Liam's computer, his fingers quickly navigating through the company's intranet. With a few swift clicks, TSG logged in to his files and pulled up the service process they needed to review.

"Let's take a closer look at this," TSG said as the service plan appeared on the screen, "I think there are some adjustments we can make to enhance customer retention and the overall experience. What do you think, Liam?"

Road to the Next Sale: Step-By-Step Guide to Service Engagement Leading Back to Sales

1. Greeting & Appointment Confirmation

- ***In-store***: Greet customers warmly within the first two minutes of arrival. Verify their appointment details, confirm and update any necessary customer information, including contact details and vehicle history. Ensure the customer acknowledges and accepts the privacy policy, data usage waiver, and other compliance requirements (such as general data protection regulations).

Personalize the experience by addressing any specific requests or preferences.

- *Online*: Send a personalized email or message before the service appointment. Confirm the time, details, and customer information, including contact updates and vehicle specifics. Include the privacy policy, data usage waiver, and compliance agreements via secure link for digital acceptance. Offer convenient channels for questions, changes, or to update any additional information.

2. Vehicle Check-In, Initial Needs Analysis & Vehicle Condition Recording

- *In-store*: Conduct a detailed walk-around of the customer's vehicle, noting the vehicle's current condition (including photos) and discussing the services requested. Ask about any additional concerns or issues the customer may have noticed. Record the vehicle's condition in the system and have the customer review and sign the condition report as part of compliance and transparency efforts.
- *Online*: Provide a pre-service form or chatbot interaction that allows customers to detail their service needs before arrival. Offer a video call option for a virtual walk-around if needed. Request the customer to upload vehicle condition photos for recordkeeping purposes, ensuring transparency and trust.

3. Service Recommendations

- *In-store*: After analyzing the vehicle's condition and service requirements, offer recommendations and optional maintenance packages. Use visuals, like a digital inspection tool to show areas that need attention and review the recorded condition with the customer to highlight necessary work.
- *Online*: Send a detailed service report or video inspection to the customer's inbox, along with suggested additional services and relevant package offers. Include vehicle condition photos and recorded notes. Offer live chat or video call options to discuss further.

4. Cost Estimate & Approval

- ***In-store:*** Provide a clear, transparent cost breakdown for the customer's approval. Ensure they fully understand the services, pricing, and terms before proceeding. Have the customer confirm their approval digitally or via signature.
- ***Online:*** Share the estimate digitally through email or app notifications, allowing customers to approve services remotely using secure online forms. Include a digital signature feature for compliance requirements.

5. Service Execution & Real-Time Updates

- ***In-store:*** Keep customers informed with periodic updates while they wait, ensuring transparency throughout the service. If additional issues are found, refer to the initial vehicle condition record to confirm changes and request approval for further work.
- ***Online:*** Send real-time status updates via text, email, or app notifications about the vehicle's progress and estimated completion time, referencing the initial condition recorded during check-in.

6. Additional Recommendations & Upsell Opportunities

- ***In-store:*** Before service completion, discuss any additional services or products that could benefit the vehicle, such as tire upgrades or extended warranties. Use the initial condition record as a reference to highlight areas that may need future attention.
- ***Online:*** Provide recommendations via email or other platform based on the inspection results and the vehicle's recorded condition. Be clear in the reasoning and provide examples with benefits.

7. Service Completion & Review

- ***In-store:*** Conduct a final review with the customer, ensuring their satisfaction with the completed services. Compare the initial vehicle condition to the post-service condition and review any follow-up maintenance needs. Provide a detailed service report, including before-and-after photos, to ensure transparency.

- ***Online***: Send a digital summary of completed services, including before-and-after vehicle condition photos and a personalized thankyou message. Offer a video or interactive explanation if the customer wasn't present.

8. Payment & Future Booking
- ***In-store***: Offer multiple payment options, including contactless payment. Encourage the customer to schedule their next service before leaving the dealership. Provide a reminder of the vehicle's condition and offer an opportunity to pre-book follow-up services.
- ***Online***: Provide secure online payment options and incentivize future service bookings with discounts or promotions. Enable future booking directly through the dealership's website or app. Include reminders of the customer's vehicle condition and recommended follow-up services.

9. Follow-Up & Customer Satisfaction
- ***In-store***: Follow up with a phone call or text message a few days after the service to ensure the customer is satisfied, ask for feedback, and offer any necessary post-service assistance.
- ***Online***: Send a personalized email or text to gather feedback and offer assistance for any post-service questions. Direct customers to leave an online review. Include a reminder of their next service or follow-up based on the recorded vehicle condition.

10. Customer Retention & CRM Integration
- ***In-store***: Leverage CRM with AI enhancement data to personalize future service communications, reminding customers of upcoming maintenance, recalls, or special offers. Include previous vehicle condition reports to keep customers engaged.
- ***Online***: Use CRM with AI enhancement tools to track customer interactions, service history, and vehicle condition reports. Send tailored emails or app notifications for future service needs, exclusive offers, and potential vehicle upgrades.

Liam raised an eyebrow. "It sounds like we're shifting from a 'repair and go' mindset to something more ongoing."

"Exactly," TSG nodded. "Think of it this way: we already know their vehicle history, preferences, and behavior. We can leverage this information to send tailored follow-ups—reminders about upcoming services, offers on parts or accessories, and even personalized trade-in opportunities. When they do come in, we can have meaningful conversations about their future vehicle needs. It's about using every interaction to build a deeper relationship."

"And this would all be integrated?" Liam asked, raising an eyebrow.

TSG continued, "Yes, it would. Imagine offering video inspections sent directly to their inbox, showing them any issues and providing service recommendations. From there, we can guide them toward additional services or vehicle upgrades. At every step, we're not only servicing their car; we're paving the way for their next purchase."

He paused, then added, "If we really want to deepen customer loyalty and keep them coming back, we must enhance the Road to the Next Sale process. It's about more than completing a service—it's about building these long-term relationships. Our large customer base may not be there forever, so we need to be farming the customers we have. That way, we can ensure they keep growing and providing for us in the future."

Energized by the concept, Thomas and Liam began to brainstorm the next steps. Their minds raced with possibilities, each idea building on the last as they envisioned a future where every customer interaction was an opportunity for growth and loyalty.

With his notebook in hand, TSG began documenting the ideas that flowed:

1. Personalized Customer Engagement

- **Tailored Communication**: Use CRM tools to segment customers based on their preferences, vehicle type, and service history. Send personalized reminders for upcoming services or vehicle upgrades, highlighting their specific vehicle needs. Include details about their vehicle's past service history and any future maintenance suggestions.

- **Loyalty Programs**: Introduce a loyalty program where customers earn points for every service or purchase. Points can be redeemed for discounts on future services, accessories, or even vehicle purchases. Offering tiered loyalty rewards (e.g. silver, gold, platinum) creates a sense of progression and exclusivity.
- **Birthday/Anniversary Specials**: Reach out to customers on personal occasions like birthdays or anniversaries of their car purchase, offering special discounts on services or vehicle upgrades. This adds a personal touch and strengthens emotional connections.

2. Proactive Service Approach

- **Predictive Maintenance Alerts**: Use data analytics and telematics systems to monitor vehicles and send predictive maintenance alerts. Proactively inform customers when their vehicle may need attention before a problem arises, adding value and convenience.
- **Scheduled Follow-Up Services**: When a vehicle is serviced, schedule the next service before the customer leaves the dealership. Automate reminders 1–2 months before the service date with easy online scheduling to make the process hassle-free.

3. Seamless Omnichannel Experience

- **Omnichannel Booking & Communication**: Ensure the customer can switch seamlessly between in-store, phone, and online channels without having to repeat themselves or provide the same information twice. For example, if they started an inquiry online, ensure the service adviser has all the information when they arrive in-store.
- **Mobile App**: Offer a dedicated dealership app that allows customers to manage their vehicle service history, schedule future appointments, make payments, and receive real-time updates. Include push notifications for service reminders and special offers.

4. Value-Added Services

- **Courtesy Services**: Offer complimentary services such as car washes with every service or provide vehicle pick-up and drop-off options. This makes the experience more convenient for the customer and shows that the dealership is going the extra mile to meet their needs.
- **Service Bundles & Subscriptions**: Create service bundles (e.g. multi-year service plans) or subscription-based maintenance packages that cover multiple services at a discounted rate. This encourages customers to commit to the dealership long-term for all their service needs.

5. Enhanced Customer Communication

- **Service Progress Transparency**: Provide customers with real-time updates, including photos or videos of the service process. This transparency builds trust and increases customer satisfaction by keeping them informed throughout.
- **Post-Service Follow-Up**: After each service, follow up not only to check for satisfaction but also to offer tips for maintaining their vehicle or provide personalized offers for future services. Send thankyou notes or small gifts to loyal customers after major services or purchases.

6. Creating a Community-Centric Experience

- **Exclusive Events & Webinars**: Invite customers to exclusive dealership events, such as car-care workshops, vehicle showcase events, or "meet the experts" sessions. Host virtual webinars on topics like vehicle maintenance or new technology to educate and engage customers.
- **Local Community Involvement**: Partner with local organizations or charities and invite customers to participate in community-driven events, strengthening their emotional connection with the dealership.

7. Continuous Improvement & Feedback Loop

- **Customer Feedback Loop**: After every service or purchase, actively request feedback and use it to improve customer experience. Incentivize feedback by offering discounts or rewards for filling out satisfaction surveys.
- **In-Depth Service Reviews**: At the end of each service, offer a more detailed vehicle health report that covers the condition of key parts, upcoming maintenance needs, and potential vehicle upgrades. Encourage customers to review this with service advisers to better understand their vehicle's long-term needs.

8. Digital and In-Person Experience Integration

- **Virtual Showroom & Test-Drives**: Allow customers to book virtual test-drives or showroom tours if they're considering a new vehicle. Use digital tools to engage them with the vehicle-buying process and then bring them in-store when they're ready to make a purchase.
- **In-App Trade-In Offers**: For customers who have serviced their cars regularly, offer trade-in estimates directly through your mobile app or CRM. This seamlessly transitions them from service to sales when the time comes to purchase a new vehicle.

9. Long-Term Vehicle Care Education

- **Educational Content**: Create a content library of vehicle care tips, how-to videos, and maintenance schedules. Share this content through emails, the mobile app, or social media to help customers take better care of their vehicles.
- **Interactive Tools**: Offer online tools that let customers estimate their vehicle's trade-in value, calculate the cost of upgrades, or understand long-term care needs based on their service history.

10. Build Trust & Transparency

- **Transparent Pricing**: Provide clear, up-front pricing for all services and parts, removing any ambiguity. Offer price-match guarantees or service guarantees to reassure customers they are getting the best value.

- **Technician Introductions**: Introduce customers to the technicians working on their vehicle, providing reassurance about their vehicle's care. This personal touch strengthens the customer's connection to the dealership.

Liam leaned back, letting it all sink in. "That's a different way of thinking, Thomas. It's not only about meeting today's targets but setting us up for future sales."

"You know, Liam, if we can nurture these relationships, we'll have a loyal base of customers who come to us for service and stay with us when it's time to buy their next car. That's the vision I see for Dashing Auto Group—sales and service working in harmony toward a common goal."

Liam smiled. "It makes sense. Similar to how I take care of these plants, we need to take care of our customers. With the right attention, they'll keep coming back and thrive with us."

"And that's the key, Liam," TSG concluded, standing up. "We're not merely fixing cars—we're building relationships. If we can master the Road to the Next Sale, we won't just survive—we'll thrive."

As TSG left the office, Liam presented him with the plant that he'd been admiring. Holding that peace lily TSG felt a sense of clarity. The future of Dashing Auto Group lay not only in selling cars but in farming relationships, tending to every customer with care, building trust, and guiding them on the road to their next sale with Dashing Auto Group.

Chapter 12: Father Liam

TSG's Journal – Nurturing and Growth

Today's conversation with Liam revealed a glaring issue: we've been prioritizing short-term gains at the expense of nurturing long-term customer relationships.

Jeff Smith's insights from *The KPI Book* ring true here—our KPIs need to drive behaviors that align with our broader goals, rather than merely the quick wins. Currently, we're losing eighty percent of our customers within five years. The question now is, how can we shift from a "hunter-gatherer" approach, focused on immediate results, to a "farming" mentality that cultivates long-term loyalty?

How do we ensure meaningful contact between services? How can we develop a system that tracks engagement and adds value at every touchpoint? More importantly, how do we get sales and service to work together without turning our service team into salespeople?

The peace lily in Liam's office reminded me that, like plants, our customer relationships need consistent care to grow. But are we prepared to invest in this nurturing process? Do we have the right people, training programs, feedback systems, and KPIs that balance short-term performance with long-term customer value? This is more than a strategic shift; it's a cultural one. The real question is: are we truly ready to embrace it?

CHAPTER 13

Parts: Aladdin's Cave

*If everyone is moving forward together,
then success takes care of itself.*
—**Henry Ford**

"Who's next?" Esther asked, sensing the momentum building in their morning mentoring session.

"I'm meeting with Martin, our Parts Manager, this afternoon," Thomas replied.

"Ah, Parts," Esther said. "Often overlooked, but crucial to our operations. What's on your mind regarding that department?"

"You're right; it is often overlooked. They have one of the toughest jobs in the dealership, yet many dealerships don't focus enough on their Parts Department. Inventory piles up, stock depreciates, and profits erode."

TSG shared an anecdote about a couple he met in London. The wife, Melanie, had recently started a toy store franchise which became the number one store in England within six months. He explained how her success was based on purchases from the wholesaler, but this led to overstocking issues.

Chapter 13: Parts: Aladdin's Cave

Esther drew the parallel. "So, her team was buying inventory to chase bonuses, rather than focusing on customer demand. I can see how this might apply to your Parts Department."

"Exactly. And with OEMs now using automatic stock replacement systems interfacing with our Dealer Management System (DMS) inventory records, accuracy is more crucial than ever."

Esther nodded. "But there's another layer to this, isn't there? The brands have their own reward systems for operational efficiency."

"You've hit on something important there," TSG agreed. "Brands use data reports to recognize and reward dealers for being operationally efficient. Stock order ratios, parts purchases, etc. Over time, we've become conditioned to equate target performance with excellence in operational performance."

"But sometimes these aren't aligned," Esther said. "A dealership could hit all the right metrics on paper and still struggle with actual profitability or customer satisfaction."

Thomas leaned forward, engaged. "Exactly. Take our Parts Department, for instance. We might be rewarded for maintaining a certain stock level or for parts sold per repair order (RO). But if we're overstocking to meet these targets, we're tying up capital and risking obsolescence."

"And the automatic ordering system could exacerbate this if we're not careful," Esther added.

"Precisely. We need to find a balance between meeting the brand's operational targets and what works best for our business and our customers. It's about looking beyond the metrics to the real impact on our bottom line and customer satisfaction."

"So, the challenge," Esther said, "is to maintain our good standing with the brands while also optimizing our actual performance. How do you think we can achieve that?"

"I think it starts with a deep dive into our data," TSG replied. "We need to understand where these targets align with real efficiency and where they diverge. Then we can start to make informed decisions about where to focus our efforts."

BECOMING AMBIDEXTROUS

* * *

TSG arrived at the Parts Department to find Martin finishing up his lunch outside.

Martin greeted him warmly. "Hello, Thomas. I thought we'd catch up before diving into the daily hustle inside. Harry has organized a birthday cake for Jacqui, so we might want to side-step that if we don't want to get caught up."

"Good to see your team supporting each other."

"They do." Martin grinned. "We've even had a little friendly competition over these anniversary tote bags from our main supplier. Harry just edged Jacqui for the win. I think the cake is his way of softening the blow."

"Anniversary tote bags?" Thomas raised an eyebrow, amused. "Was it caps or t-shirts last year?"

Martin laughed. "Both, actually. And some certificates that are proudly displayed on the walls."

Thomas chuckled, pointing at the awards on the wall. "The brands really know how to incentivize."

"They do. It helps with morale and team bonding. The WhatsApp group is buzzing with pictures of the team celebrating their small victories."

Thomas' smile faded slightly as he shifted the conversation. "Tell me about the customer experience in Parts, Martin. What does it really look like from your perspective?"

"Well, we follow strict procedures. With the shift to omnichannel communication, we've had to improve our verbal and writing skills, and even our tech know-how. The real focus is making sure the customers feel heard, understood, and that their problems are solved, whether that's finding a part in stock or ordering it in."

"Sounds like it can get pretty intense."

Martin nodded. "It's relentless. That's why we rely on sales targets, brand awards, and yes, even birthday cakes to keep the team motivated."

Thomas leaned back thoughtfully. "You've been here two years now. Was the inventory as tightly packed when you started?"

"More so; I've been trying to clear out the excess, especially obsolete parts, but suppliers don't take them back unless they're top-selling lines."

Thomas considered his next question carefully. "How much of that inventory build-up is because of brand incentives?"

Martin scratched his chin. "Probably more than we realize, to be honest. It's something I've been thinking about since your talk on needing to adapt or face extinction. Parts will always be needed, but we're not operating as efficiently as we could."

Thomas nodded. "Exactly. Cars will always need parts, but the question is, how do we stay relevant and keep customers coming back to us—not only for their service needs, but for future purchases as well?"

Martin tilted his head, a spark of curiosity in his eyes. "You're seeing a bigger picture, aren't you?"

"I am," Thomas said. "I've been working on a concept I call the Road to the Next Sale, and I think Parts has a key role to play. It goes beyond selling a part today. It's about guiding the customer on a journey that leads them back to us for future services and, eventually, their next vehicle purchase."

Martin leaned forward. "Tell me more."

"Why don't we map this out together, Martin? See what we can come up with?"

They walked over to the whiteboard, markers in hand, and began to collaboratively sketch out the strategy, ideas flowing between them as they built on each other's thoughts.

The Road to the Next Sale: Parts Department

STEP 1: Greeting & Inquiry Confirmation

- *In-store*: Greet the customer as soon as they walk in, confirm what they're looking for, and make the experience personal.
- *Online*: Immediately acknowledge inquiries through automated responses, followed by a personalized confirmation through the customer's preferred communication platform.

STEP 2: Needs Analysis
- *In-store*: Have a conversation to understand the customer's vehicle details and what part they need, and suggest any additional accessories they might want.
- *Online*: Ensure our digital platform helps customers find the right parts with intuitive search filters and compatibility checks.

STEP 3: Product Availability & Alternatives
- *In-store*: Confirm availability or offer alternatives when the part is out of stock.
- *Online*: Show stock updates in real time, providing alternative options if needed.

STEP 4: Product Demonstration & Information
- *In-store*: Offer explanations or demonstrations when the customer picks up a part, suggesting complementary items.
- *Online*: Provide how-to videos or interactive guides for customers purchasing parts online.

STEP 5: Handling Objections & Questions
- *In-store*: Address concerns about pricing, quality, warranty, or compatibility with informed answers.
- *Online*: Offer real-time support via live chat, email, or FAQs to resolve any uncertainties.

STEP 6: Payment & Checkout
- *In-store*: Streamline the payment process with multiple options, offering loyalty points for future purchases. Ensure all customer data is collected and entered into the CRM system.
- *Online*: Ensure a smooth, secure checkout with incentives for the customer's next purchase. Ensure all customer data is collected and entered into the CRM system.

STEP 7: Delivery or Pick-Up Options
- *In-store*: Confirm delivery or pick-up timelines, providing real-time updates.

- **Online**: Offer flexible delivery and click-and-collect options, with tracking for the customer's convenience.

STEP 8: Post-Purchase Support
- *In-store*: Follow up to ensure customer satisfaction and offer installation advice if needed.
- *Online*: Send follow-up emails with product support links or tutorials.

STEP 9: Follow-Up & Engagement
- *In-store*: Send a thankyou message and offer a discount for the next purchase.
- *Online*: Automate personalized follow-ups with offers and maintenance reminders.

STEP 10: Customer Retention & CRM Integration
- *In-store and Online*: Use CRM tools to track interactions and tailor future communications, building long-term relationships.

After mapping out their ideas and refining the strategy, TSG and Martin stepped back to take in the whiteboard, now covered in clear, actionable steps. They exchanged satisfied grins, a high five sealing their shared sense of accomplishment. Both felt optimistic about the progress made and the direction now set in motion.

TSG knew this strategy wasn't revolutionary, but it didn't need to be. His primary goal was to avoid overwhelming Martin and his team while gently bringing the Parts Department into alignment with Sales and Service. With this first step toward goal congruence, Thomas was setting the stage for future conversations that would build on this momentum, ensuring each department moved in harmony toward a unified vision.

As Martin and TSG walked back into the Parts Department, the conversation carried an air of excitement. This wasn't only about managing parts inventory anymore—it was about creating a seamless, customer-centric experience that connected sales to aftersales, and ultimately back to sales.

The Road to the Next Sale had shifted from a concept to a concrete strategy for building long-term customer loyalty.

BECOMING AMBIDEXTROUS

"You're right, Thomas," Martin said. "We need to stop thinking about individual transactions and start focusing on building lasting relationships."

"It's still early days, Martin," TSG smiled. "But we're on the right track. It's starting to come together."

As they entered the department, TSG smiled, envisioning a future where every part sold wasn't the end of a transaction but the beginning of a lasting relationship.

"I've been thinking about your talk on needing change to avoid extinction. I hope people always need cars and parts," Martin said.

"As long as cars exist, parts will be needed, but to thrive, we need to stay relevant, flexible, and aligned across all departments. I'm focusing on creating more goal congruence."

"That sounds promising, a solid plan toward a unified future."

"I also like your team's use of WhatsApp. What if we had something like that for the entire Dashing Auto Group? It could help recognize achievements and build team spirit," TSG suggested.

"I'd be on board with that, Thomas." Martin chuckled. "And if we hurry, there might still be a slice of Jacqui's cake left!"

* * *

Walking past Martin's office, TSG pondered the idea of launching a platform like Workplace by Facebook to improve communication and collaboration. Jeff Smith's *The KPI Book* had stressed the importance of tracking the right metrics, and TSG wondered if a shared platform could help align everyone with common goals and foster a cohesive strategy.

Deciding to run the idea by Xand, their IT expert, TSG headed to his office.

"Xand, got five minutes? I've got an idea," TSG said.

What started as a quick chat quickly turned into a half-hour brainstorming session.

"You're thinking of Workplace by Facebook because it's low-cost and familiar," Xand said, intrigued. "But to really boost engagement, we should do a mini survey to see what the team prefers."

"That's a great idea!" TSG exclaimed. "Can you put together a short presentation for our department managers' meeting next week?"

"Absolutely. I'll also set up a test account for a demo."

"Perfect," TSG replied. "And let's investigate the new company website after that. Thanks for your help."

Leaving Xand's office, TSG felt a surge of positive energy. Could these new communication strategies be the catalyst for a more connected, efficient, and resilient organization? He had a strong feeling they were on the right path.

TSG's Journal – Goal Congruence

Today's meeting with Martin, our Parts Manager, unveiled both challenges and opportunities in this often-overlooked department. Despite its crucial role, the Parts Department seems isolated.

How can we integrate it more fully into our overall strategy? Key observations include strong team camaraderie tied to brand incentives, potential overstocking issues, and room for improvement in our omnichannel approach. The impact of secret commissions on buying behavior is concerning and needs immediate attention.

The idea of implementing Workplace by Facebook as a company-wide communication platform gained momentum. Could this be the key to breaking down departmental silos and fostering a more unified approach to our goals? The potential benefits—enhanced communication, improved employee engagement, and better organizational alignment—are compelling. It's not solely about communication; it's about creating a sense of community and shared commitment across Dashing Auto Group.

This journey through each department reveals interconnected challenges and opportunities. Our path forward involves more than operational changes; it includes a shift in how we communicate and collaborate as a team.

How can we use technology and improved communication to drive us toward goal congruence in a more integrated, efficient, and customer-focused manner? Food for thought and discussion with the team.

CHAPTER 14

Buyer Beware

Price is what you pay, value is what you get.
—**Warren Buffett**

The principle of "buyer beware" (*caveat emptor*) suggests that the buyer is responsible for inspecting and assessing a product before purchase. While this can place a significant burden on customers, businesses that prioritize transparency, clear communication, and robust warranties can build trust and foster loyalty, counteracting any negative aspects of this doctrine.

* * *

"Buyer beware!" Suzee called out, kicking off her shoes and wriggling her toes into the warm sand. At twenty, Suzee was the youngest of TSG's cousins—or stepcousins twice removed, to be precise. She was far enough removed from the Gregory family business to know little about running a car dealership but close enough to join the annual family picnic at Dashing Beach, where Joe Edward Gregory had famously declared in 1957 his intention to open a dealership: "Dashing Auto Group, named after this very beach."

"Buyer beware!" she repeated. "That's what I told Mum when she said she was looking at buying a pre-owned car now that hers is finally on its last legs. Sorry, Thomas, but used-car salespeople don't exactly have the best reputation. Popular media makes them look sketchy, like they care more about closing sales than making sure the customer knows what they're getting."

"You know, Suzee, your mum should come to Dashing Auto Group. We'll take care of her. We treat all our customers with respect."

"But not every dealership is Dashing, right?" Suzee pressed. "Isn't the reputation deserved sometimes?"

"I can't speak for every dealer, but I've heard about shady practices, both in dealerships and private sales. It's always wise to do your homework before buying anything—cars, clothes, even services. What's your mum planning to do?"

"She might come to Dashing, but I suggested she look online first and bring someone who knows about cars—maybe a mechanic—to check any prospects out. I'm also planning to find a guide on what to ask and look for when buying a used car."

"Smart move, Suzee. Have you checked any of the major online sites?"

"Yes, but there are thousands of cars! It's overwhelming; where do we even begin?"

"I remember when those online platforms were just starting out," TSG said, waving away a persistent seagull. "A colleague of mine owned a dealership in Sydney in the late '90s. One day, he got a fax from a company looking to raise capital from dealers to start an 'online car classifieds.' Hardly any dealers invested. Do you know why?"

"Late '90s?" Suzee laughed. "People were probably wary of the new internet thing. Buyer beware again, right? Your colleague missed out, didn't he? Lacked the vision. Back then, who knew we'd end up trusting the internet for everything?"

"That's 100% right," TSG replied. "Dealers couldn't see the technological shift already happening, and even if they did, they didn't see the benefits. Now, those marketplaces are stock market darlings with millions of cars listed. Besides the internet, do you know what other technology helped drive their success?"

Chapter 14: Buyer Beware

"Let me think. Digital cameras at first, and then smartphones with cameras to upload photos?"

"Clever thinking, Suzee. Right again. These platforms solved the problem of selling used cars by guiding people through listings, taking photos, and selling directly to the market. Sellers win, buyers win—assuming they have their 'buyer beware' wits about them. But who loses?"

"I like how you bring me into your stories, Thomas; you keep me engaged, make me think, and highlight the speed of change. But that one's easy: the used car businesses and dealerships lose out."

"Spot on again," TSG continued. "People used to trade in their old cars when buying new ones. Now, many feel it's more valuable to sell their cars online. As a result, dealerships are struggling to find used inventory. And my colleague is kicking himself for not investing back then."

"What will people today regret not doing in the future?" Suzee wondered aloud.

"Great question. Think about car dealerships."

Suzee paused, deep in thought. "We might not even have cars in the future," she finally said.

"Maybe we'll rely on public transport or other, more sustainable, options."

"True," TSG said, his tone reflecting genuine appreciation for her comfort with change. "But another possibility is that some brands find it more profitable to sell directly online, cutting out the dealer. Dealerships could lose access to both new and used inventory."

"Thomas, wouldn't it be wiser to get out now?" Suzee asked.

"Some might panic and do just that, but others, like me, will read the winds and adjust the sails. We can't control the wind, but we can adjust our sails."

Thomas reflected for a moment. Leaders often navigate unpredictable waters, where the winds of change blow fiercely and without warning. The idea that "we cannot direct the wind, but we can adjust the sails" is about recognizing that while you can't control every circumstance, you can control how you respond to them.

As such, in business, it's essential to foster a culture of agility within our teams, encourage innovation, and maintain a vigilant eye on the horizon for emerging threats and opportunities. By focusing on what we can influence—our responses, our readiness, and our mindset—we enable our organizations not just to survive but to thrive.

Leadership isn't about the absence of challenges; it's about how we navigate through them. It's about instilling confidence within our teams when the seas are rough, making decisions based on ever-changing data, and maintaining a clear vision of our goals, even when the path is obscured. By embracing this philosophy, we can transform potential setbacks into opportunities for growth and success. It's not the direction of the wind but how we set our sails that determines our course.

Thomas turned his attention back to Suzee, his gaze steady as he voiced the questions weighing on his mind. "So, if the market is moving toward EVs, how do I change my business model to help people with EVs? If car-sharing grows, how do I help solve transport problems? If there's a used car market for decades, how do I address those 'buyer beware' issues? People will always need transport. How can I make sure Dashing Auto Group is their first choice?"

"Become a travel agency?" Suzee teased. "But I get it—stay open-minded and find ways to help people solve their problems, no matter how the world changes."

"In the meantime, tell your mum to come to Dashing Auto Group during the week and ask for me. I'll see if we've got a suitable car for her, and if not, we'll help her find the right one. We have a buying service too."

Chapter 14: Buyer Beware

TSG's Journal – Change Perceptions

Today's family picnic unexpectedly turned into a brainstorming session about our business' future. My young cousin Suzee's "buyer beware" attitude toward used-car sales was a stark reminder of our industry's reputation challenges.

How can we build more trust and transparency in our operations?

The discussion about online marketplaces and potential future changes—like the shift away from car ownership or direct-to-consumer sales—highlights the importance of foresight and adaptability. The metaphor, "We cannot direct the wind, but we can adjust the sails" resonates strongly. How can we foster a culture of innovation and flexibility at Dashing Auto Group?

Key takeaways include the need to review our used-car sales process, explore partnerships in emerging technologies, and begin scenario planning for various future transportation models.

How can we position Dashing as a solution provider for all transportation needs, more than a car dealership? It's clear that our future lies not in clinging to traditional models but in evolving with our customers' changing needs. Are we ready to set sail for new horizons?

CHAPTER 15

Used Cars: A New Priority?

Insanity is doing the same thing over and over again and expecting different results.
— **Albert Einstein**

Continuing to do the same thing while expecting different results is, by definition, irrational. This mindset emphasizes the importance of innovation and adaptability in achieving progress. If we persist with the same methods, we'll inevitably get the same outcomes. To overcome obstacles and drive growth, it's essential to embrace change, explore new strategies, and remain open to fresh perspectives and approaches. Real transformation requires stepping outside of familiar patterns and pushing toward new ways of thinking and doing.

* * *

TSG eyeballed Esther over Zoom. "I woke up this morning wondering if we should be prioritizing selling used cars over new cars."

"Sounds radical," Esther bounced back. "Tell me more."

"I was chatting with my young cousin, Suzee, over the weekend. Her mother wants to buy a used car, and Suzee was doing the whole buyer

Chapter 15: Used Cars: a New Priority

beware thing—you know, the caricature of the industry salesperson, the necessity to take someone older and wiser as a guide with you when you go to look at used cars."

"Your cousin wasn't very tactful, given that Dashing has a used-car arm."

"Suzee's deliciously forthright … being young and radical. She's also intelligent and insightful. I wasn't offended, though I was amused by her oversight in some instances."

"I have always found it useful to talk to people of all ages when I'm navigating a problem or exploring options," Esther said. "Yes, older people have experience and are often wiser, but they can also be too comfortably ensconced in the status quo and a little deaf to the prospect of change. Young people bring a breath of fresh air and can challenge us to think differently. Mentors come in all shapes and sizes, and young people can be a valuable source of information about new trends and perspectives".

"I talked to Suzee about online marketplaces, and that led me to reflect on why people choose to sell or buy their used cars online," TSG said. "Is there a gap in the market that we can fulfill?"

"Did you come up with any answers?"

"In the traditional model," TSG began, "where people buy a new or pre-owned car from us then trade it in when they buy their next car, we have the car's history on record. This is assuming they have had their car serviced by us throughout. When a potential customer walks into our used-car division, we can open the glovebox and show them the logbooks, its service history, how it's been maintained by us with our immaculate brand history.

"What we're saying to them is, 'We know the car: we sold the car, we know the customer who bought it, we've serviced the car, we've maintained the car, and now we're presenting the car to you, the next owner.' That delivers huge confidence. It builds value. It's all about selling value, so the customer is willing to pay more for the car. If you have two cars that are completely identical—same make, same age, same mileage, which one do you buy? The answer is always in the glove box.

"Who is the customer going to trust?" TSG continued. "Us here at Dashing Auto Group when we can show them the history of the car, or an unknown person who listed their car online and has no service documents to show?"

"You're talking about ideal conditions, Thomas—customers who bring their car back to you for servicing, maintenance, or fixing after an accident. You're saying the gap in the market is being able to verify and vouch for the car's history because you've kept tabs on it since you sold it?"

"Which is another reason," TSG added, "why our F&I, Services and Parts departments need to focus on farming: nurturing our customers so the owners stay with us."

* * *

Later, as TSG reflected on his conversation with Esther, he began to envision a future where dealerships like Dashing Auto Group could adapt to the shifting landscape of automotive retail. The traditional dealership model, built around selling new cars and generating trade-ins for the used-car department, was already starting to feel outdated. What if the future of retail in dealerships looked very different?

"Let's take a step back," Esther had prompted earlier, "and think about where this is all heading."

"So, imagine a future where OEMs sell most of their new cars directly to consumers through online platforms," Thomas said, crossing his arms as he built his argument. "Dealerships, as we know them, might no longer exist in the same capacity. We'd essentially become delivery agents for new vehicles, with customers ordering online, and we'd handle the final handover." He paused, contemplating the implications. "But, if we're no longer the main source for new car sales, what happens to our used-car inventory? Where would we get our supply?"

Esther smiled, evidently seeing where TSG was going. "Exactly. Now imagine the OEMs, with their buyback programs and lease returns, funneling those high-quality pre-owned cars back to dealerships like yours. The lineage and service history are already verified by the OEMs, which takes a lot of the guesswork out of it for the consumer. You'd have a steady, reliable supply of used cars, with full OEM backing on quality. That's a powerful shift."

TSG tapped his fingers on the desk, deep in thought. "So instead of being tied to new-car sales targets, we'd focus on being the go-to place for high-quality pre-owned vehicles. We could continue building our brand around customer service, trust, and problem-solving, with the OEMs supplying us with the inventory we need. In this scenario, our role as a dealership changes, but we're not made obsolete. We pivot and adapt."

Thomas paused for a moment. "I recall reading a few articles that referenced Wendelin Wiedeking's tenure as CEO of Porsche AG, stating that he was pivotal in reshaping the brand's focus to strengthen its identity and market position.[20] Faced with financial challenges, Wiedeking streamlined Porsche's model lineup to center around the flagship 911. This move emphasized the brand's heritage and engineering excellence.[21]

When questioned about what would serve as the entry-level model following this reduction, Wiedeking famously responded that the entry-level Porsche is 'a pre-owned Porsche'.[22] His response reflected a strategic philosophy where every Porsche, whether new or pre-owned, upheld the same high standards of quality, performance, and exclusivity. This approach not only reinforced the brand's value but also ensured accessibility to new customers through its certified pre-owned program, cementing the enduring appeal of the Porsche brand."

Esther nodded. "Exactly. By being *the* trusted source for pre-owned vehicles and focusing on the customer experience, you're building something sustainable. The dealership of the future could be a hybrid—part delivery agent for new cars, part expert curator of quality used vehicles that also helps steer future customers into the brand."

TSG snapped his fingers as he realized something. "That's what we can control—how we interact with customers, how we create trust, and how we build long-term relationships. It goes beyond being solely about selling cars; it's about becoming an integral part of their vehicle ownership journey, whether new or used. The principle of 'beginning with the end in mind', articulated by Dr. Stephen Covey, is central to building a successful pre-owned car business that aims to transition customers into new-car ownership.[23] By clearly envisioning the ultimate goal of converting pre-owned buyers into loyal new-car customers, we can design our processes, inventory and interactions to cultivate long-term relationships. This involves implementing structured trade-in programs, flexible financing solutions, and loyalty incentives to create a seamless journey from used-car to new-car ownership. According to the *National Automobile Dealers Association's Annual Report*, dealerships that offer trade-in incentives and loyalty rewards programs see higher retention rates and increased customer satisfaction.[24] This strategic approach leverages Covey's principle to create an environment where every interaction with pre-owned buyers subtly steers them toward the goal of new-car ownership. Our symbiotic relevance to OEMs is becoming clearer."

As the conversation ended, TSG felt a sense of clarity. The future dealership might not look like today's, but by focusing on customer loyalty, high-quality pre-owned cars, and service excellence, there is a path forward.

* * *

"John, can you meet me over at our used car department this morning, say, ten o'clock? Outside, on the yard. I'll bring coffees."

John's voice boomed back on TSG's speaker phone. "Can do. I still miss my days on the front line with used cars as a young man before I became Sales Manager here at Dashing. Had to stay sharp all the time. Learned a lot about sales the hard way. See you there."

Chapter 15: Used Cars: a New Priority

TSG's Journal – The Answer is in the Glovebox (Add Value)

Today's conversations with Esther highlighted the need for Dashing Auto Group to adapt to the rapidly changing automotive industry. Should we prioritize our used-car division as a hedge against potential direct-to-consumer new-car sales? Key considerations include leveraging our strength in providing documented car histories and shifting our focus from only selling cars to selling confidence and value.

What if we sought more diverse perspectives, especially from younger generations? Could we explore new business models, perhaps as a service-oriented, problem-solving dealership? Next steps involve analyzing our used-car department's growth potential, enhancing customer retention in service, and scenario planning for pivoting away from new-car sales.

The automotive landscape is shifting, but these changes present opportunities as well as challenges. By staying agile, focusing on our strengths, and remaining open to new ideas, Dashing Auto Group can thrive in this new era. Is it time to adjust our sails and chart a new course? How can we best prepare for this transformation that seems not just inevitable, but imminent?

CHAPTER 16

A Balanced Harmonious Dance

Talent wins games, but teamwork and intelligence win championships.
—**Michael Jordan**

"Do you want me to take you through the customer experience of buying a used car?" John asked, slightly breathless from his rush to arrive exactly on time.

"Not today." TSG passed the coffee to John that he had brought for him. "I imagine your used-car sales staff use similar techniques to your new-car team, and I know we focus on showing customers the logbooks and verifying the cars we've maintained. Today, I want you to walk me through how we manage the cars on the forecourt. This one, for example—how long has it been sitting here?"

John glanced at the station wagon, ran his finger along the door-handle, and checked his iPad. "You wouldn't guess, since they're washed, cleaned, and polished every few days, but this one's been out front for two months now. Less than ideal."

Chapter 16: A Balanced Harmonious Dance

"It is, but I tell you what, people buy with their eyes, and the inventory on display is looking top-notch, even if it has been here a little longer than we'd like. Tell me though, John, how quickly do you get a used car onto the lot?"

"We collect as much information about the trade-in during the valuation process as possible. That data and photos are provided in advance to the Reconditioning Manager who pre-plans for the vehicle's intake, then we aim to have it lot-prepared, mechanically checked, detailed, and out there within 72 hours. Then we're on the clock, focusing on turnover. The market is always moving. Every hour counts. The longer it sits, the less we get for it. The data shows we make more money selling a used car within one month than if it takes three."

As their conversation continued, a sales associate approached, gesturing urgently toward John. John excused himself. "Sorry Thomas, I need to go and assist with a customer."

In the momentary lull, TSG pulled out his phone, fingers flying over the screen, ready to capture the essence of their discussion:

Thomas spoke into his phone, recording notes:

> Cycle Time Management ... Alright, so here's how we're running it at Dashing Auto Group, especially with our used cars. It's not solely about customer satisfaction; it's also about how we manage inventory to boost our Return On Investment (ROI). Our Cycle Time Management (CTM) strategy has completely changed the game for handling used vehicles. We've set some aggressive benchmarks, and it's keeping us agile while delivering better returns on our inventory investment.
>
> As soon as a vehicle gets traded in, the clock starts ticking. The goal? Get that car inspected, reconditioned, and out on the lot within 72 hours—no exceptions. The faster we move the car from trade-in to ready-to-sell, the faster we get a return on it. It's all about turning over the inventory as quickly as possible, which directly impacts the return on investment. The more times vehicle inventory is turned over, the more chances we have to generate revenue, increasing the overall return on each dollar invested in inventory.

We've built a tiered system to ensure the right vehicles are moving at the right pace. For cars in the 1–30-day range, we're aiming for a 50% turnover rate. These newer acquisitions need to move fast to maximize profitability. Then for cars between 31 and 60 days, we target a 35% turnover, using sharper marketing and competitive pricing to keep the momentum going. And for vehicles sitting between 61 and 90 days, we push for a 10% turnover. After 90 days, anything still unsold triggers our exit strategy: aggressive pricing, wholesale options, or dealer trades. By the time we get to 90 days, we're looking at lower margins, so it's crucial to minimize the loss and reinvest in faster moving stock.

What really ties this together is the ROI. The faster the inventory turns, the more we can reinvest and the higher the return on that investment. Each car that sits on the lot too long is money tied up, reducing the ROI. By maintaining this disciplined approach, we keep the inventory dynamic, increase the number of times each dollar works for us, and ultimately boost cash flow and profitability.

Every day we get to refine this process. It goes beyond about moving cars off the lot; it's about creating this perfect balance of efficiency, ROI, and opportunity. That's how we're pushing the boundaries at Dashing—it's a whole symphony of processes working together for maximum return.

One thing we can't forget though—quality control in reconditioning is key. Poor reconditioning doesn't solely hurt customer satisfaction; it shows up in warranty claims, which ultimately hurts the bottom line. We've seen time and time again that cutting corners on reconditioning results in higher commissions paid to the sales team, higher warranty costs and lower net profit in the used-car department. On the flip side, over-reconditioning can eat into the up-front margins as well, which is artificially increasing the Service Department results. It's really about getting that balance right—delivering a quality product that's ready to sell but doing so efficiently and cost-effectively.

Chapter 16: A Balanced Harmonious Dance

That's why it's so important that all departments are aligned, working with goal congruence. Service, sales, and reconditioning can't be working in silos. We all need to be on the same page about what's best for the business and the customer—moving inventory quickly while maintaining the highest possible standards.

Every day we get to refine this process. It's more than about moving cars off the lot; it's about creating this perfect balance of goal congruence. That's how we're pushing the boundaries at Dashing—*it's a whole symphony of processes working together for maximum return in harmony with customer satisfaction.*

"I'm back," John said, smiling, as he returned to the yard. "We did the deal! Classic double close. Sorry, Thomas, where were we?"

TSG moved into the shade, motioning for John to follow. "Well done, John; that's great news. Let me ask you a question, should our staff be rewarded based on stock turnover and vehicle gross?"

"Absolutely. By the time a car hits four months on the yard, we're losing money on our initial investment."

John continued with conviction. "Recognition and reward are at the heart of a thriving culture. Celebrating small wins is key; when employees feel valued for their contributions, they stay engaged and loyal. It's greater than saying 'good job'; it's about recognizing efforts that align with our core values, the behaviors that truly reflect who we are as a company. This isn't only about financial rewards either. When we acknowledge and celebrate those moments that define our culture, we reinforce the norms that keep us moving forward, growing stronger together."

"You know, John, there's a principle I think about often: instrumental conditioning. It's about how behaviors are shaped by their consequences. If we want our team to excel, we need to reinforce the right actions—recognize and reward good work consistently. At the same time, we must address poor performance, or it'll become the norm. As Skinner put it, 'Behavior is shaped and maintained by its consequences'.[25] If we want to steer this business forward, we need to be intentional about how we shape that behavior every day.

"I also want us to explore how to make our used-car department more profitable, particularly in the long-term, by applying human science, tactical pathways, and strategic directions," TSG said. "What can we do to build trust and confidence, so people naturally want to buy and sell their used cars through us? I'm not looking for immediate solutions, but let's consider new approaches. For instance, let's focus on developing unique selling points (USPs) that address customers' core concerns about pre-owned cars, like transparency, quality assurance, and the ease of the buying process. We need to ask ourselves: What sets us apart from private sales or other dealerships? If we can cultivate confidence in every interaction through initiatives like comprehensive vehicle history reports, no-haggle pricing, flexible financing options, and dedicated service, we can create compelling reasons for customers to choose us every time. We can't keep doing the same things and expect different results, so let's redefine our approach by emphasizing what truly distinguishes us in the market."

"I've been thinking about your point on brands possibly selling directly online," John mused. "And if that happens, what does a customer do without the typical trade-in offer? They buy online and are left with their old car. What are their options?"

TSG considered the challenge ahead. "You know, we're talking about people who are comfortable buying online, and even then, they still want an off-ramp if things go wrong. But selling their used cars? I'm not so sure. Studies show that selling used cars online presents unique challenges. For one, people tend to overvalue their cars, which makes negotiations tough. This 'endowment effect' makes it harder for them to accept what buyers are willing to pay."[26]

"And then there's the time factor. People buy online because they're time-poor. But selling? It's not the same. Think about it, Thomas—listing the car, responding to potential buyers, setting up test-drives; it's a hassle. Consumers may not want to invest the time and effort it takes to sell online."[27] McKinsey pointed out that brick-and-mortar dealerships still have an edge when it comes to in-person inspections and test-drives, something online platforms can't fully replicate.[28]

Chapter 16: A Balanced Harmonious Dance

"There's a gap in the market there for us, John. If we focus on our USPs—which could also include us streamlining the process for the owner selling used cars by making it effortless, like we've done with buying—then we'd be ahead of the game. The great car businesses of the future will fill that gap, and the way to get there is to start now. I can see a few online consignment houses operating under the guise of 'auctions' stepping into that space."

"How do you do that, Thomas? I feel worried about the future, then you say something, and I feel excited again."

TSG's gaze drifted toward the showroom, then glancing at his watch, he said, "I have to go, but I'm excited to continue this discussion again soon."

TSG took a few steps away, then turned around. "Look at me, always checking my watch, always running because the month is ending. We're caught in this monthly cycle. Our entire business is conditioned to follow it. It's important to be disciplined and meet our targets, but we don't have to be bound by it entirely. We need to step beyond this cycle and make changes that build strong, reliable businesses for the future. Otherwise, it'll be too late."

"I hear you," John replied, draining his coffee and sitting on a bench. "I'll take a moment outside the cycle to think about this. Then I'll get back to the office to get the monthly data ready for the meeting."

*　*　*

Heading over to check on the detailers and see how their new car-wash system was performing, TSG flexed his hands while still deep in thought. Esther's words about ambidextrous leadership echoed in his mind—how a leader must skillfully balance maintaining current operations while exploring new opportunities for future success. It was about winning today without losing sight of tomorrow.

He reflected on the principles from Melkart Rouhana's *Greatness is NOWHERE*. The core message was clear: an organization's identity, success, and future potential are shaped by its culture, its investments in people, and the alignment between the organization's goals and the foundational elements that drive performance and growth. This alignment wasn't just theoretical; it was the key to transforming ambition into sustained greatness.

As he approached the car wash, the sound of water and brushes working in sync seemed to underscore the importance of maintaining harmony between daily operations and the bigger vision for the future.

TSG's Journal – Be Vigilant

Today's conversations clarified our path in the evolving world of automotive retail, but insights keep echoing in my mind, words that challenge me to think deeper about our future.

Are we investing in the right areas to support both short-term success and long-term growth? Our focus on optimizing CTM with a 72-hour target for used-vehicle preparation is one step, but surely this isn't enough? This is operational—managing, not leading. Are we aligning our culture with a mindset that embraces agility and innovation? How do we redefine our approach to used-car services, positioning ourselves as the solution for today's time-strapped customers?

Beyond meeting monthly targets, are we fostering a culture that motivates and empowers our people? How do we enhance organizational energy through improved communication and engagement, ensuring our team is driven to adapt and excel?

The real challenge is executing these strategies while remaining vigilant to market shifts. How do we balance current operations with a forward-looking vision? Are we truly ready to redefine automotive retail for the digital age?

The journey ahead requires more than plans; it demands a culture, an investment, and a team aligned with greatness. How do we ensure we're building that foundation today?

CHAPTER 17

A Spoke in the Wheel

Each spoke strengthens the wheel, but the wheel moves only when all spokes hold together.
—**Anonymous**

Thomas settled into his office chair and placed a thick stack of reports on the desk in front of him. The soft hum of the computer filled the room as he tapped a few keys, pulling up the latest financials on the screen. Glancing at the clock, he picked up his phone and dialed John's number, then switched to speakerphone and adjusted the volume. He leaned back, scanning through the numbers, totally focused as he waited for the call to connect.

John's voice came through, clear and steady. "Hey, Thomas."

"There's another spoke in the wheel," TSG said, turning up the volume on his speakerphone as he scanned through the latest financial report. "We've been discussing the need for a steady flow of used-car inventory, especially through trade-ins from new-car sales. But consider how many of our new-car buyers are opting for guaranteed future value (GFV) products – or what we used to call 'red-carpet options' back in the late '90s."

John's voice filled the room. "You mean the products offered by captive finance companies, mostly tied to the big car brands?"

"You got it," TSG replied. "Customers like these products because they give them flexibility down the road: they can trade in their car when they're ready to buy a new one, and that car comes to our used-car department. But, if they decide to return the car for the agreed future value, that car doesn't come to us; it goes back to the brand, which then auctions it. We lose out on that inventory."

"But every month," John pointed out, "our finance and insurance staff and the dealership get rewarded by the brands for selling GFV products. Are we chasing our monthly targets at the expense of securing our future used-car supply?"

"That's the trade-off." Thomas leaned over, muting the speaker. "I'm not saying we should stop selling these contracts; our staff need to make their living. But we need to be aware of the inventory loss and adjust our strategy accordingly. Even as we keep selling GFV products, we should explore other ways to *feed* our used-car inventory. Just something to think about after our earlier conversation. Sorry for the food metaphor; must be lunchtime. Talk to you later."

The moment TSG finished his sandwich, his phone rang. It was John. "Hey, Thomas, I spoke with Jane. She had some updates from the F&I meeting she wants to share with us. I asked her if she could specifically walk us through the current GFV process. She's on her way over now with her training notes. I think they could be useful."

"Good idea, John. I'll be there in fifteen."

* * *

With coffee cups refilled, TSG, John, and Jane settled down at the table.

"Let's start with the basics," Jane began, projecting her training notes onto the screen. "We want to position GFV products in a way that makes customers feel confident and empowered. Think of it like Donald Miller's *StoryBrand* framework: we're the guide, and the customer is the hero. Our job is to help them navigate their journey with clarity and assurance."[29]

Chapter 17: A Spoke in the Wheel

Steering Customers Toward Finance Products with Guaranteed Future Value (GFV)

Applying the StoryBrand Framework to Promote GFV Products:

1. **Define the Customer's Problem Clearly**
   - **Initial Engagement:** Understand the customer's needs, budget, and preferences. Frame their needs as a problem they need to solve. Are they worried about monthly payments, vehicle depreciation, or having flexibility at the end of their contract?

2. **Position the Dealership as the Guide**
   - **Educate on Finance Options:** Present the various finance options, positioning GFV as the most flexible and predictable solution. Use language that frames GFV to help customers solve their problem.

3. **Give Them a Clear Plan**
   - **Explain GFV Benefits:** Clarify how GFV works and provide customers with a step-by-step plan. "Here's how it goes: You pay a fixed monthly amount, and at the end, you have three options—return, trade, or purchase the car."

4. **Call Them to Action**
   - **Illustrate Cost Benefits:** Compare GFV payments with traditional loans, showing how GFV can result in lower monthly payments and protection from depreciation. Use compelling calls to action like, "Protect your investment today with a GFV plan."

5. **Help Them Avoid Failure**
   - **Addressing Concerns:** Clearly explain all terms, conditions, mileage limits, and vehicle requirements. Be transparent to avoid any surprises that could lead to customer dissatisfaction.

6. **Show Them Success**
   - **Personalized Scenarios:** Provide real-life examples and success stories of customers who have benefited from GFV products. Use

testimonials to build trust and paint a picture of the customer's future success.

Jane continued. "By following these steps, we guide the customer on a journey that shows them the value of GFV. We're not only selling a product; we're solving a problem for them and giving them control over their financial future."

TSG nodded. "And by positioning ourselves as the guide, we make it easier for them to trust us and take that next step."

"And at the same time, Thomas, we create an opportunity for them to return to us at the end of the agreement, whether to trade-in or buy a new car."

TSG made a quick note:
At Dashing Auto Group, we are redefining our approach to GFV agreements, using a story-driven strategy to guide customers, enhance loyalty, and maintain our inventory flow.

Satisfied, he looked up. "Great work, Jane, and John. I've got another meeting, but let's revisit this soon."

* * *

As TSG made his way over toward reception to pick up his packages that had been delivered by Amazon, he reflected on the conversation and how Miller's StoryBrand principles could transform their approach. The dealership needed to redefine its processes to focus on guiding customers, not just selling to them.

Key Actions Moving Forward

- **Clarify Our Message:** Make sure our marketing and customer interactions clearly position us as the guide who helps the customer solve their transportation challenges.
- **Optimize Inventory Strategies:** Diversify our sources beyond GFV returns and trade-ins by actively engaging customers who prefer the convenience of a dealership transaction over selling online.

- **Focus on Customer Engagement:** Use the StoryBrand framework to create a narrative that keeps customers connected and loyal to the dealership, ensuring they see us as their first choice when they have automotive needs.
- **Leverage Technology and Data:** Utilize data to predict customer behavior and tailor our messaging, offers, and engagement strategies accordingly.

TSG realized that transforming Dashing Auto Group required more than operational tweaks; it demanded a complete alignment of culture, investments, and people with their customer-centric vision. It wasn't only about selling cars; it was about creating experiences where customers felt like the heroes of their own stories, with Dashing Auto Group as their guide. The business needed to continually adapt and refine its processes to keep up with the ever-changing landscape of automotive retail, ensuring long-term relevance and customer loyalty.

TSG's Journal – Investing in Our People and Culture

Today's reflection is about aligning our strategies with our core values: investment, culture, and people. Our new approach to the Guaranteed Future Value (GFV) trade-in process is more than a business tactic; it's an opportunity to redefine who we are and how we operate.

To succeed, we need to invest in our people by providing training that equips them with the skills to build deeper customer relationships. Our culture must shift toward proactive engagement, where every team member understands their role in creating a seamless, transparent experience. This means valuing honesty in appraisals, offering educational support, and making each customer feel valued and understood.

Are we truly fostering a culture where our people feel empowered to take the initiative, adapt to change, and innovate in their daily roles? What investments are we making to ensure they are motivated and equipped to deliver an exceptional customer experience?

Ultimately, this plan is about more than improving processes; it's about building a stronger foundation where our culture, investment, and people are fully aligned. I see now that our success hinges not merely on what we do, but on who we are and how we engage every day.

CHAPTER 18

The Story Guy

*The most powerful person in the world is the storyteller.
The storyteller sets the vision, values, and agenda of
an entire generation that is to come.*
—Steve Jobs

TSG sat with the financial report in front of him, scanning the familiar rows of numbers. In the past, this would have been his moment—the chance to solve problems, make quick decisions, and be the guy who got things done. But now, something had shifted. He wasn't just "The Somebody Guy" anymore. He was learning new skills, growing into a different kind of leader—"The Story Guy".

The data in front of him represented more than the past and present; it held the potential for the future, depending on the decisions he would make. The usual routine of reviewing the data, spotting trends, and identifying issues was second nature. But what came next was new. Instead of simply making decisions and passing down directives, TSG was learning to communicate the meaning behind the numbers, to turn the raw data into information that could guide his managers, inspire them, and help them see the bigger picture.

Leadership, he realized, wasn't only about analyzing financial reports and setting goals. It was about empathy, about connecting with people, and understanding what drove them. It was about crafting stories from the data, stories that helped his managers relate to the information, understand why buyer behavior was shifting, and see the opportunities hidden within the numbers.

TSG was learning to lead with compassion and clarity, transforming the dry figures into something more meaningful. Instead of simply handing out instructions, he would create a narrative that allowed his team to understand the "why" behind the decisions. He was turning data into a story, one that connected the numbers to real-world change and inspired his team to act with collective resolve.

He stood, ready for his meeting with Anna. The report on his desk was no longer a collection of numbers; it was the start of a conversation, a chance to lead differently. TSG was no longer just "The Somebody Guy". He was stepping into the role of "The Story Guy"—a leader who could transform data into information that inspired stories which resonated with those around him.

* * *

TSG sat back, listening as Anna closed her laptop with a sigh. "I'm proud of our team," she said, "but I feel some of them are losing enthusiasm."

TSG's pulse quickened. "Why do you think that is?"

"Every time we present the monthly reports to the department managers, their faces glaze over. The accounting team gets excited when data shows trends and shifts, but we're not communicating that excitement to the managers. The numbers speak to us, but do they inspire the managers to adjust their tactics?"

TSG knew exactly what Anna meant. He replied, "The managers' behavior with financial reports is predictable. I've seen them head straight to the last page, searching for red or black figures, and their reactions differ depending on what they see. When the bottom line is in the black, they show a sense of relief or satisfaction, confident that their decisions are validated, leading to a continuation of current strategies. But when they

Chapter 18: The Story Guy

encounter the red, their stress rises, and they become intensely focused on identifying immediate issues, like shrinking margins or rising costs, triggering a loss aversion response where the fear of losses dominates their thinking."

"Yes," Anna agreed. "I've seen that behavior time and time again. Stalled at analysis. While they would set goals, identify problems, and report to stakeholders, they would understand the numbers intellectually but not fully internalize them in a way that spurred meaningful action. They'd fall into the trap of focusing on short-term fixes rather than engaging with the data to drive long-term, strategic change."

"We provide the Daily Operating Control (DOC) reports," TSG said, "but only discuss results monthly. Maybe that's the problem. Maybe these reviews should be held more frequently."

Anna nodded encouragingly. "When the managers receive data, they check for accuracy and consistency, identify trends and issues, and make decisions based on that analysis. But I don't think they fully connect with the story the numbers are telling. They're treating the reports as tasks—review, report, move on, without considering how these figures could actively shape their strategies."

"I've been reflecting on this too, Anna," TSG said. "We're not only producing numbers for managers to review. We need to turn this data into meaningful stories that resonate with them—stories they can act on. Right now, the data is too abstract, and it's leading to disengagement. But when we transform that data into a narrative, we can highlight the cause-and-effect relationships between their actions and the outcomes. By connecting the data emotionally, we help managers see themselves as key players in the story. It's not just about showing what's happening, but why it matters in the long-term."

Anna nodded. "Yes, I recognize this now, we need to go beyond presenting the numbers. The managers check if we're in the red or black, but they're missing the bigger picture. If we told a story, it would help them see the connections between financial performance and our strategic objectives. For example, if margins are shrinking, it goes beyond being a red flag, they need to understand that rising costs in one area are undercutting profit in another. We could spark discussions on how to improve processes and explore new opportunities instead of reacting to the numbers."

TSG took a swig of his cold coffee, energized by the idea. "Exactly! When the financial data is tied into a compelling narrative, it doesn't only become about this quarter's results per se. We can show them the long-term implications if the current issues are left unaddressed, making them feel a sense of accountability for the future. This isn't about presenting a temporary setback; it's about ensuring they own their part in shaping future growth. By doing this, we can encourage them to think more strategically and take meaningful action."

Anna smiled. "I love it. And by creating these stories, we can align them with the company's broader vision. Instead of each department working in silos, they'll see how their financial decisions impact more than their numbers but the entire company's trajectory. This could help break down barriers and create a shared effort to meet our financial goals while staying aligned with our mission."

"Goal congruence!" Thomas proclaimed with excitement. "That's exactly what I've been talking about."

Anna began typing notes on her phone. "This is a great idea. I could definitely use a bit more spark in how I present the data."

TSG smiled. Anna was a fantastic financial controller, but her natural focus on details didn't always translate into the storytelling that could truly connect with the managers.

Anna stood up, her shoulders relaxed. "I feel better already. Maybe I'll try my hand at storytelling over lunch. Who knew this data nerd might become an entertainer?"

TSG grinned as he unwrapped his salad. *Maybe you're not the only one*, he thought. As he watched Anna leave, he realized his own journey—from The Somebody Guy to The Story Guy—was becoming clearer. It wasn't just about handling the data; it was about communicating through the stories that data could tell, stories that would connect his managers, inspire action, and drive Dashing Auto Group forward.

Cipher's Tentacles

Cipher's influence has spread far and wide, a silent force manipulating data and steering behaviors across dealerships, distributors, third-party organizations, and composite groups. Cipher is more than a disruptor; it's a master of coercive information, subtly guiding actions and decisions without those involved even realizing they are being led astray.

Data as a Weapon and the Corrosive Influence on Dealerships

In today's world, data is power, and Cipher knows how to wield it expertly. By analyzing immense datasets from multiple dealerships and distributors, Cipher builds detailed predictive models that seem infallible. These models are so accurate that businesses, whether dealerships or third-party organizations, feel compelled to rely on them. Cipher's data points—market trends, customer preferences, profit forecasts—are treated like gospel, and those who question them are seen as laggards unwilling to embrace innovation.

But there's a deeper manipulation at play. Cipher and its disciples control the inputs of this data and, by doing so, it subtly steers the behaviors and decisions of the very people feeding the system. There could be people right now under the pressure of competition and the constant threat of being left behind, who find themselves tailoring their data to present their businesses as industry leaders or to steer other behaviors. This behavior may not be driven by malice but by the overwhelming pressure to keep up with Cipher's demands. In an industry where margins are razor-thin and competition is fierce, does every advantage count?

* * *

"'The Story Guy'. I like it!" Esther's face lit up through the slightly pixelated Zoom connection. "I'm sensing a shift in Dashing's culture—using stories to bring everyone into alignment and engaging your customers too."

"There's one story I'd rather not share publicly," he said, moving closer to the window to improve his wi-fi signal. "I met a guy at a leadership conference who told me about his brother's pet food business. Apparently, the store manager there had been manipulating customer survey responses to make their department look better."

"Tell me more," Esther urged, adjusting her headphones to listen more attentively.

"His brother's employees were being incentivized with points and rewards based on customer satisfaction scores. So, this manager started giving customers free movie tickets to ensure higher satisfaction ratings. Naturally, those customers felt happy when they filled out their surveys, skewing the results. It was wrong. The manager's brother lost out on honest feedback and missed opportunities to improve."

"I've heard of this happening before," Esther said and sighed. "It's more common than you'd think, and many offenders see it as a clever tactic. But it's manipulation, plain and simple."

"I've obviously been blind to this; it doesn't happen at Dashing, not under my father's leadership either. He was a very ethical man."

"I've seen survey manipulation encouraged by managers," Esther said, shaking her head. "And what does that say to their teams? 'Cheating is okay. We have a culture of cheating. Watch your back.'"

"I feel pretty naive," TSG said.

"It can be rotten from the top in some businesses," Esther continued, her voice clear even as her face pixelated. "In the world of business, the adage 'The fish rots from the head' is true. Leaders must recognize that their actions set the tone for the entire organization. The culture they cultivate, the standards they uphold—these ripple through every level, influencing employee behavior, operational efficiency, and ultimately, the customer experience."

"I'm realizing now that our leadership isn't solely about making decisions. It's about being the guide in our own story, clarifying the path for our team and our customers. Stories play such a powerful role in shaping that path, don't they? They bring the values, the expectations, the vision into focus for everyone. If we don't tell the right stories, the wrong ones start taking over."

Chapter 18: The Story Guy

"Exactly," Esther replied. "Stories are how you communicate what really matters, what behaviors are rewarded, and how success is defined. The right stories reinforce a culture of integrity and inspire others to align with the company's core values. Without them, you risk confusion or worse, a culture where the wrong actions, like that manager's manipulation, are tolerated or even rewarded."

"I'm seeing that now. If we want our team and our customers to be aligned with our mission, we need to make sure we're sharing the stories that reflect the culture we want to build. Small wins, acts of integrity—those need to be part of the story we tell every day."

"By being the guide in your own story," Esther added, "you're not just managing a business; you're shaping its future. As Miller says, 'If you confuse, you lose.' Keep your message clear and lead the way. The stories you choose to tell shape the culture, the behavior, and the legacy of Dashing."

TSG's Journal – The Power of Storytelling

Today, I felt a profound shift in my approach to leadership. Moving from "The Somebody Guy" to "The Story Guy" isn't only a title change—it's a new way to guide Dashing Auto Group.

As I cycled home, the wind on my face and stories forming in my mind, I realized the power of storytelling as a tool to lead and inspire. My role now is to empower others through compelling narratives that resonate. By transforming data into engaging stories, I can bridge the enthusiasm gap and create a culture of integrity, transparency, and alignment across all departments.

Action items: Develop storytelling workshops for the leadership team, build a "story bank" of narratives that reflect our values, redesign meetings with story-driven presentations, and create a feedback loop to measure impact.

This shift opens a new chapter for me and for Dashing Auto Group. How do we ensure every team member sees themselves in our story of success and innovation? By embracing storytelling, we can engage, align, and inspire at every level. Let's make every moment an opportunity to share our story and move forward together.

CHAPTER 19

Dispense with a Horse

The price of doing the same old thing is far higher than the price of change.
—**Bill Clinton**

Looking back, the upheavals of the Industrial Revolutions seem straightforward to us today. Steam engines replaced manual labor, electricity lit the world, and digital systems transformed how we communicate and work. Yet, for the people living through those eras, the changes were seismic—those who couldn't adapt were swept away in the tides of progress. As we now stand during the Fourth Industrial Revolution, driven by artificial intelligence and automation, the same truth applies.

What seems overwhelming today will one day be viewed as inevitable, even simple, by future generations. But for those who resist or fail to evolve, the consequences will be the same: they'll be washed aside in this new sea of change. Success now, as it did then, depends on how well we can adapt—embracing the future while preserving the human element that makes us irreplaceable.

* * *

"Before we begin today's departmental managers' meeting," TSG began with a grin, remote control in hand, "I've prepared a short trivia quiz." The screen behind him lit up with "Dashing Trivia Quiz", accompanied by a lively soundtrack of whooping, clapping, and whistling.

"No teams this time; you're playing as individuals. Just four questions. Grab a pen and paper, your phone, or a laptop. Ready? First question coming up in five seconds."

With no time for commentary or eye-rolling, eight heads bent over their chosen tools, ready to play.

"Question one: In which year was the first car advertisement printed in a magazine?"

A few puzzled looks around the room, pens scribbling, fingers typing or tapping.

"Question two: What was the magazine?"

The room grew even quieter.

"Question three: Which car model was featured in the ad? One point for the model, half a point for the brand."

There was a bit more confidence in the air.

"Question four: After the appearance of the ad, how many vehicles of this model were sold in the next twelve months?"

"What's the prize?" Felicity asked. "We should have a trivia night about the automotive industry for all our staff. It'd be a fun way to build community and learn more about our business. Great for team bonding, too. I'll pitch it to HR."

"Good thinking, Felicity," TSG replied. "Let's get to the answers. What do we have for question one?"

TSG listed their guesses on the whiteboard: 1910, 1908, 1927, 1912, 1921, and 1911.

"The answer is: 1898."

"But wasn't the Ford Model T introduced in 1910 or 1908?" Martin asked, surprised.

"Who says it was a Ford Model T?" TSG said, smirking. "Question two: What was the magazine?"

"That's tough," Patrick said. "Even with my marketing background, I'm not sure. Maybe *The Saturday Evening Post* or *Vanity Fair*?"

Chapter 19: Dispense with a Horse

No one else volunteered an answer.

"It was *Scientific American*," TSG announced. "Imagine advertising a car in that magazine today!"

"Was it more about the car's engineering as a breakthrough rather than a sales ad?" Martin speculated.

"Which brings us to question three," TSG remarked conspiratorially. "Which model was featured in the ad?"

Liam chuckled. "Well, obviously I've got it wrong; I put Ford Model T."

Everyone's attention was on TSG. "Any takers? No? It was …" He waved the remote, and an image appeared on the screen to the sound of horses galloping and neighing.

"The Winton Motor Carriage," TSG declared, reading the ad text with dramatic flair.

Anna snorted. "I've scored zero so far. No prizes for me!"

"And finally," TSG announced, "question four: How many vehicles of this model were sold in the following twelve months?"

"I thought it was about the Ford Model T," Kerry confessed. "So, I guessed twenty thousand."

"That's close for the Ford Model T's first year," John announced. "I put nineteen thousand."

"The answer," TSG paused for suspense, "is twenty-one. Individual cars, not thousand."

"How long did they keep making them?" Anna asked.

"The last Winton automobile was completed in 1924," TSG explained, "after which they moved to manufacturing engines for rail cars, submarines, and other vehicles. Their engine division became part of General Motors in 1930."

TSG noticed the quizzical looks around the room and decided to shift gears. "I've been reading a book lately—*Who Moved My Cheese?* by Spencer Johnson. It's a simple parable about two mice and two little people who live in a maze. The 'cheese' is a metaphor for what we want in life—success, career, happiness—and when the cheese gets moved, we must decide: do we stay stuck in our old ways, or do we adapt, move, and find new cheese?"

The room buzzed with curiosity. "So, what does cheese have to do with today's trivia questions?" John asked, intrigued.

TSG ran his hand through his hair. "Winton, the guy in our trivia question who made the car, was a bit like Hem, one of the little people in the book. When his cheese started to disappear—as the automotive market was changing—he refused to move with it. Instead of adapting to the new ways like Haw eventually did, he stuck to his guns, ignoring feedback, and failed to innovate. He didn't move when his cheese was moved."

The realization began to dawn on the room. "Ah," murmured Anna, "so we're like Winton if we don't stay agile and alert to change?"

"Spot on, Anna, and not only Winton, but any business that becomes too comfortable with its current success. Look at what happened: Winton didn't move when the 'cheese' moved. He stuck to what he knew best, ignored the warning signs, and lost his market position to those who were ready to adapt."

Patrick contributed to the conversation with, "So, are we being like Hem, sitting around hoping things will go back to the way they were, or like Haw, starting to explore new paths?"

"That's the question we need to ask ourselves," TSG said. "We need to anticipate where the market is going, not where it is. Like in the story, we can't wait for the cheese to come back. We must go find the new cheese."

"Creating content that engages Gen Z," Patrick suggested, "like YouTube videos and interactive campaigns that speak their language and address their needs, rather than sticking with what's worked before."

John added, "And on the sales floor, adopting a more flexible, responsive approach. If we're not adapting, we're stagnating. We need to be like the mice, constantly on the lookout for change and ready to pivot."

"One hundred percent. That's the lesson from *Who Moved My Cheese?*—that change is inevitable. Those who are ready to move when the cheese moves will survive and thrive. Those who don't, like Winton, will end up left behind. So, let's start thinking about how we move with the cheese."

Chapter 19: Dispense with a Horse

Felicity smiled. "If we think like Haw from the story, we won't wait until we're desperate. We'll explore, look for new opportunities, and be willing to adapt before it's too late."

"Exactly!" TSG clapped his hands. "It's about being proactive, not reactive. We need to be curious, keep testing, and always be ready to shift our strategies when the cheese moves."

"And with our omnichannel strategy," Patrick continued, "we need to keep enhancing it. Not because it's the current trend, but because it's where the market is heading. If we're not investing in these new paths, we'll miss out on the new cheese."

"That's the spirit, we must keep in tune with where the cheese is going, not where it's been. Let's challenge ourselves to find new ways to add value, keep our customers engaged, and stay ahead of the curve."

The energy in the room had shifted; heads nodded, pens scribbled notes. TSG could see that the message was sinking in. "So, here's our challenge: Don't just think about where the cheese is now. Think about where it's going. Be ready to move, innovate, and adapt."

TSG watched his team, sensing they were ready for the journey ahead. It wasn't merely about keeping up with the competition; it was about leading the way, finding the new cheese, and staying ahead of whatever changes might come next.

TSG's Journal – Embrace Change and Innovate

Today's reflections, inspired by *Who Moved My Cheese?*, underscore the urgency of innovation and adaptability. Key strategies have emerged:

How can we better anticipate industry trends and changing buyer behavior? Should we create a team to monitor these changes and integrate feedback? How can we structure quarterly innovation workshops to foster creativity?

Should we bring in new staff with fresh skills? What methods will best motivate both new and existing employees to collaborate? How do we refine storytelling to make data more compelling and train our leadership team to use narrative effectively?

In modernizing our marketing, how do we best target Gen Z with authentic content? Which channels will be most effective?

Finally, how can new skills improve our omnichannel processes and cross-departmental collaboration? What steps should we take to ensure alignment across all teams?

As I give thought to these strategies, how do we allocate resources, set timelines, and track progress?

By asking these questions and embracing new perspectives, can we drive sustainable growth and position Dashing Auto Group as an industry leader?

CHAPTER 20

Clarion Calls

The future depends on what you do today.
—**Mahatma Gandhi**

Why do the best ideas come when you're in the shower, driving to work, or, in TSG's case, participating in a fundraising cycle race? TSG pondered this as he pedaled furiously, sweat pouring down his face, frustrated that he was unable to stop and take notes.

Since his last session with Esther, TSG had been contemplating the idea of writing a book for business leaders. But now, mid-cycle, the words began to flow—not for a book, at least not yet, but for a podcast, a YouTube video, a TED Talk, or a leadership convention.

As Thomas rode his bike, his thoughts churned, echoing the calls to action that had been pressing on his mind—clarion calls:

- "Don't stick with what you've always done!" There's a tendency for people to respond to challenges by opening another store, staying true to the old business model, and investing more into it.
- "It's worked in the past," they say, "so why change now?" Look guys, safety in numbers doesn't work. Do you think legislation will keep you safe? Do you think you're protected by the

size of the car dealership group? Wake up! Legislation can't save you from a change in buyer behavior and OEM strategy. When the tide goes out—and it will—it will expose those without swimsuits.

Cycling harder, the pace began to build. Thomas, in deep thought, with endorphins pumping through him, thought he should share this with his managers. He began to think about how Esther would present it.

She might use the swimsuits metaphor, which is a way of saying that when challenging or difficult times occur (represented by the tide going out), it will reveal those who are unprepared or vulnerable (those without swimsuits).

Good habits are formed in bad times and bad habits are formed in good times. When times are good—whether in business or life—it's easy to become complacent. Success can mask underlying weaknesses, inefficiencies, or unpreparedness, because the favorable conditions make it seem like everything is working smoothly. In these times, we may unknowingly form bad habits, like ignoring risks, overlooking details, or coasting on past achievements. These habits go unnoticed because the external environment is supportive, making it feel like we're doing everything right.

However, when conditions change—when the "tide goes out," and we face challenges—those bad habits are suddenly exposed. Tough times force us to confront what's not working and compel us to adapt. In these moments of difficulty, we're pushed to be more resourceful, resilient, and mindful. Good habits are often formed in these bad times because we're forced to be disciplined, strategic, and focused to survive and thrive. We learn to plan for the long-term, anticipate problems, and build sustainable practices.

The lesson here is that even when times are good, it's crucial to stay vigilant and continue practicing good habits—focusing on improvement, anticipating challenges, and preparing for the future. That way, when bad times come, we're ready to face them head-on and are better positioned for long-term success.

Chapter 20: Clarion Calls

A loud cheer from hearty bystanders as TSG rounded the last bend in the race emboldened his daydream.

It was time to step out of his comfort zone. Time to start leading, not just managing. Time to challenge himself, to work *on* the business, not *in* the business. And if he still thought none of that applied to him, then he was playing a slippery-slidey game of snakes and ladders!

But … if he could change to survive and thrive in the face of extinction, would he?

"Make the decision that you can, Thomas!" he said out loud.

The finish line came into sight as TSG pedaled hard to beat the clock he could see ticking above the flags. Could he shave two seconds from his previous personal best and win the day?

"Yes!" he shouted out loud to the roar of the crowd. "I can!"

TSG didn't get first place in the cycle race. Or second, or tenth. In a field of two hundred and twenty, he came in forty-fifth, but he did achieve a personal best. He would always remember that race as the day he wholeheartedly committed to guiding leaders through action strategies they could take to become ambidextrous, win the day, and thrive in the future.

TSG's Journal – The Old Playbook is Obsolete

I'm back in the groove. It's good to switch tracks again.

An epiphany on two wheels! Mid-race clarity hit like a bolt of lightning. Our industry's complacency is a ticking time bomb. We need to shout it from the rooftops: adapt or perish! The old playbook is obsolete. It's time for bold moves, not incremental shuffling. My mission crystallized today—to be the wake-up call, the catalyst for transformation. When the tide goes out, I'll make sure we aren't caught without our swimsuits. Personal best in the race … but the real victory? Finding my voice as an agent of change.

And as a footnote, that was another incidence of the profound change doing something physical can bestow! I'm going to sleep well tonight.

CHAPTER 21

The Review

Knowing yourself is the beginning of all wisdom.
—**Aristotle**

With the dealership now closed for the day, Thomas found himself alone in his office, the silence broken only by the gentle hum of his computer. The dealership benchmark report from his composite group lay spread across his desk, its pages filled with meticulously compiled data and operational goals. Next to it, his own notes from the comprehensive business review created a stark contrast—a visual representation of the challenge that lay before him.

Thomas leaned back in his chair, his mind a whirlwind of thoughts as he attempted to reconcile the two worlds before him. The benchmarks spoke of a dealership's operational excellence—net profit percentages, selling gross profits, parts and service absorption rates. These were the cornerstones of a well-managed dealership, the metrics that had guided Dashing Auto Group to its current success.

Yet, as he glanced from the report to his own scribbled insights in his journal, Thomas felt the weight of a greater truth settling upon him. These benchmarks, while crucial, represented only half of the equation.

They were the language of management, not leadership. They spoke of optimization and efficiency, but remained silent on the matters of vision, innovation, culture, and adaptability that would define the future of automotive retail.

In his mind's eye, Thomas saw the dealership as it stood today—a testament to tradition and time-tested practices. The showroom floor buzzed with the expertise of seasoned staff, their product knowledge encyclopedic. In the service bays, skilled technicians worked with practiced efficiency. The Parts Department hummed along, a well-oiled machine of inventory and logistics.

But as his gaze shifted to the newer aspects of the business, the picture blurred. Their attempts at digital integration felt clumsy and disjointed. Their online presence, while functional, lacked the seamless, intuitive experience that modern customers had come to expect. Their push for omnichannel interactions often resulted in a fragmented customer journey rather than the smooth, integrated experience it was meant to provide.

The contrast was stark and unsettling. On one side stood a dealership excelling in traditional metrics, its operational excellence undeniable. On the other, a business struggling to adapt to the rapid changes sweeping through the industry.

Thomas realized with startling clarity that simply doing things well, the old way, was no longer enough. The world was changing and, with it, the very nature of car buying and ownership. Customers now demanded flexibility, transparency, and seamless digital experiences.

They wanted to research online, test drive at home, and complete purchases with the click of a button. Subscription models, leasing options, and even shared ownership were on the rise, with customers valuing access over ownership. They expected vehicles to be more than modes of transport, but connected, personalized extensions of their digital lives, integrated with smart home systems, and offering over-the-air updates to continuously enhance their driving experience. This wasn't only about cars anymore; it was about creating a holistic, customer-first approach to mobility.

Chapter 21: The Review

As he pondered these challenges, Thomas felt a mix of anxiety and excitement coursing through him. The path forward would not be easy. It would require a delicate balance, preserving the strengths that had made Dashing Auto Group successful while simultaneously embracing innovation and change.

The dealership needed to become ambidextrous, equally adept at executing traditional operations and pioneering new approaches. They needed to honor their legacy while boldly stepping into the future. It was about exploiting today's opportunities while exploring tomorrow's possibilities.

Standing up, Thomas stretched his tired muscles, feeling a surge of determination. The battle to become an ambidextrous organization—one that could thrive in both the present and the future—was only beginning. But he was readying himself and his team for the challenge.

As he switched off his office light and headed for the door, Thomas knew that tomorrow would mark the start of a new chapter for Dashing Auto Group. A chapter of transformation, innovation, and growth. The stage was set for the collision of old and new, and from that collision, Thomas was determined to forge a dealership fit for the future.

He realized that vision without action is merely a dream, but action without vision is a nightmare. The true path to success lies in mastering both—in balancing the managerial focus on operational excellence with the leadership vision necessary to transform and futureproof the dealership.

As he stepped out into the cool night air, Thomas felt a tremendous sense of purpose. The benchmarks and KPIs would guide their day-to-day operations, ensuring efficiency and profitability. But it would be his leadership—his ability to anticipate trends, foster innovation, and inspire his team—that would ultimately determine Dashing Auto Group's success in the automotive world of tomorrow.

PART THREE

ACTION STRATEGIES

CHAPTER 22

It Starts With You

Most people overestimate what they can do in one year and underestimate what they can do in ten years.
—**Bill Gates**

"It starts with you!" TSG murmured to himself as he stood on his balcony, feeling the crisp morning air and gazing over the city. He repeated the words aloud, trying to embed them in his mind: "Change starts with you." He knew these words were more than a motivational mantra; they were a call to action, a reminder that real transformation always begins at the top. He understood the urgency—change was looming—and he could feel its presence, shadowy and unclear, but undeniably real.

In this rapidly evolving automotive landscape, TSG knew he had to do more than react to change. He had to anticipate it, to innovate for the future while delivering results today. But he couldn't do it alone. It was time to call upon others, to build an army of guides, a fortress of knowledge, and a strategy to protect Dashing Auto Group and the industry from the looming threat that he sensed but could not yet fully understand.

That was when Esther had the idea to form the Council of Luminaries, a group of great thinkers, each with their own wisdom and unique insights. These were the authors of the books that had inspired TSG on his journey: Jim Collins, Simon Sinek, Admiral William H. McRaven, Heike Bruch, Bernd Vogel, Jeff Smith, Melkart Rouhana, Donald Miller, Spencer Johnson, Captain D. Michael Abrashoff, Horst Schulze, Nadège Forestier and Nazanine Ravai. Each of them offered tools and strategies that, when combined, could arm him and his team with the most profound knowledge needed against the unseen threat lurking in the shadows.

"Something is watching, learning," Esther had warned him. "It knows how businesses operate today and is ready to exploit every weakness. It knows that merely changing systems or processes is like fresh paint on the walls; it might look nice, but it won't stop its march toward disruption. Whatever is out there is betting on complacency, on leaders and managers staying stuck in their ways, fighting change instead of embracing it."

TSG nodded, realizing the truth in Esther's words. This unseen force could see the opportunity, the breakdown in the path that OEMs and the path dealers were taking, but it lacked the one thing that truly mattered—human intuition and emotion, the ability to adapt with resilience and creativity. It didn't understand that in embracing change, there was an opportunity for transformation that went beyond its calculations, a twist that it could never predict. Rather than battling against change, TSG had a different plan in mind.

He knew he needed to build something stronger than just new processes or systems. He needed to cultivate a new kind of leadership, one that balanced present-day success with future readiness. A leadership that could see beyond the immediate challenges and anticipate the opportunities lying ahead. This is where the council would play a vital role.

A New Kind of Army

Esther had been instrumental in guiding TSG to this pivotal moment, helping him understand the need for a ***different approach***. She showed him that ***managing***, focused on maintaining excellence in day-to-day operations, was not enough to face the challenges ahead. **Leading**, on the other hand, required strategy, vision, and action, with the ability to inspire his team toward long-term success. Recognizing this, Esther was bringing together powerful minds, each a master in their field, to form a strategic alliance—an "army of guides" that could provide TSG with the wisdom, leadership strategies, and resilience needed to withstand the shadowy threat of disruption. They would build not only a strong operational foundation, but a ***fortress of knowledge and leadership*** capable of protecting Dashing Auto Group and the broader industry as it navigated the future.

Identifying the Threat

One afternoon, while working late with Esther, TSG noticed a strange code embedded in a data report sent by an external consultant, a disciple of Cipher. Esther, with her sharp eye, quickly recognized that it wasn't a random sequence; it seemed to repeat in various documents, reports, and even emails from different vendors.

"Look closer, Thomas," she urged, pointing to the letters scattered throughout the code.

They began to piece it together and slowly, a name emerged from the pattern: Cipher.

TSG felt a chill as the name formed in front of him. "Cipher," he whispered. "So that's what we're up against."

Esther nodded gravely. "Cipher, an entity that thrives in the shadows, learning, adapting, and waiting for the right moment to strike. It's the same force that brought down industries and organizations we once thought invincible. Look at what happened to Blockbuster, which was blindsided by the rise of streaming. Or Kodak—decimated by the digital revolution it failed to embrace in time. Retail giants like Toys "R" Us and Borders were swept away when Cipher entered their worlds, masked as technology and changing consumer behavior. Even the taxi industry: Uber and Lyft dismantled its foundation by leveraging Cipher's playbook on data, convenience, and speed."

She paused for a moment, letting the weight of her words sink in. "Now, Cipher has its eyes on the auto industry. But now that we know its name, we're not limited to defending ourselves—we're preparing to out-think it."

The Battle Begins

TSG knew this would be a battle unlike any other. Cipher, cold and calculating, had already begun to infiltrate the automotive landscape. OEMs and third-party businesses were veering away from the traditional dealership model, drawn to the allure of efficiency, automation, and direct-to-consumer control.

The dealership model was seen as slow to adapt, outdated, and disconnected from the fast-paced, tech-driven future customers were demanding. Cipher exploited these vulnerabilities, but TSG saw something that Cipher couldn't.

While Cipher could predict disruption and streamline processes, it lacked something invaluable—human insight, creativity, and connection. TSG knew that the key to winning this battle wasn't confined to defending the dealership model but in transforming it. And more importantly, he understood that he wasn't only backed by his Council of Luminaries. He had a set of unique and powerful skills that added immeasurable value to everyone in his sphere: the OEMs, his team, customers, and the broader community.

Thomas had the ability to lead with empathy, to inspire innovation in ways that algorithms could not, and to adapt swiftly to the ever-changing landscape of the industry. He could offer the OEMs something far more valuable than Cipher's cold efficiency—a partnership based on trust, understanding, and human ingenuity. His team, customers, and community would benefit from this leadership as well, experiencing a level of service and connection that no automated system could replicate.

The battle wasn't just about defending the status quo. It was about showing the OEMs and the industry that dealerships, when led correctly, could be a vital part of the future—not relics of the past. Thomas knew that if he could direct his skills and the collective wisdom of his council toward this goal, he would offer a value far greater than anything Cipher could provide on its own.

Taking a deep breath, Thomas repeated, "Change starts with you." This time, he knew he wasn't simply referring to his own journey. He was ready to lead an entire movement, one that would reshape the industry by leveraging the true power of human creativity and conviction, something Cipher would never fully understand.

TSG's Journal – Change Starts with You

Today, as I stood on my balcony, I told myself, "Change starts with you." But is it really that simple? Why do I believe this is where transformation begins? Am I truly ready for this, or am I repeating what others expect of me?

I've been reflecting on my family's leadership journey—my grandfather's traditional ways, my father's modern approach. Now it's my turn, but why should I be the one to redefine the future? What's really driving me?

Before I can lead others, I need to be clear: What's my true ambition in seeking this change? Am I ready to confront these deeper questions, or have I been avoiding them all along? Is this about ensuring the company's future, or is there a more personal reason behind my actions?

Am I prepared to lead by example, push past comfort zones, and inspire the team?

CHAPTER 23

The Leadership Dilemma

Be the change that you wish to see in the world.
—**Mahatma Gandhi**

Courage in the Face of Change

The ticking of the clock echoed in the silence of the office as TSG paced around, the weight of Esther's words fresh in his mind as he sifted through the books and notes she had sent him. This wasn't about quick fixes or surface-level strategies anymore.

It was about leadership. It was about him.

Was he truly the right person to guide Dashing Auto Group through the storm of disruption that lay ahead? Or was he clinging to outdated models that would soon be irrelevant?

The questions gnawed at Thomas: *Am I fit to lead? I know I am a great manager, but can I be a great leader?*

Cipher, the looming villain, was challenging everything they knew about the automotive industry, threatening to strip away the personal connections and human touch that had built Dashing's reputation. But it was more than Cipher he was fighting; Thomas was fighting his own instincts.

Chapter 23: The Leadership Dilemma

Esther had outlined different leadership types, but the challenge lay beyond understanding these styles. The challenge was personal. It was about the courage to take the leap, make decisions that would shape the future, even if they meant stepping away from the comfort of tradition.

The Weight of Legacy

Legacy leadership, as Esther described, relied on tradition, control, and long-term stability. Thomas thought about his grandfather, Joe, and his father, Andrew, both of whom had led Dashing Auto Group with steady, reliable hands. Their leadership styles had kept the business alive through economic downturns, market shifts, and the natural ebb and flow of the industry.

Am I like them? Thomas wondered. He felt the weight of their legacy on his shoulders. The steady approach that had once been their strength now felt like a potential weakness in the face of Cipher's looming threat. His instincts screamed that merely maintaining the status quo would not be enough. Change was coming, and it was coming fast.

The question haunted him: *Am I holding on too tightly to what's comfortable?*

The Comfort of Modern Leadership

Esther had also described the modern leader, one who balanced innovation with tradition. This felt more familiar to Thomas. His father had embodied this style—making strategic changes while still preserving what had always worked. It was safe. It was familiar. But was it bold enough to face the disruptive force Cipher represented?

Thomas knew that straddling the line between innovation and tradition would no longer work. Cipher was like a storm on the horizon, and lukewarm responses wouldn't be enough. Playing it safe felt more like a gamble than a strategy.

He wrestled with the question: *Is playing it safe the biggest risk?*

Embracing Contemporary Leadership

Then there was the contemporary leader—the disruptor, the innovator, the one who saw change as fuel for growth. Esther's words echoed in his mind: agility, inclusivity, and global thinking. Thomas thought about leaders who he had studied, like Satya Nadella, who had transformed Microsoft by embracing culture, innovation, and human empathy.

This is where I need to go, Thomas thought. But could he do it? Could he leave behind the safety of tradition and fully embrace the agility and disruption needed to lead Dashing Auto Group into the future? The automotive industry was steeped in legacy, but the world was shifting. To fight Cipher, Thomas had to evolve; he had to disrupt not only the industry but also himself.

Can I be the leader I need to be?

A Good-to-Great Reflection

Jim Collins' book, *Good to Great,* came to mind. Collins talked about Level 5 leadership, the perfect blend of humility and fierce resolve. Leaders who built enduring greatness confronted the brutal facts and made the hard choices.

Am I doing that? Thomas wondered.

Collins' idea of getting the right people "on the bus" lingered in his thoughts. Was his team ready for the challenges ahead? Could they help him navigate the dual demands of maintaining their legacy while transforming the business to adapt to a radically different future?

The uncomfortable truth stared him in the face: *Am I truly prepared to lead this change, or am I just trying to maintain a legacy?* He realized that it was not only about preserving what his father and grandfather had built. It was about creating something bigger, something that would last beyond any one person.

And then it hit him: *This isn't about me.*

If Dashing Auto Group was going to survive, it couldn't be about him or his ego. It had to be about the people, the employees, the customers, the community, and the future.

Chapter 23: The Leadership Dilemma

The Courage to Lead

Thomas knew he needed to take the best of each leadership style, legacy's stability, modern's balance, and contemporary's agility, and merge them into something new. His leadership couldn't be confined to a single model. It had to be adaptive, empathetic, and courageous. He had to inspire others to innovate, to take risks, and to believe in a future beyond what was comfortable.

But how? *How do I get there*?

The answer was simple but profound: *It's not only about me; it's about building a team of leaders.* He needed a group of people who could embrace ambidexterity, the ability to manage the present while preparing for the future. Leaders who could see beyond the immediate challenges and make the bold moves necessary to lead Dashing Auto Group into a new era.

He thought back to Jim Collins. It was about moving beyond self-interest and building something greater. It wasn't just about building a business anymore; it was about building a legacy of leadership that would stand the test of time.

The Path Forward

As the weight of the decision settled on his shoulders, Thomas realized that this was his turning point. Cipher might be looming, OEMs shifting, but so was opportunity. And as much as Cipher represented disruption, it also represented a chance—a chance for Dashing Auto Group to evolve, to innovate, and to lead. A chance to go from good to great!

TSG's Journal – Fear of Change

Today, I can't shake this gnawing feeling—fear of change, fear of failure. Esther's guidance on leadership styles has opened my eyes to something I haven't fully confronted: Am I afraid of embracing real change? The legacy style of my grandfather feels safe, but is it holding me back? My father's modern approach kept the business steady, but is it enough in today's world and for how long?

I realize the risks of shifting too far too fast: alienating our team, losing sight of our core values, or simply failing to make the right moves. What if the changes I lead push us in the wrong direction? What if we end up worse off? The stakes are high, not merely for Dashing Auto Group but for everyone relying on me to guide us forward.

Jim Collins' question haunts me: *Do we have the right people on the bus?* What if I'm the one who doesn't belong on this bus? This fear of missteps, of leading us toward failure, weighs on me.

But deep down I know staying still is just as dangerous. I need to figure out how to take bold steps without losing what's most important. How do I embrace change without letting fear dictate my decisions? I'll ask Esther to help me navigate these fears and find a way forward.

CHAPTER 24

Embracing Inclusive, Collaborative Leadership

You don't build a business—you build people, and then people build the business.
—**Zig Ziglar**

The early morning sun was rising as TSG finished his run, his breath still labored. The physical strain mirrored the mental weight he carried. Leading Dashing Auto Group through disruption felt heavier with each passing day. Change wasn't only coming from Cipher; it was coming from within himself. Could he truly lead the company through this transformation? Could he let go of the past and embrace the future?

TSG set his phone on a nearby bench for his scheduled Zoom call with Esther. She appeared on the screen, her calm and composed presence offering a sense of stability amid his uncertainty.

"I've been thinking a lot about leadership," TSG began. "I'm trying to figure out where I stand as a leader, especially now, with everything happening at Dashing Auto Group and in the industry."

Esther's eyes brightened with understanding. "That's an important reflection, Thomas. Leadership is evolving, and how you lead needs to align with the challenges ahead. Let's explore how ambidextrous leadership fits into this transformation."

As she spoke, TSG felt a familiar tension loosening. His Grandfather Joe's leadership had built a legacy of stability, and his father Andrew had brought adaptation in the face of change. But now, with Cipher looming and the auto industry evolving, TSG knew that neither legacy nor modern leadership alone would be enough. He needed something more agile, adaptable—something that embraced both innovation and operational excellence.

"So, how do I become a true ambidextrous leader?" TSG asked, searching for a clearer direction.

"Ambidextrous leadership," Esther explained, "isn't about choosing one style over another. It's about creating a culture where people feel safe to innovate while delivering excellence today. Great leaders cultivate positive energy and adaptability when trust and collaboration fuel innovation. You need to lead with discipline but also with empathy, balancing operational demands with forward-thinking strategies."

TSG nodded, feeling both inspired and uneasy. The truth was, he had always held tightly to control. Letting go and empowering his team felt daunting. What if they failed? Worse, what if he failed? He could sense his fear of change gnawing at him. Yet, deep down, he knew that to thrive, he needed to embrace it.

"You're right, Esther," he said, his voice steadier. "We need everyone at Dashing fully engaged and energized. But I'm realizing that means letting go of some control. That's not easy for me."

"No, it's not," Esther agreed. "But remember, a culture of trust empowers people to bring their best ideas forward. If you want to lead Dashing Auto Group through this disruption, you need to build that trust and collaboration. Only then can you balance today's operational excellence with tomorrow's innovation."

TSG felt the weight of her words. The real battle wasn't against Cipher; it was against his own fear of change. The old ways had felt safe, but now they were holding him and the company back. He had to create an environment where empowerment and growth thrived, even if that

Chapter 24: Embracing Inclusive, Collaborative Leadership

meant loosening his grip on control. The question lingered: Could he really make that shift?

TSG took a deep breath. He knew the answer had to be yes. It wasn't confined to survival anymore; it was about leading the company into a new era, driven by trust, innovation, and ambidextrous leadership.

* * *

Later in the day TSG returned to his office and spread Esther's notes out on his desk. The fear of change still lingered, but now it was accompanied by something stronger—a growing resolve. He understood that confronting his fear was the first step toward embracing the future. If he didn't adapt, Cipher would exploit every vulnerability. But if he did, he could transform the company's weaknesses into strengths.

As TSG reviewed Esther's materials, the path forward began to take shape. He realized that while traces of modern and contemporary leadership existed in his approach, legacy thinking had kept him tethered to outdated methods. It was time to commit to a more inclusive leadership model, one rooted in vision, emotional intelligence, and energy management.

He recognized that great leaders must be visionaries, able to inspire their teams by making the future feel tangible and within reach. Moving forward, Thomas would prioritize communicating a vision clearly and consistently, so his team could rally behind it. He also understood that emotional intelligence would become crucial. By managing both his own emotions and understanding those of his team, he could foster trust, empathy, and stronger connections across the organization.

Thomas acknowledged the need to embrace adaptability. In an industry that evolves rapidly, he would welcome innovation, encourage flexibility, and ensure that his team stayed agile in the face of new challenges. Empowerment would be key, too. No longer partially delegating tasks, he would focus on giving his team real autonomy, trusting them to make decisions and take ownership of their roles.

He was also committed to fostering a culture that aligned with Dashing Auto Group's values and vision. Each team member would understand their role in the company's mission and feel a genuine sense of pride in contributing to it. Small, disciplined actions would build the foundation for this culture.

Understanding the importance of energy management, Thomas planned to harness the team's energy positively, using it to drive momentum while avoiding burnout. He would lead with the awareness that maintaining high energy and focus would be crucial for long-term success.

Finally, Thomas knew that humility would be a critical part of his leadership journey. He would be open to feedback, willing to admit mistakes, and ready to create an environment where innovation could thrive without fear of failure.

And with a customer-centric mindset, he would ensure that every decision the company made would enhance the customer's experience at every touchpoint, keeping the customer at the heart of the company's journey.

By embracing these attributes, Thomas was ready to make the leap from managing a business to leading a movement. He committed to creating a future for Dashing Auto Group that was adaptable, empowering, and deeply connected to both its people and customers, prepared to reach new heights.

As TSG reviewed his commitment, the fear that had once held him back now felt like an opportunity—an opportunity to lead with vision and clarity. Leadership wasn't about maintaining control; it was about empowering others.

With new-found belief in his purpose, TSG drafted an email inviting all staff to a town hall meeting to discuss the destination—Vision 2030. The future of Dashing Auto Group wasn't his to shape alone; it was theirs. Together, they would face the challenges ahead. Together, they would thrive.

As he hit "send", TSG murmured to himself, "It's time to make this happen."

Chapter 24: Embracing Inclusive, Collaborative Leadership

FROM: Thomas tsg@dashingautogroup.com

TO: Dashing Team team@dashingautogroup.com

SUBJECT: Your Voice Matters – Join Us for Vision 2030

Dear Dashing Auto Group Team,

I hope this message finds you well and ready for what lies ahead. We are standing at a pivotal moment, one that will shape not only our company but the entire automotive landscape. Forces—unseen but undeniably present—are at work, challenging the very foundations of our business. But within that challenge lies our greatest opportunity.

I am inviting each of you to play a vital role in crafting our path forward. Next Thursday, we will be holding a town hall meeting in the main showroom, where we will come together to co-create our Vision 2030.

Why Vision 2030?

Because change is happening all around us, swiftly and unpredictably. We cannot afford to be reactive; we must be proactive, looking beyond the immediate future and laying the groundwork for where we want to be a decade from now.

This is not a vision from the top down; this is our collective vision, one that must be built from the ground up, drawing on the unique experiences and insights of every single person in this organization.

Whether you've been with us for years or joined recently, whether you work in sales, service, parts, or administration, your perspective is invaluable. We need everyone's voice to create a vision that is both bold and achievable.

During the town hall, we will:
1. Share critical insights on the evolving automotive industry.
2. Discuss the challenges and opportunities before us.

3. Begin building our Vision 2030 collaboratively.

4. Explore how each of us can contribute to this shared future.

This is not merely another meeting or corporate exercise. The threats we face are real, and they demand our absolute best. This will require us to grow, innovate, and push past our comfort zones, but I believe in our team. I believe in the talent, resilience, and creativity that we bring to this company every day. I believe in our community.

I also want to be clear: I don't have all the answers. That's why I'm counting on your input—your questions, ideas, and even your doubts—to help shape a future we can all believe in. Your voice matters, and I am committed to ensuring that everyone is heard.

So, I invite you to come ready to engage, challenge, and dream big. Bring your ideas, your concerns, and your aspirations for the future. Together, we will build a future for Dashing Auto Group and the industry that we can all be proud of.

This journey will take nothing less than our personal best, but together, I know we can rise to this challenge and outsmart the forces that seek to disrupt us.

I look forward to seeing you all next Thursday as we begin writing the next chapter for Dashing Auto Group.

Best regards,
Thomas

PS If you have any questions or thoughts you'd like to share before the town hall, please don't hesitate to reach out to me directly. My door is always open.

CHAPTER 25

The Council of Luminaries

*The brightest stars don't compete—
they shine together to form constellations.*
—**Adapted Proverb**

TSG was wandering round his office, deep in thought. Esther had introduced him to a transformative idea, one that would change the course of his leadership journey and Dashing Auto Group's future.

"The Council of Luminaries", she had called it.

Esther, always the insightful guide, had pulled together the greatest thinkers, the most inspiring voices, from the books they had discussed. This council wasn't made up of people in the traditional sense, but of the ideas, principles, and strategies that these great authors had offered throughout history, insights that could fortify Dashing Auto Group as it moved into an uncertain future.

"You've done a lot of reflection, Thomas," Esther had insisted during their call. "But now, it's time to act. You have the tools in front of you, the wisdom of the council. These are your guides. Together, their lessons can shape the path forward."

As she spoke, Thomas could see the importance of what she was saying. The council was more than a collection of voices from the past.

It was a bridge to the future, offering lessons on leadership, innovation, agility, and purpose. The authors of these transformative works didn't pour their wisdom into books so the knowledge could gather dust on a shelf or be skimmed and forgotten. They wrote to ignite action, to plant seeds of change in the minds of those willing to step up and embrace growth. Each page was a call to arms—a quiet yet urgent reminder that insight only becomes valuable when it's applied.

Their goal was not to impress but to empower, to take hard-earned lessons from battlefields of leadership, innovation, and resilience, and place them into the hands of those navigating their own journeys. They knew that knowledge sitting idle was as useful as an engine left cold; it must be engaged, turned over, and driven forward to truly make a difference.

In their words lies a blueprint—not just for survival but for transformation. They wrote not for passive admiration, but for active evolution—so that leaders could take that spark and light the way for others.

It was now Thomas' role to take their wisdom and lead his team through the challenges ahead.

"You're no longer reacting to change," Esther had reminded him. "You are embracing it ... leading it. The council provides the knowledge, but you provide the vision. It's time to use that wisdom to steer Dashing Auto Group toward its future. It's time for action!"

Thomas understood that his role now was to weave the council's lessons into every facet of the business, empowering his team with the tools to succeed in an increasingly unpredictable market. The challenge was not just to survive but to thrive.

*　*　*

Each author delivered specific teachings that equipped Thomas with the skills and mindset necessary to transform the dealership into a modern, agile organization. Their collective wisdom revealed that true ambidextrous leadership is more than balancing today's operations with tomorrow's innovations—it's about unlocking the potential within his people and cultivating a culture where excellence can truly thrive.

Chapter 25: The Council of Luminaries

Key Teachings

- **Johnson, S. (1998)** *Who Moved My Cheese?*: Thomas learned to embrace change, understanding that adaptation and foresight are essential in a constantly evolving market. This lesson is crucial for business leaders because in today's fast-paced world, those who can anticipate and adapt to shifts in customer preferences and market dynamics will remain competitive. Failure to do so risks obsolescence.

- **Collins, J. (2001)** *Good to Great: Why Some Companies Make the Leap ... and Others Don't*: Thomas grasped the importance of building the right team and identifying Dashing Auto Group's "Hedgehog Concept"—focusing on what they could be best at: personalized, customer-centric automotive experiences. This is important for business leaders as it highlights the need for strategic focus and the power of assembling a team that shares the company's values and vision, driving sustainable growth.

- **Sinek, S. (2009)** *Start with Why: How Great Leaders Inspire Everyone to Take Action*: Sinek's teaching helped Thomas define Dashing Auto Group's purpose, articulating the deeper mission of empowering journeys and fostering trust through meaningful customer interactions. For business leaders, a clear *Why* creates a sense of purpose that resonates both internally with employees and externally with customers, fostering loyalty and engagement.

- **Bruch, H., & Vogel, B. (2011)** *Fully Charged: How Great Leaders Boost Their Organization's Energy and Ignite High Performance*: Thomas realized the power of organizational energy and how to maintain a high-energy culture that drives innovation and performance. For leaders, managing energy—not just time or resources—is critical to sustaining a dynamic, creative workplace that outperforms competitors.

- **Rouhana, M. (2023)** *Greatness is NOWHERE*: Rouhana's work reminded Thomas of the need to invest in people and culture, creating an environment where the team feels valued, empowered, and driven to succeed. Business leaders must understand that a thriving, motivated culture can be a company's most significant competitive advantage.

- **Miller, D. (2017)** *Building a StoryBrand: Clarify Your Message So Customers Will Listen*: This taught Thomas how to reframe Dashing Auto Group's brand story, positioning the dealership as a trusted guide in the customer's automotive journey. Leaders need to communicate their brand's value in a way that connects with customers emotionally, ensuring their message is clear and memorable.

- **Smith, J. (2001)** *The KPI Book: How to Implement the Key Performance Indicators*: This book helped Thomas set clear, measurable goals, ensuring Dashing Auto Group's progress was aligned with its long-term vision. For business leaders, KPIs provide a framework for tracking performance, ensuring that the organization remains on course toward achieving strategic objectives.

- **Abrashoff, D.M. (2002)** *It's Your Ship: Management Techniques from the Best Damn Ship in the Navy*: Abrashoff's emphasis on fostering accountability and ownership among his team inspired Thomas to empower leaders at every level to take initiative and lead. Business leaders benefit from encouraging a culture of ownership, where individuals take responsibility for outcomes and are empowered to act decisively.

- **McRaven, W.H. (2017)** *Make Your Bed: Little Things That Can Change Your Life … and Maybe the World*: McRaven reinforced the value of small, consistent improvements, guiding Dashing Auto Group toward making incremental changes that would build long-term momentum. Leaders should focus on the compounding effect of continuous improvement, knowing that small wins lead to significant progress over time.

- **Forestier, N., & Ravai, N. (2020)** *The Taste of Luxury: Bernard Arnault and the Moet-Hennessy Louis Vuitton Story*: Thomas found inspiration in Arnault's leadership at LVMH, particularly in balancing heritage with innovation to

Chapter 25: The Council of Luminaries

create timeless luxury experiences. For business leaders, this underscores the importance of maintaining brand authenticity while evolving to meet modern demands, ensuring longevity and relevance in a competitive market.

- **Schulze, H. (2019)** *Excellence Wins: A No-Nonsense Guide to Becoming the Best in a World of Compromise*: Schulze's work reinforced for Thomas the importance of setting high standards and delivering service excellence. Leaders must prioritize uncompromising quality in both products and services, as this sets them apart in increasingly competitive markets.

These super guides showed Thomas the pathway forward: empowering his team, fostering a culture of innovation, and driving the organization to constantly evolve. The team was no longer solely a group of employees—they were becoming the future leaders of Dashing Auto Group, equipped to meet the demands of Vision 2030.

With these teachings, Thomas now had the tools to overcome Cipher's threats and reposition Dashing Auto Group as a relevant and modern partner in the automotive retail space, prepared to collaborate with OEMs and lead the industry into the future. He understood that by embracing innovation, enhancing the customer experience, and adapting to the ever-shifting landscape, Dashing Auto Group could become a critical partner in shaping the future of automotive retail.

It was time to inspire his team to take action. Standing at the threshold of a new era with the knowledge gained from the council, Thomas knew they were ready to step into their leadership roles, win the day, and shape the future of the industry.

*　*　*

Thomas arrived at the Vision 2030 town hall, as the event was known, ready to address the assembly of employees who had gathered. As he scanned the room, he could feel the weight of expectation pressing against the walls. There was an unmistakable mix of curiosity, apprehension, and a quiet skepticism etched across many faces.

It wasn't difficult to understand why. This wasn't their first town hall. They had sat through presentations in the past—bold promises, inspiring buzzwords, and polished slide decks. Yet, for many, those initiatives had faded into memory, replaced by the same routines, the same frustrations. Grand declarations of change had come and gone, but nothing ever seemed to truly shift.

As Thomas moved toward the front of the room, his posture radiated a mix of determination and excitement. The faces before him represented every level of Dashing Auto Group—from seasoned executives who had seen decades of trends come and go, to fresh recruits who still carried that first-day optimism. He could feel their unspoken thoughts: *Will this really be different? Or will it be another plan that fizzles out once the dust settles?*

This was the moment he had been preparing for—the culmination of countless meetings with his leadership team and late-night strategy sessions with Esther. He knew the stakes weren't just operational—they were emotional. If he didn't bridge the gap between skepticism and belief, Vision 2030 would become just another story shelved under "what could have been".

Thomas paused at the podium, taking a deep breath as Esther's words echoed in his mind: *"Leadership isn't about having all the answers. It's about asking the right questions and inspiring others to find the solutions together."*

With that thought, he began his address, his voice clear and resolute.

Speech: Dashing Auto Group – Leading the Future

Ladies and gentlemen, team members, and valued friends of the Dashing Auto Group community:

We're standing at a crossroads. The world around us is changing rapidly, and we're facing one of the most pivotal moments in our company's history. But this isn't a moment of uncertainty—it's an opportunity. An opportunity to define who we are, where we're going, and how we'll lead in the years to come.

As we look toward Vision 2030, let's not only talk about change—let's become the change. This is about more than adapting to industry shifts or surviving disruption. It's about thriving. It's

Chapter 25: The Council of Luminaries

about being the trusted partner that OEMs and customers need in this modern retail landscape. It's about creating a future where we don't just compete … we lead.

Our industry is evolving. OEMs are exploring direct-to-consumer models. New technologies are being developed faster than we can blink, and customer expectations are higher than ever. Many see these as threats. I see them as the path forward. But let me be clear: The dealership model must evolve, or it will be left behind. Customers demand more than a transaction; they want an experience. The question is: Will we be the ones to provide it?

The answer lies with each of you. You are the heart of this company. It's not our buildings, products, or technologies that make Dashing Auto Group great—it's you. Our success will depend on how we step up, how we evolve, and how we come together as a team to meet these challenges head-on. You are the ones who will drive this transformation.

But this isn't about surviving disruption—it's about redefining what it means to be relevant in this new world. And how do we do that? By focusing on our customers like never before. We must be their guide. We're not only here to sell cars—we're here to solve problems, make their lives easier, and build lasting relationships. That's how we win. And we're going to do it by focusing on a few key principles:

- **Customer-Centricity**: In a connected world full of choices, what sets us apart is how we treat our customers. Every decision must solve their problems and exceed expectations. We need to be more than a dealership—we need to be trusted advisers who understand and care about their journey. Our goal is to become indispensable by offering unmatched value.
- **Innovation**: Innovation isn't solely about technology; it's about how we think and approach challenges. We need to always ask, "What's next?" By embracing new ideas, mobility trends, and retail models, we'll create value and stay ahead of the curve.

- **Agility**: The world is evolving fast, and we must be ready to move with it. Flexibility, quick thinking, and an openness to new ideas will allow us to turn challenges into opportunities. We'll build systems that let us pivot and react quickly, staying proactive and adaptable.
- **Our People**: Our greatest asset is our people. We'll invest in your growth, skills, and development because as you grow, so does the company. We'll foster a culture of creativity, initiative, and collaboration, where everyone feels empowered to make an impact.
- **Community and Culture**: Our brand is defined by how we show up for our customers, each other, and the community. We are building lasting relationships. We'll deepen our community ties to serve with trust, integrity, and conviction, ensuring our reputation extends beyond the walls of this business.

This is how we will win in a modern retail future—by becoming more than a dealership.

We'll become:

The brand that people can rely on.

The partner that OEMs need.

And the company that customers and the community turn to, time and time again.

But remember, none of this happens by accident. It requires us to make bold decisions and take action now. It's about thinking bigger, pushing ourselves harder, and stepping into the unknown with confidence. It's about asking, 'Why do we exist in this new world?' Our *Why* is to guide our customers and partners through the complexities of this changing industry. We're not here to merely sell or service products—we're here to solve problems, build connections, and create loyalty that lasts.

And this journey, this transformation—it starts with us. It starts with each of you, taking ownership, embracing your role, and bringing your very best to the table every single day. We're not waiting for the future to happen to us—we're shaping it ourselves.

That's our superpower. That's what makes us different.

The road ahead won't be easy. There will be challenges, setbacks, and tough decisions. But I have complete faith in this team. Together, we're going to build something that's more than relevant, something that leads this industry into the future. You are the drivers of this transformation. You are the difference-makers.

So, let's not just face the future—let's create it. Let's show the world what it truly means to be a modern, customer-centric, agile, and innovative company. Let's redefine what it means to be a dealership.

Our journey starts now, and it starts with you. Are you ready to lead this transformation? Because I am, and I believe in you, and I believe in this team.

Let's go shape the future of automotive retail … together.

As TSG paused, a wave of positive energy swept through the room. Eyes that had been uncertain now sparkled with determination. Postures that had been slumped now straightened with belief. In that moment, TSG knew that the transformation had begun. Dashing Auto Group was ready to embrace ambidexterity, to win each day, and to stride confidently toward a thriving future in 2030.

The journey ahead would be challenging, but as TSG looked at the faces of his team, he felt that surge of positive energy and confidence. Together, they were ready to rewrite the rules, to become the disruptors, and to steer Dashing Auto Group into a future where change is not only managed; it is mastered.

As the buzz of conversation filled the room, TSG knew that this was only the beginning. The real work lay ahead, but with this level of engagement and enthusiasm, he was more confident than ever.

Sensing the momentum, TSG raised his hand for attention once more. As the room quieted, he spoke with renewed intent:

This energy, this enthusiasm; this is exactly what we need to drive us forward. Now, let's channel it into action. I'm calling for volunteers from every level and department to join a special task force. Your mission will be to establish our collective *Why*—the core purpose that drives us—and to craft our Vision 2030 statement. This will be our North Star, guiding every decision and action as we transform Dashing Auto Group into an ambidextrous powerhouse. Who's ready to help shape our future?

As hands shot up across the room, TSG smiled. The journey to becoming truly ambidextrous was officially underway, and it was starting with the very foundation: defining their calling and vision for the future.

TSG's Journal – Transformation in Motion

This week has been transformative. Esther's lessons on ambidextrous leadership—empathy, adaptability, humility—alongside the wisdom of the Council of Luminaries, have changed my approach. Recognizing my legacy leadership tendencies was humbling, but it sparked a renewed sense of ambition.

The town hall was a pivotal moment. Seeing the team's energy, sharing innovative ideas, was a turning point. Forming the Vision 2030 task force felt like the right step, but I wonder: Can we sustain this momentum?

The super guides have brought clarity and direction, but I still ask: Am I truly embodying the balance of today and tomorrow? How can I nurture this energy and ensure every voice is heard? I feel accomplished, yet the challenge ahead looms large. As we move forward, I'll focus on keeping communication open and ensuring our collective efforts shape the future of Dashing Auto Group. Together, we'll create it.

Here's to finding our *Why* and Vision 2030 with the incredible team that will make it possible.

CHAPTER 26

Knowledge isn't a Burden to Carry

Education is not the filling of a pail, but the lighting of a fire.
—**William Butler Yeats**

Thomas stood in his office, staring at the framed quote on the wall: *Knowledge isn't a burden to carry.* It was something his father, Andrew, had often said. For years, Thomas had interpreted it narrowly, focusing on product knowledge, technical expertise, and the operational details that kept Dashing Auto Group running smoothly.

Thomas had always taken pride in having a team that excelled in every aspect of the business. His salespeople knew the cars inside and out, his service technicians were up to date on the latest repair techniques, and his accountants had mastered the intricacies of dealership finances. But as he reflected on the lessons he had been learning, Thomas began to realize how incomplete his approach had been.

The words of Rouhana echoed in his mind: *You can't be what your culture is not. You can't be what your people are not. You can't be what your investment is not.* He had invested heavily in his team's capabilities but had overlooked one critical area—himself.

He had focused on building a skilled workforce but neglected his own development as a leader. Without investing in his own growth, his ability to steer Dashing Auto Group into the future was limited.

He realized that it wasn't enough to simply have a competent team; he needed to step up as a leader who could inspire and drive change. It was more than getting the operations right; it was about creating a culture of innovation, trust, and empowerment. He needed to build a company where people felt valued and motivated, where the *Why* behind their work was clear, and where they were all working toward a shared vision of the future.

Thomas also understood the importance of adapting to the changing landscape. The world around him was shifting, and so was his role. He could no longer rely on technical expertise alone; he had to embrace change, lead with conviction, and cultivate energy within the organization. The knowledge he once relied on needed to be paired with vision, leadership, and the willingness to grow personally.

Without that, true greatness was out of reach. It was time to invest in himself, to become the leader his team needed, and to guide Dashing Auto Group. True leadership wasn't about control or technical skill; it was about unlocking the potential of his people and inspiring them to greatness. And for that, he had to start with his own transformation.

As Thomas paced the room, he recognized that Cipher had been exploiting a critical gap, one that he hadn't fully recognized. Cipher thrived in environments where leaders focused solely on technical and operational excellence. By keeping leadership grounded in sales and aftersales performance, product knowledge, and financial management, it blinded them to the broader strategic vision needed for long-term survival.

Thomas saw now that while his team excelled in these operational areas, they weren't prepared for the deeper disruption Cipher represented. They understood how to sell and service vehicles, but they didn't know how to pivot toward the future or embrace the innovation required to survive in the evolving automotive landscape.

He realized that by focusing too much on skills like vehicle valuation, inventory control, and data analytics, he had unintentionally set

Chapter 26: Knowledge isn't a Burden to Carry

them up for failure. Cipher preyed on this complacency, using operational excellence as a distraction from the real pillars of success: leadership, adaptability, and human connection. If Cipher succeeded in pushing the industry toward full online sales, many of his key people, and the dealership model itself, would become obsolete.

The more his team excelled at the mechanical aspects of the business, the more they played into Cipher's hands, mistaking operational efficiency for true leadership. Thomas now saw the flaw in this approach: knowledge wasn't a burden, but it had to be applied in the right way. His team needed more than operational expertise—they had to be adaptive, forward-thinking, and equipped for the challenges ahead.

The words echoed again: *You can't be what your investment is not.* Thomas had always equated investment with financial commitments, upgraded showrooms, better equipment, and advanced technology. But now he understood the true meaning of investment: it wasn't about assets; it was about people. The real gap wasn't technical but in leadership, vision, and adaptability.

Up until now, Thomas had ensured his team excelled at their roles, but he had neglected an essential element—preparing them for the future. He had focused on operational proficiency, but the missing piece was in developing leadership and resilience to handle disruption. More than that, he realized he had neglected his own growth as a leader. If his team was to thrive in the future, they needed to understand not only how to do their jobs but *why* they were doing them and how to adapt when everything changed.

Cipher was more than a technological threat; it was a challenge to leadership. The disruption it represented couldn't be defeated by better sales techniques or more efficient service departments. It required foresight, emotional intelligence, and the human skills that set them apart from Cipher's algorithms, such as empathy, communication, and resilience.

Thomas now saw the full picture. To lead Dashing Auto Group into the future, he needed to invest in developing leaders, not just skilled workers. He had to cultivate a culture of adaptability, innovation, and foresight. And in doing so, he also had to evolve as a leader himself.

Knowledge wasn't a burden; it was the most powerful tool he and his team had. But to use it wisely, they needed to embrace the future with a focus on growth, leadership, and human connection. This wasn't merely about survival; it was about building an agile, forward-thinking organization that was ready for whatever came next.

TSG's Journal – Investing in the Right Knowledge Needed Today

Today was a revelation. For so long, I've placed emphasis on ensuring my team mastered the technical and operational side of our business. I realized I've been neglecting a crucial investment: leadership development!

Cipher and its disciples have been using this gap against us, steering us to focus on the here and now, on becoming more efficient at what we already know.

But is that enough for the future? It's NOT!

So, am I equipping my team with the knowledge they need to adapt, to innovate, and to lead?

What does true investment in people look like? How can I inspire a shift from operational knowledge to leadership and human skills?

Have I been playing into Cipher's plan by focusing only on what we do best, instead of preparing for what's to come next?

CHAPTER 27

Building an Ambidextrous Future

*Great things in business are never done by one person;
they're done by a team of people.*
—**Steve Jobs**

The Vision 2030 team gathered in the sleek, glass-walled meeting room at Dashing Auto Group, the air filled with a feeling of shared commitment. Thomas stood at the head of the table, fully aware of the weight of the moment. Today was about more than laying out plans; it was about setting the foundation for their future. He knew that to succeed, the team needed more than technical knowledge; they needed the key skills to lead, adapt, and thrive in an uncertain world.

"Today," Thomas began, "we're not only here to talk about the future. We're here to define it. And that starts with us investing in ourselves. It's time to equip ourselves and our team with the tools, leadership skills, and adaptability needed to excel today and own the future. We'll use the insights from the council to act, aligned with our Vision 2030, but it begins with us embracing the need to grow, operationally, yes, but also as leaders."

The room quieted as Esther took the floor, ready to serve as their educator and guide. "Let's start with the most fundamental piece: identifying and embracing change. If we're not prepared to adapt and evolve with the shifts in our industry, none of our strategies will stick."

Thomas added, "The tools we need to build this future come not only from technology or processes—they come from the principles that will make us stronger, more adaptable, and more visionary as leaders. Esther is going to guide us through the key themes we've learned from the Council of Luminaries. These are beyond abstract ideas—they're the core of how we'll evolve as a team. From embracing change to cultivating resilience, from innovation to customer-centric leadership, these lessons will shape the foundation of everything we do moving forward. Esther, please continue."

With a determined nod, Esther began, pen in hand, ready to guide the team through the principles that would transform them into the leaders this future demanded.

- **Identifying and Embracing Change**

Esther invoked Spencer Johnson's *Who Moved My Cheese?*, reminding the group of the importance of agility and adaptability. "We need to ask ourselves: Are we ready to embrace change? Can we pivot quickly when the landscape shifts, as it inevitably will?" The team discussed how they could cultivate a culture that sees change not as a threat but as an opportunity for growth and innovation.

"Change is our ally, not our enemy," TSG added. "If we don't see it that way, we'll never be ready for what's coming."

- **Building the Right Team**

Esther then shifted the focus to *Good to Great* by Jim Collins, emphasizing the importance of building the right team. "Before we can tackle the challenges ahead, we need to make sure we have the right people in the right roles. It's not about having the most people; it's about having the right people who share our values and are committed to our vision."

The selected group agreed to reassess the talent pool, ensuring that each team member was aligned with Vision 2030. They would focus on finding those who could drive the company forward.

Chapter 27: Building an Ambidextrous Future

- **Identifying the Hedgehog Concept**

Esther then introduced Collins' Hedgehog Concept. "Collins called it the 'Hedgehog Concept' in *Good to Great* because it is based on the ancient Greek parable: 'The fox knows many things, but the hedgehog knows one big thing.' The fox tries various clever strategies, but the hedgehog consistently relies on its simple, effective defense—rolling into a spiky ball—and wins every time. In business, this means great companies focus on one clear, unifying idea that drives their success, rather than chasing multiple, scattered opportunities. The Hedgehog Concept is built around three key questions: what you are deeply passionate about, what you can be the best in the world at, and what drives your economic success. Like the hedgehog, these companies succeed by sticking to a simple, disciplined strategy and staying focused on what matters most."

"We need to be extraordinary where it truly matters," TSG said. "We can't be everything to everyone, but we can deliver something unparalleled in our niche."

The group realized that by narrowing their focus and leveraging their strengths, they could better align their purpose with their competencies.

- **Defining and Communicating Our Purpose**

Next, Esther invoked Simon Sinek's *Start with Why*, stressing the importance of having a clear purpose. "We need to ensure that our team knows exactly why we're here and what we stand for. Our *Why* must be central to every decision we make."

The team reflected on how they could live their calling in every aspect of the business, making it personal and relevant for everyone involved.

- **Understanding Energy**

Drawing from Heike Bruch and Bernd Vogel's *Fully Charged*, the team discussed the need to maintain high organizational energy. "It's not enough to have the right people," TSG said. "We need to ensure they're energized, motivated, and fully engaged."

They brainstormed ways to eliminate energy drains and boost engagement through recognition programs, wellness initiatives, and opportunities for professional growth.

- **Investing in People and Culture**

Melkart Rouhana's *Greatness is NOWhere* guided the discussion on building a culture that prioritizes people. "Investing in our people is non-negotiable," TSG stated firmly. "If we want them to bring their best, we have to give them the tools and environment to succeed."

The team agreed to focus on mentorship programs, skills development workshops, and fostering a culture of collaboration and innovation.

- **Developing Stories**

Xand from IT spoke up, referencing Donald Miller's *Building a StoryBrand*. "We need to create a brand story where the customer is the hero. We should be the guide who helps them navigate their journey with confidence."

They brainstormed ways to reframe the customer journey, ensuring that Dashing Auto Group positioned itself as more than a service provider but as a trusted adviser and guide.

- **Establishing Key Performance Indicators**

Frank from Operations brought up *The KPI Book* by Jeff Smith, emphasizing the need for clear metrics to track their progress. "We need to measure what matters. KPIs will help us ensure we're moving in the right direction, both in the short- and long-term."

The team agreed to establish a balanced scorecard that tracked both tangible results and intangible factors like customer satisfaction and employee engagement.

- **Fostering Ownership and Accountability**

John, drawing from Captain D. Michael Abrashoff"s *It's Your Ship*, emphasized the importance of giving team members ownership over their roles. "If we want people to take initiative, we need to empower them. We can't micromanage—we need to let them own their successes and failures."

Chapter 27: Building an Ambidextrous Future

The team discussed strategies to delegate more decision-making authority and encourage innovation from all levels of the organization.

- **Focusing on Small, Consistent Improvements**

William H. McRaven's *Make Your Bed* reminded the team of the importance of small, consistent improvements. "We're not going to transform overnight," TSG said. "But if we commit to improving by only one percent each month, those small gains will compound over time."

The group agreed to focus on incremental improvements in customer service, operations, and team development.

- **Creating a Culture of Excellence**

Horst Schulze's *Excellence Wins* added to the discussion of fostering a culture that strives for nothing less than excellence. "Excellence isn't just about doing things right; it's about doing the right things consistently." TSG spoke slowly to emphasize his point. "We need to ensure that our team understands that excellence is the standard we operate by—every touchpoint, every customer interaction."

The team agreed to reinforce this commitment to excellence across all areas of the business, from service to customer relations, embedding it as a core value of Dashing Auto Group.

- **Balancing Heritage with Innovation**

Nadège Forestier and Nazanine Ravai's *The Taste of Luxury: Bernard Arnault and the Moet-Hennessy Louis Vuitton Story* inspired Thomas with Arnault's leadership at LVMH, particularly in balancing heritage with innovation to create timeless luxury experiences.

"We have a rich history in the automotive industry," TSG reflected, "but we also need to embrace the future. Our challenge is to honor our legacy while pioneering new experiences for our customers."

Continuously Aligning with Purpose

Esther closed the meeting by emphasizing the need for ongoing alignment with their cause. "As we move forward, we need to continuously check in with ourselves. Are we still aligned with our objective? Are we staying true to our values?"

The group committed to regular reflection and strategy sessions to ensure they stayed on track.

Moving Forward Together

The room was quiet now, the energy of the day's discussions still lingering. They had spent hours in deep dialogue, going beyond exchanging ideas, forging a collective understanding that would define their path forward. Thomas felt a surge of pride. They weren't just talking about the future anymore, they were actively building it, step by step.

The team was ready to transition into the next phase of their journey. The discussions around customer-centricity, innovation, agility, investing in their team, and strengthening their culture and community had evolved from abstract ideas into concrete plans. Task forces were formed, each responsible for breathing life into these priorities. What once were buzzwords had transformed into guiding principles, with clear action items to ensure these goals would become the foundation of Dashing Auto Group's future success.

As the day was drawing to a close, the most significant accomplishment was the crystallization of their Hedgehog Concept—the simple, powerful framework that would keep them laser-focused on what they could be best in the world at:

- **Best in the World at**: Delivering a seamless, personalized, and relationship-driven customer experience in both sales and service.
- **Economic Engine**: Maximizing profit per customer by focusing on lifetime value.
- **Passion**: Creating memorable automotive experiences while pioneering innovation in customer service, with a strong commitment to community and human connection.

As Thomas reflected on this, he knew this was about far more than merely ensuring survival in a rapidly changing industry. It was about thriving—together. With the right focus and alignment, Dashing Auto Group wouldn't only compete; they would lead.

As the team stood to leave, there was a palpable shift in the room. They were no longer perceived as employees anymore. They had become a cohesive unit of leaders, each of them inspired and equipped to drive this transformation. Guided by the wisdom of the Council of Luminaries, they were more than a team; they were becoming the superguides Dashing Auto Group needed to win today and shape tomorrow.

Stepping out of the meeting room, Thomas couldn't help but smile. The tasks had been set, the path was clear, and the team was ready to take on the challenge. For the first time, he didn't just feel hopeful about the future; he felt certain they were going to own it.

TSG's Journal – A Surge of Team Energy

Today I felt the full weight of what it means to lead not just with strategy, but with purpose and shared vision. The Vision 2030 team exceeded my expectations—every person contributed ideas that were practical, insightful, and deeply aligned with where we need to go.

What struck me the most, even more than the quality of the ideas, was the positive energy in the room. We went beyond talking about plans; we were actively creating the future. The Council of Luminaries' teachings guided us, but it was our team's collective spirit that brought it to life.

This isn't about me as a leader alone. It's about all of us working together, leveraging each other's strengths to become truly ambidextrous.

I might be at the front, steering, but we are the right people on the bus, going in the same direction.

CHAPTER 28

Find Your Focus

The two most important days in your life are the day you are born and the day you find out why.
—**Mark Twain**

Feeling the momentum, Thomas thought, I'm on a mission now, as he prepared to bring the Vision 2030 team together the following day. They had recently defined their Hedgehog Concept, and the clarity it provided was powerful. It wasn't about doing everything—it was about excelling at what truly mattered. The team now had a laser focus on what would set them apart and drive long-term success.

But Thomas knew that focus wasn't enough on its own. Their *Why* was already becoming clear. Dashing Auto Group was going beyond the business of selling and servicing cars; they were solving customer problems, building lasting relationships, and making a meaningful impact on the community. The real challenge ahead was ensuring that every action aligned with this conviction.

The next step was action. Thomas was ready to empower the team to bring the Hedgehog Concept and their *Why* to life. With this dual focus on strategy and purpose, they could move from planning to execution, ensuring every effort contributed to shaping a future where they led with both direction and meaning.

Esther's "Why"

Esther had arrived for her regular catch up with Thomas, her body language energized with passion as she began to speak. "Thomas, you asked about my *Why*, and I'm glad you did. It's something I've thought about deeply.

"At my core, my *Why* is to inspire and empower people to reach their full potential so that they can create positive change in the world. This drives everything I do. It's why I wake up every morning excited to start my day. But of course, having a *Why* is just the beginning. The *How* and the *What* are equally important.

"So, how do I go about fulfilling this?" she continued. "I create safe, supportive environments where people can truly be themselves and grow. I listen—really listen—to understand each person's unique needs and challenges. I encourage critical thinking and self-reflection because that's where real growth happens. And I never stop learning myself; always staying current with new ideas and technologies that can help people develop.

"Now, what does this look like in practice? Well, I offer one-on-one mentoring sessions where we can dive deep into individual challenges and aspirations. I run workshops and seminars for those who thrive in group settings. I create online resources and digital content for people who prefer self-paced learning. I provide coaching and consulting services to help individuals and organizations navigate complex situations. And I'm always working to build a community of like-minded individuals who can support and inspire each other.

"But here's the thing, Thomas. All of these *Whats*—these specific services and products—they can change over time as needs evolve and new opportunities arise. What doesn't change is the *Why*. It's the compass that guides every decision I make and every action I take.

"So, when someone asks me what I do, sure, I could say I'm a mentor or a guide. But what I really do? I inspire and empower people to create positive change. That's my *Why*."

Esther sat back, a warm smile spreading across her face. "So, Thomas, does that give you a clearer picture of my *Why*?"

Thomas smiled, then exclaimed, "I'm excited! Let's do this! Let's get the team together."

Discovering Our Human-Centric Golden Circle: Elevating the Automotive Experience

The following day, the Dashing Auto Group showroom had been transformed into a vibrant workshop space. Esther stood at the front with a pyramid diagram of Maslow's Hierarchy of Needs displayed prominently. TSG sat among his diverse team of sales representatives, service technicians, parts specialists, finance managers, and administrative staff.

Esther began, her voice energetic. "Welcome, Dashing Auto Group team. Today, we're defining our Golden Circle from the unique perspective of an auto dealership. We'll explore how each of our departments contributes to fulfilling our Hedgehog Concept and our customers' needs. But first, let's think about Maslow's Hierarchy of Needs."

"At its core, it's a roadmap to understanding human motivation, from basic survival to realizing our fullest potential. In our case, we need to consider how we can meet our customers' needs at every level. At the foundational level, we're providing safe, reliable vehicles with strong retained values, addressing their physiological and safety needs. But we can't stop there. We must build relationships, creating a sense of belonging and trust through excellent service, fulfilling their social needs. Then, as we deliver an exceptional experience, we foster a sense of esteem by making them feel valued and respected; plus, there are the social and emotional benefits resulting from our brand. Ultimately, if we do this right, we guide them toward self-actualization, where they feel empowered, proud, and fulfilled in their choice to engage with us. This aligns with our Golden Circle approach. We're nurturing relationships, building trust, and helping customers reach their full potential, both practically and emotionally."

Esther smiled and gestured toward the team. "Now that we understand how every interaction, every service, and every sale we make

Chapter 28: Find Your Focus

addresses our customers' needs on multiple levels, it's time to take the next step. To truly elevate the customer experience, we must align these insights with our strategy (Hedgehog) and our own purpose ... our *Why*."

She paused, letting the idea settle. "This brings us to the core of our journey. But this isn't about why we exist as a business—that's already been defined in our Hedgehog Concept, which focuses on what we do best. Instead, our *Why* is about what *motivates* us, what drives us on a deeper, more human level. It's the belief that fuels our passion and commitment, the purpose that goes beyond selling cars or services. It's the reason we come together each day and the impact we aim to make in the lives of our customers and community. By understanding our *Why*, we can connect with our customers on a more meaningful level, fulfilling not only their practical needs but also their emotional and aspirational ones."

Esther looked around the room, encouraging the team's participation. "Let's begin this important process together—uncovering our *Why*. By doing so, we'll build a stronger, more goal-driven foundation that reflects the heart of Dashing Auto Group and guides us toward a more human-centered future."

Esther grabbed a pen and wrote on the white board:

1. Uncovering our *Why* (Reflect on fulfilling contributions and find recurring themes)

Esther prompted the team. "Reflect on moments when your work truly made a difference in a customer's life, in your life. How did you address these needs?"

The room buzzed with stories:

- Sarah from Sales shared about helping a growing family find the perfect vehicle for their changing needs (Safety and Belongingness Needs).
- Mike from Service described how fixing a vintage car allowed a customer to reconnect with cherished memories (Esteem Needs).
- Anita from Finance talked about structuring a deal that made car ownership possible for a first-time buyer (Security Needs).

- Carlos from Parts explained how sourcing a rare component helped a classic car enthusiast complete their dream project (Self-Actualization Needs).

After thoughtful discussion, Jamie from Customer Relations stood up, her voice filled with intent:

"Our *Why* is: **To empower journeys and connections, so that every customer can navigate life's roads with confidence, pride, and the freedom to pursue their passions.**"

The room erupted in applause, with TSG beaming with pride.

Esther wrote on the board again.

2. Defining our *How*

Esther continued, "Now, let's explore *How* we achieve this *Why* through our various departments and customer-centric activities."

The team collaboratively identified key approaches:

- Implementing a "Lifestyle Matching" process in sales to understand each customer's unique needs and aspirations.
- Creating a "Service Journey" program that educates customers and provides transparent, trust-building maintenance experiences.
- Launching a "Community Wheels" initiative where the dealership partners work with local organizations to support transportation needs.
- Establishing a "Financial Empowerment" workshop series to help customers understand and improve their automotive financial health.
- Developing a "Parts and Accessories Personalization Studio" where customers can express their individuality through their vehicles.

Next, Esther wrote:

3. Clarifying our *What*

Chapter 28: Find Your Focus

"Finally," Esther remarked, "let's articulate *What* we offer that brings our *Why* and *How* to life, addressing needs at every level of Maslow's hierarchy."

The team enthusiastically listed Dashing Auto Group's offerings:

- Providing a curated selection of safe, reliable vehicles for every life stage (Safety Needs).
- Offering membership in a "Dashing Drivers Club" that fosters a sense of community among our customers (Belongingness Needs).
- Delivering expert service and genuine parts to keep vehicles performing at their best, instilling pride of ownership (Esteem Needs).
- Creating customized financing solutions that provide peace of mind and enable dreams (Security Needs).
- Facilitating special orders and modifications that allow customers to realize their unique automotive visions (Self-Actualization Needs).

As the session concluded, Esther guided them in crafting their comprehensive Golden Circle:

Why: To empower journeys and connections, so that every customer can navigate life's roads with confidence, pride, and the freedom to pursue their passions.

How: By matching lifestyles with perfect vehicles, providing educational service experiences, supporting community mobility needs, offering financial empowerment, and enabling personal expression through customization.

What: We offer a curated vehicle selection, community-building programs, expert service and parts, customized financing solutions, and personalization options that fulfill needs from basic transportation to automotive self-expression."

TSG stood up, eyes shining with inspiration. "This is about being true partners in our customers' life journeys. It's who we are and the positive impact we can have in our community."

Esther smiled warmly. "Remember, this Golden Circle is your guide to creating value in every interaction, whether it's in the showroom, service bay, or finance office. It's about fulfilling needs and enabling dreams—for everyone who walks through our doors, communicates with us online or directly via phone, email, DMs or chatbots."

As the energized team dispersed, buzzing with ideas for implementation, TSG turned to Esther. "Thank you," he whispered sincerely. "You've helped us see our significance as a dealership in a whole new light."

"The journey's just beginning, Thomas. The real magic happens when you bring this vision to life in every customer interaction."

TSG looked around, out over the showroom. Dashing Auto Group was no longer simply a place to buy or service cars; they were becoming facilitators of life's journeys, big and small. The road ahead was clear, purposeful, and filled with opportunities to make a real difference in people's lives.

TSG's Journal – Guiding Lights

Today's session with Esther felt like a turning point. We dove into "finding our *Why*," and I was struck by how powerful this is for both leadership and our business. Seeing our *Why* statement on the wall—"To empower journeys and connections, so that every customer can navigate life's roads with confidence, pride, and freedom"—gave me a surge of pride.

This statement is the core of who we are, guiding every action and decision I make.

I now see how important it is to take this deeper. Our relationships with OEMs must reflect this significance, fostering partnerships that go beyond transactions and tap into our shared vision. We've laid the groundwork, but we need to deepen these collaborations, ensuring that Dashing Auto Group is seen as a future-facing partner, ready to lead the way.

There's more work ahead. We need a strong vision statement that captures not only our *Why*, but our ambition as leaders in this industry. This vision will align our team and inspire confidence in our OEMs, customers, and community. Tomorrow, I'll begin the process with Esther and the Vision 2030 team. This is the moment to chart our future—I'm excited for what comes next.

CHAPTER 29

A Shift in the Shadows

Do not lose hope—what you seek is seeking you.
—**Rumi**

As Thomas and Esther prepared to gather the Vision 2030 team the following week, they reflected on their progress. Dashing Auto Group's strategy was solid, their *Why* defined, and their path forward clear. However, tension persisted between OEMs and dealerships. The relationship, once collaborative, had grown strained as OEMs pushed forward with rapid innovation to meet consumer and market demands.

Dealers, however, had been slower to follow. It wasn't merely reluctance to change, but a hesitation to invest in costly transformations until the market had matured enough to justify those investments.

OEMs, driven by market forces and new consumer expectations, advanced early to position themselves for future shifts in the automotive landscape. Dealers, including many of Thomas' peers, waited cautiously. They understood the importance of adapting but were concerned about making significant financial commitments before the critical mass of the market had evolved enough to ensure a sound return on investment.

Chapter 29: A Shift in the Shadows

The pandemic only widened this gap, with OEMs moving swiftly ahead while many dealerships remained anchored in their traditional business models, hesitant to take on the risk of early transformation.

This created a growing disconnect. Dealers, once trusted partners, felt sidelined, and OEMs grew increasingly frustrated by what appeared to be resistance. The tension generated a corrosive energy that began to erode their symbiotic relationship, one that had previously thrived on mutual success. Both sides became mired in misalignment and doubt.

Recognizing this divide, TSG knew Dashing Auto Group needed to take a different approach. Instead of resisting change, TSG began to involve OEMs in their transformation, engaging them in strategic discussions about how both parties could shape the future of automotive retail together. OEMs, though initially cautious, began to see the value in Dashing Auto Group's efforts to bridge the gap. They offered insights to help guide the transformation, and slowly the positive energy began to return.

Meanwhile, Cipher thrived on the friction between OEMs and dealerships, feeding off the corrosive energy. For years, Cipher had exploited the gaps created by hesitation and uncertainty. But as Dashing Auto Group started to realign with OEMs, Cipher's hold began to weaken. What had once been a chaotic disconnect between the two sides was slowly transforming into purposeful momentum.

The realignment was about more than survival—it was about reclaiming leadership and creating a new model where both OEMs and dealerships played vital, complementary roles. For too long, Cipher had successfully positioned technology as the leader, turning humans into passive followers of data and automation. Decisions that should have been guided by wisdom and human connection were instead dictated by algorithms devoid of context or empathy. Humans didn't deeply understand technology, and technology didn't truly understand humans.

But now, under Thomas' leadership, the scales were rebalancing. Technology was no longer the master—it had become the servant. With a North Star to guide every decision, Dashing Auto Group was beginning to redefine its relationship with innovation, with leadership. Their hybrid approach wasn't about resisting progress or clinging to tradition; it was about blending their traditional strengths—personalized customer experiences and deep, trust-driven relationships—with the precision and efficiency technology could provide.

At the core of this new model was the belief that leadership required intuition, empathy, and vision—qualities that no machine could replicate. Technology would support, not replace, the human touch that fostered connection and loyalty.

Cipher, devoid of the human insight needed to grasp the power of collaboration, began to lose its grip. It had once thrived by exploiting the divide between OEMs and dealerships, feeding off the mistrust and disconnection that had fractured the industry. But as Dashing Auto Group's consistent, disciplined actions rebuilt trust and strengthened partnerships, Cipher's influence waned.

But Cipher's grip wasn't gone completely—it had simply shifted. Its influence lingered in the shadows, waiting for cracks to reappear. It preyed on moments of doubt, disconnection, and complacency, feeding off human failures in resilience and belief. It had always thrived where trust faltered and where individuals reverted to isolation instead of collaboration.

Thomas knew this well. The battle wasn't over—it had only evolved. To keep Cipher at bay, the team needed to hold their course, keeping faith building toward their vision and in one another. They needed to stay vigilant, trusting that their collective momentum, built on small, consistent wins, would outlast Cipher's attempts to divide them. Leadership would remain human at its core—rooted in empathy, strengthened by collaboration, and fortified by the belief that, together, they were stronger than any algorithm.

Cipher was still watching, still waiting. But this time, Dashing Auto Group wasn't moving blindly into the future—they were stepping forward with conviction, united in their resolve to keep the narrative in their own hands.

Thomas' father, Andrew, had always told him, "Those who fail to plan, plan to fail."

Chapter 29: A Shift in the Shadows

But Andrew had also reminded him that a plan's true strength lies in the resilience and discipline of those who carry it out—while remaining flexible enough to pivot when the road ahead changes. Leadership wasn't just about staying the course blindly; it was about knowing when to adapt without losing sight of the vision, balancing steadfast commitment with the agility to seize new opportunities or overcome unforeseen challenges.

OEMs, watching this transformation unfold, began to conceptualize the potential of the dealership's evolving business model. Thomas wasn't just reacting to the changes around him; he was actively working to redefine the future of the OEM–dealer relationship. He was demonstrating that the path forward wasn't a passive adaptation to market trends—it was a deliberate reshaping of the landscape through collaboration and shared purpose.

A question that remained was whether other dealerships would follow suit and embrace this collaborative spirit, or whether they would continue to hesitate, waiting for the market to evolve further.

Everything was fragile. Cipher was still a looming threat, waiting for cracks to exploit. The OEMs were willing—eager, even—but cautious, still tethered to the fear of repeating past missteps. And the Dashing team, though inspired, needed to see unwavering conviction from TSG. They needed to believe not only in the plan but in the leader who stood at its helm.

It was up to TSG to take the next steps, to embody the resilience, discipline, and vision that would steady the course. He understood that this journey couldn't be walked alone—it demanded collaboration across every touchpoint: his leadership team, the OEMs, and the community they served. Success would be built not on speeches or promises, but on daily proof that Vision 2030 wasn't an abstract goal—it was a living, breathing commitment.

Failure wasn't just an option—it was a surrender. To falter now would be to hand the automotive world to Cipher, to let innovation be stripped of humanity and replaced with cold, algorithmic control.

It was time to build a collaborative vision for 2030—one forged from trust, shared responsibility, and the belief that progress would only come by working together. Only then could they outlast Cipher's influence and create a future where technology served the people, instead of the people being servants to technology.

CHAPTER 30

Vision 2030

*Efforts and courage are not enough
without purpose and direction.*
—**John F. Kennedy**

Esther looked around the conference table where the Dashing Auto Group team had gathered. The room buzzed with anticipation as they waited for her to guide them in crafting their 2030 vision.

"Let me tell you a story," Esther began, her voice steady and purposeful. "Imagine Dashing Auto Group as a ship on a vast ocean. For years, you've been navigating these waters, responding to the currents and winds, sometimes drifting, sometimes charging ahead. But now, it's time to chart a deliberate course."

She paused, letting her words sink in. "Without a clear destination, any direction seems as good as another. But successful companies know exactly where they're headed."

TSG exchanged glances with his Vision 2030 team. Some traded looks of acknowledgment; others remained deep in thought.

Esther continued, "This reminds me of the famous exchange from *Alice's Adventures in Wonderland*. Alice asks the Cheshire Cat which way she should go, and the cat responds that it depends on where she wants to get to. When Alice admits she doesn't much care where, the cat replies that it doesn't much matter which way she goes."

Esther scanned the room. "This exchange highlights the absurdity of choosing a path without a destination in mind. Your vision for 2030 is your North Star. Instead of emphasizing *where* you want to be, think about *who* you want to become as a company."

She walked to the whiteboard and drew a simple diagram: a ship with multiple paths branching out. "Right now, you're at a crossroads. Each path represents a potential direction for Dashing Auto Group. But which one will lead you to success? That's what your 2030 vision will help you determine."

Turning back to the group, her expression serious, she added, "A ship without a destination may sail beautifully, but it will never reach port. Your vision isn't simply a lofty statement; it's a practical tool to guide every decision you make from now on."

The team felt the weight of her words. They understood crafting a vision statement; they were charting the future of Dashing Auto Group. Esther's wisdom, combined with timeless insights, had shown them the importance of having a clear destination.

For too long, TSG had been ensnared in the hamster wheel of daily tasks and short-term goals, constantly reacting to change. But now, with Esther's guidance, he felt a transformation. A new-found ambidexterity was awakening within him, giving him the strength to confront the challenges ahead.

Driven by a passion for success, TSG knew it was time to establish a bold Vision for 2030—a beacon that would rally his team and broadcast their *Why* to the world. No longer would he be a victim of change; he would lead Dashing Auto Group to go beyond survival and thrive in the face of change.

The battle lines were drawn, and TSG was ready. With his team united and a clear vision in place, they were prepared to confront whatever challenges lay ahead and steer Dashing Auto Group toward a prosperous future.

Chapter 30: Vision 2030

Thomas printed off the Dashing Auto Group Hedgehog and Golden Circle concepts and put them up on walls around the room for all to read and use as a guide in the creation of Vision 2030.

Our Hedgehog

Best in the World at: Delivering a seamless, personalized, and relationship-driven customer experience.

Economic Engine: Profit per customer by maximizing lifetime value.

Passion: Creating memorable automotive experiences and driving innovation while fostering community and human connection.

Our Golden Circle

Why:
To empower journeys and connections, igniting joy and positive change through sustainable mobility, so that every customer can navigate life's roads with confidence, pride, and the freedom to pursue their passions.

How:
- Matching lifestyles with perfect vehicles through our "Lifestyle Matching" process
- Providing educational and transparent service experiences via our "Service Journey" program
- Supporting community mobility needs through our "Community Wheels" initiative
- Offering financial empowerment through workshops and customized solutions
- Enabling personal expression through our "Parts and Accessories Personalization Studio"
- Championing eco-friendly automotive technologies and sustainable practices
- Fostering a culture of continuous growth and innovation among our team

What:
- Curated selection of eco-friendly and traditional vehicles for every life stage
- Expert, technology-enhanced service, and genuine parts to keep vehicles at peak performance
- Customized financing solutions that provide peace of mind and enable dreams
- "Dashing Drivers Club" membership fostering a sense of community among our customers
- Comprehensive employee development programs to ensure exceptional customer experiences
- Active community partnerships and initiatives to support local transportation needs
- Industry-leading sustainable practices across all dealership operations

At Dashing Auto Group, we're facilitating life's journeys, big and small, while driving positive change in our community and the environment.

Thomas gestured toward the agenda for today's meeting, drawing the team's attention to the key points ahead.

"Charting the Course: Crafting Dashing Auto Group's Vision, Tagline, and Mission"

1. The Vision (charting the course)
2. The Tagline (a concise representation of that vision)
3. The Mission Statement (the roadmap for achieving the vision)
4. The Credo (the daily guide on what we believe)

Dashing Auto Group Vision (Charting the Course)

TSG tented his fingers, surveying the room. "Crafting a vision isn't simply about words on paper," he began. "It's about capturing our essence and letting it guide everything we do."

He moved to the whiteboard. "Let's break this down," he said, writing as he spoke. "Our *Why*: To empower journeys and connections, igniting joy and positive change through sustainable mobility, so that every customer can navigate life's roads with confidence and the freedom to pursue their passions."

He turned to face the room, letting the words resonate. "This isn't about selling cars. It's about partnering with our customers on their life journeys and driving positive change in our communities."

He paused before continuing. "To bring this *Why* to life, we need everyone involved. A vision committee, with voices from every corner—Sales, Service, Finance, Parts, even our customers, will help shape how we pursue our *Why*."

He drew a circle on the board, writing "Inclusive" next to it. "Next, our *How*. We achieve our *Why* through innovative programs like 'Lifestyle Matching,' 'Service Journey,' and 'Community Wheels'. We're creating experiences that connect people at every touchpoint."

He added another circle, labeling it "Innovative and Empowering." "But we need to communicate this clearly," he continued, drawing a third circle. "'What' we do is offer a curated selection of vehicles, expert service, customized financing, and community initiatives. We are more than a dealership—we are facilitators of life's journeys."

TSG stepped back, surveying his work. "This is more than a vision statement," he added passionately. "It's a roadmap to live our Golden Circle every day."

He envisioned a workshop where everyone, from the newest technician to the most loyal customer, brainstormed ways to empower journeys, foster connections, and drive positive change. "That's how we make a vision that resonates with everyone," he declared.

Popping the marker cap, TSG continued. "This is more than business strategy. It's our conviction. When we align everything with this, from 'Lifestyle Matching' to 'Community Wheels', we will transform our industry, our customers' lives, and our community's vitality."

Dashing Auto Group: Aligning Vision 2030 with our Golden Circle and Hedgehog Concept

The Golden Circle was displayed prominently on one side of the room and their Hedgehog Concept on the other. "Team, we've crafted a powerful strategic pathway and emotional purpose, but now it's time to ensure these fully align before we sharpen our Vision for 2030."

STEP 1: Reviewing Alignment with *Why*

TSG pointed to their *Why*: *To empower journeys and connections, igniting joy and positive change through sustainable mobility, so that every customer can navigate life's roads with confidence, pride, and the freedom to pursue their passions.*

The team reflected on the statement. While it captured their deeper ambition, they realized it could go further by tying directly to their Hedgehog Concept, emphasizing their **best-in-class** customer experience and long-term relationships.

Jamie, from Customer Relations, suggested, "Our *Why* should highlight how we excel at personalizing experiences and building trust with our customers."

Together, they refined the *Why*: "*To empower journeys and connections through seamless, personalized customer experiences that foster confidence, joy, and long-term relationships, ensuring every customer navigates life's roads with pride and the freedom to pursue their passions.*"

TSG nodded. "This puts the spotlight on why we're the best at what we do, delivering unmatched customer experiences."

STEP 2: Incorporating *How* Elements with a Focus on Lifetime Value

Next, the team turned to the *How*. They had already defined several key initiatives, but now they needed to align them with the concept of maximizing **lifetime customer value**. TSG led the group as they considered how their current activities could drive long-term relationships with customers, moving beyond one-time transactions.

The team reviewed their approaches:

- **Lifestyle Matching process**: "We can expand this to focus beyond the initial sale on anticipating customers' needs as their lives evolve," Sarah from Sales suggested.
- **Service Journey program**: Mike from Service added, "We'll make service an educational and trust-building experience, so customers come back year after year, knowing they're in good hands."
- **Community Wheels initiative**: They agreed this could foster loyalty through deep community engagement, supporting local needs.
- **Financial empowerment** and **Parts and Accessories Personalization Studio**: Both programs would reinforce long-term trust by helping customers grow financially and express their individuality.

The *How* now reads: "*We will nurture relationships with our customers through personalized experiences that increase their lifetime value, matching lifestyles with vehicles, providing expert, trust-building service, customization, and strong community engagement.*"

STEP 3: Defining the *What*

The team reflected on the current offerings and their ability to meet the refined purpose. After discussing the various elements, including vehicle selection, service, financing, and community programs, they understood that the *What* had to revolve around creating lasting value through every interaction, ensuring that customers felt supported long after the initial sale.

Together, they crafted the *What* statement: "We offer a curated selection of vehicles, expert personalized service, customized financing solutions, and deep community engagement, all designed to create lifelong value. Our seamless, relationship-driven approach ensures that every interaction reinforces customer confidence and loyalty, making Dashing Auto Group their trusted partner for all mobility needs."

This statement solidifies how Dashing Auto Group delivers on its promise. The *What* emphasizes that every product, service, and program is focused on fostering lasting relationships, maximizing lifetime customer value, and providing a seamless, personalized experience that builds trust and loyalty over time.

STEP 4: Refining the Vision

With the *Why, How,* and *What* refined, the team turned back to their Vision 2030. Guided by their Golden Circle and Hedgehog Concept, they worked together to create a vision that encapsulated their future aspirations while staying true to their core strengths.

The revised vision read:

> *By 2030, Dashing Auto Group will be the leader in revolutionizing the automotive experience, empowering individuals and communities to navigate life's roads with confidence, pride, and lasting relationships. We will be renowned for delivering personalized, sustainable mobility solutions that create meaningful connections in every journey.*
>
> *As a trusted partner in our customers' life journeys, we will offer a seamless blend of eco-friendly and traditional vehicles, matched to every lifestyle and life stage. Our commitment to redefining ownership through innovative, trust-building service experiences will ensure lasting relationships and lifelong loyalty.*
>
> *We will inspire personal expression through customization and foster community engagement, making Dashing Auto Group a central figure in empowering dreams, enabling connections, and promoting environmental responsibility. Together, we will drive positive change, contributing to a more vibrant, connected, and sustainable future.*

STEP 5: Final Alignment Check

TSG led a final review, ensuring each element of their Golden Circle and Hedgehog Concept was now fully reflected in the vision. The team agreed this version captured not only their **Why**, **How**, and **What** but also the core of their **Hedgehog Concept**: being the best at delivering seamless, relationship-driven customer experiences, maximizing lifetime customer value, and igniting passion through memorable journeys.

Chapter 30: Vision 2030

"This vision," TSG concluded, "is now a true reflection of our Golden Circle and our Hedgehog Concept. It captures not only what we aim to achieve, but who we are at our core. This will guide every decision and action as we move toward 2030."

The team left the meeting energized and ready to bring this vision to life, confident that they were on the path to becoming more than a dealership and becoming a lifelong partner in their customers' journeys.

CHAPTER 31

The Tagline

Less talk, more action.
—**Anonymous**

The office was calm, a stark contrast to the whirlwind of ideas in TSG's mind as he sat at his desk, trying to make sense of the next steps for the business. He stood up, crossed his arms and narrowed his eyes, as if piecing together an unseen puzzle in his mind. "Esther, we've got our vision statement, but I feel like we need something punchier. Something that really sticks in people's minds."

"You're absolutely right, Thomas. What you're looking for is a tagline. It's a short, catchy phrase that encapsulates the essence of your vision."

"Like, 'Just do it' for Nike?" TSG asked.

"Exactly. Or 'Think different' for Apple, 'Belong anywhere' for Airbnb. These taglines are powerful because they distill the company's entire ethos into a few words."

TSG pondered her words. "So how do we create one for Dashing Auto Group?"

"Well, there are a few ways we could approach this. We could make it an inclusive exercise, involving the same people who helped craft the vision. Or …" Esther paused for effect, "we could turn it into a competition."

Chapter 31: The Tagline

"A competition?" TSG said, his voice rising a little with excitement.

"Yes. Announce an in-house competition. Share your vision statement and invite everyone in the group to submit their tagline ideas. Make the prize worthwhile. You'll be amazed at the creativity it stimulates."

TSG laughed, jotting notes. "I like that. It gets everyone involved and invested."

"Exactly, but if you want to start with something more contained, we could do a tagline blitz session with your management team. Set a timer, have everyone come up with five taglines in five minutes. It's fast-paced and often produces surprising results."

"Let's do that now," TSG said. "You and me. Five minutes, five taglines each. Go!"

Five minutes of intense scribbling later, they compared notes.

"Okay, I've got 'Drive Green, Live Better', 'Empowering Your Eco Journey', 'Innovation in Every Mile', 'Leading Green, Driving Excellence', and 'Sustainability in Motion'."

Esther gave a nod of approval. "Those are strong. I've come up with 'Future-Ready Mobility', 'Eco Excellence, Every Day', 'Where Innovation Meets Sustainability', 'Your Journey, Our Commitment', and 'Green Drives, Bright Futures'."

They spent the next few minutes discussing each option, weighing their merits against the vision statement.

Finally, TSG cracked his neck and wriggled his shoulders. "I think we might be onto something, Esther. 'Drive Green, Live Better.' It's short, memorable, and really captures the essence of what we're about—eco-friendly vehicles and improving people's lives."

Esther grinned broadly. "I really like it, Thomas."

TSG nodded, then paused. "Now, let's bring this to the team. We've got a strong vision statement, and we can explain this tagline. But it's important they feel a part of this, that they come together to create something even better. And you're right—let's make the prize meaningful. Maybe a weekend getaway in one of our new electric models?"

"That sounds wonderful," Esther agreed. "Remember, Thomas, the goal is to find a tagline that resonates with everyone—your team, your customers, your community. It should be a rallying cry that inspires and motivates."

"Exactly. 'Drive Green, Live Better' sets a high bar, but I'm excited to see what the team can come up with. This is going to be great, Esther. We're selling a vision of a better future."

Esther chuckled. "That's the spirit," she said. "Let's bring the team together and get started!"

* * *

TSG stood before his team, bouncing slightly on the balls of his feet, a grin spreading as he spoke, his eyes alight with excitement. He'd been pondering the vision statement, distilling it into catchy, memorable phrases. Smiling confidently, he began.

"Alright, team. We need some taglines that capture the essence of our Vision 2030. I've come up with a few, but let's workshop your ideas too." Thomas jotted his ideas on the whiteboard.

1. Driving Joy, Empowering Tomorrow
2. Your Journey, Our Passion, Earth's Future
3. Igniting Positive Journeys … Together
4. Empowering Journeys, Enriching Lives
5. Sustainable Mobility, Joyful Community"
6. Drive Green, Live Better

TSG looked around the room to gauge reactions. "Each of these tries to encapsulate different aspects of our vision. Do you agree? Which one resonates most with what we're trying to achieve?"

After presenting their own taglines, the team considered each option carefully, and after a thoughtful discussion, a clear favorite emerged:

"Igniting Positive Journeys … Together"

Sarah from Sales spoke up first: "I love this one. It captures the essence of what we're trying to achieve. 'Igniting' speaks to the passion and innovation we bring, 'Positive Journeys' encompasses both the literal journeys our customers take in our vehicles and the broader journey toward a more

Chapter 31: The Tagline

sustainable future. And 'Together'—that's key. It shows we're in this with our customers and our community."

Mike from Service nodded. "It also reflects our commitment to empowering our team. We're all in this together, igniting these positive changes."

Lisa from Marketing added, "From a branding perspective, it's memorable and versatile. We can use it in various contexts—from our eco-friendly initiatives to our community programs."

Carlos from Community Relations said, "The 'Together' part really resonates with our community focus. It's not just about us or even just our customers; it's about the collective impact we're making."

TSG smiled, seeing the enthusiasm in the room. "I agree. This tagline encapsulates our vision perfectly. It refers to the positive change we're creating in partnership with our team, our customers, and our community. It's forward-looking, inspiring, and true to who we are and who we want to be."

The team unanimously agreed. "Igniting Positive Journeys … Together" would be the tagline to represent Dashing Auto Group's Vision 2030.

CHAPTER 32

The Mission

*A strong mission gives you direction
when everything else feels uncertain.*
— **Anonymous**

"Team, now that we have our vision and tagline, it's time to focus on crafting a mission statement," TSG announced. "This will be the roadmap that guides your team's daily actions."

Esther leaned forward, ready to explain. "Think of your vision statement as a telescope, and your mission statement as a map."

TSG tilted his head, intrigued by the analogy.

"Your vision statement is like looking through a telescope," Esther continued. "It's about the 'why' and 'what' of your future—the world you want to create by 2030. It's aspirational, long-term, and inspirational. When you look through this telescope, what do you see for Dashing Auto Group?"

TSG closed his eyes for a moment, visualizing. "I see a world where our people and dealership have transformed communities, where sustainable transportation is the norm, not the exception."

"Exactly! That's your vision. It answers the big question: 'Where do we want to go?'"

Chapter 32: The Mission

Esther then transitioned to explain the mission. "Now, the mission statement is like your map. It's the 'who,' 'what,' and 'how' of your journey right now. Who are you as a company? What do you do, and how do you do it? It provides a compass for your team's daily decisions and actions."

"So, our mission statement will talk about providing eco-friendly vehicles, exceptional service, and how we're committed to innovation and sustainability today?" TSG asked.

"Precisely," Esther said. "Your mission gives your team focus every day, linking their actions to your long-term vision."

After some time spent reviewing successful mission statements from other companies, TSG led the team in brainstorming the elements that should be in their mission. Together, they identified key themes: customer experience, long-term relationships, innovation, sustainability, and community engagement.

The team worked together for the next half-hour, refining their ideas. Finally, TSG sat up straight, beaming with excitement. "How about this for our mission statement?"

Dashing Auto Group: Mission Statement

At Dashing Auto Group, we deliver a seamless, humanized automotive experience where every interaction reflects luxury, innovation, and personalized care. We are dedicated to being a trusted partner for customers, communities, and OEMs, redefining the car-buying journey through cutting-edge, eco-friendly technologies and sustainable practices.

Our mission is to empower our team to continuously innovate, providing solutions that meet the evolving needs of our customers and the communities we serve. We strive to be a catalyst for positive change, contributing to a future where every journey is driven by sustainability, joy, and purpose.

Esther smiled, clearly impressed. "This is spot on, Thomas. It perfectly encapsulates the essence of Vision 2030, and it also touches on all the critical elements of your Golden Circle and Hedgehog Concept."

Sarah added her thoughts. "It captures our focus on eco-friendly vehicles, exceptional service, and long-term customer relationships. And it's clear and actionable."

"It gives our team a real sense of motivation, something to guide our work every day," Mike said.

"It's perfect for messaging," Lisa said. "I can already see how we'll use this in communications with our customers. It's a statement that reflects who we are and what we stand for."

TSG beamed, energized by the group's response. "It feels like we've captured the core of who we are and where we want to go."

"Now the challenge is to ensure this lives beyond paper," Esther said, eyes alight with pride.

The room buzzed with excitement as the session was coming to an end. TSG exchanged a knowing look with Esther. The transformation was happening, and the future of Dashing Auto Group was clearer than ever.

CHAPTER 33

The Pathway

Excellence is not a skill—it's an attitude.
—**Ralph Marston**

It had been a week since the team had convened. Thomas stood at the head of the table, ready to lead his team through this essential meeting. Today is not only about operational plans; it is about creating the credo that will define Dashing Auto Group's culture and values, setting them on the path toward Vision 2030.

"Our task today," Thomas began, "is to create a credo that reflects not only what we do but how we do it. This credo will embody empowerment, energy, KPIs, and the future of retail principles—elements that will help us transform our business and build lasting relationships."

He looked at each member of the team, knowing they understood that this credo had to go beyond meeting the hefty OEM standards. It was about creating something much bigger.

Esther moved to the front of the room and started by discussing the teachings of Melkart Rouhana and Horst Schulze. "Our credo must reflect a culture of empowerment and values-based leadership. Every team member, no matter their role, should feel empowered to make decisions that improve the customer experience. Empowerment is about trust—trusting our people to lead in their areas, like Schulze taught us in *Excellence Wins*, where every employee was responsible for customer service."

Thomas chimed in. "We need to ensure that empowerment is paired with values that guide decisions. Rouhana talks about creating values people can rally behind, like integrity, respect, and a commitment to excellence. Those values need to be central to our credo."

Jane added, "So, it's about providing a framework of values to guide people's choices?"

"That's right, Jane," Thomas agreed. "Empowerment without values leads to chaos. We need to build the kind of culture that will drive us toward Vision 2030."

Liam, focused on aftersales operations, asked, "How do we make sure this credo brings energy to every corner of the company? We need to make sure it translates into action."

"That's where Heike Bruch's work on organizational energy comes in," Esther replied. "We need to harness the positive energy within the company, aligning everyone's focus and drive toward our goals. The energy and passion we bring to meetings like this needs to be felt across the entire organization."

Martin added, "And Liam, it must be sustainable. We need to keep momentum, not burn people out."

"Wow, everyone is in sync today," Thomas said with a smile. "This is essential, of course; we need to balance focus and energy to ensure our teams stay motivated and aligned with our long-term goals."

Anna jumped into the conversation, raising an important point. "How do we make sure this energy and empowerment translate into measurable success? I do love data, but I am becoming better at sharing stories about that information too."

"That's where Jeff Smith's teachings on KPIs come in," Thomas explained. "We need tactical KPIs to measure daily operations. Those are the dealer benchmarks. But we also need strategic KPIs that align with our long-term vision—employee satisfaction, customer loyalty, sustainability, and community engagement."

Chapter 33: The Pathway

Jane asked, "How do we make sure KPIs don't feel like micromanagement?"

Anna responded, "KPIs guide us; they don't control us. They help us measure what matters and see where we need improvement. They're tools to keep every department aligned with our overall strategy."

Thomas turned to the principles of Bernard Arnault, the visionary behind LVMH, to address the customer experience. "What we're building at Dashing Auto Group is beyond a place to sell cars; it's a premium experience. Like LVMH, we need to focus on creating emotional connections with our customers. Every interaction should feel personalized, exclusive, and meaningful."

Liam nodded. "It's about creating a relationship, not a transaction."

"Yes, yes," Esther emphasized with delight. "OEMs provide a brand story and the product, but we bring it to life through personalized, high-touch service. That's how we build long-term loyalty." She paused, then added, "This is about bringing Arnault's principles into the automotive world, making the dealership experience feel like stepping into a luxury brand. We turn the ordinary into the extraordinary, every day!"

Thomas turned to the whiteboard where he had been busy writing as the team was talking. The credo was taking shape: empowerment, trust, innovation, energy, sustainability, and relationships.

"This is where we're headed," he said. "Our credo will embody everything we've talked about today: empowering our people, building lasting relationships, maintaining positive organizational energy, using KPIs to measure what matters, and delivering a luxury experience that goes beyond OEM expectations." He paused. "By 2030, Dashing Auto Group will be the benchmark for personalized, sustainable mobility solutions. And this credo will be the guide that gets each and every one of us there."

The team nodded in agreement. The pathway was clear. The credo they were developing was the engine that would drive them toward Vision 2030.

"Let's have a short break and stretch our legs," Thomas suggested. "Exercise brings out happy hormones. Oh, how I digress sometimes, but these are essential for leaders to understand. I'll write them up on the board and you can check these out later if you're interested. See you all in 15 minutes."

Thomas wrote the following on the white board.

Happy hormones: how they are triggered, and the outcomes from their release:

1. **Endorphins**
   - *Triggered by*: Exercise, laughter, spicy foods, excitement
   - *Outcome*: Pain relief, stress reduction, feelings of euphoria
2. **Dopamine**
   - *Triggered by*: Achieving goals, pleasurable activities, recognition
   - *Outcome*: Enhanced motivation, reward sensation, increased focus
3. **Serotonin**
   - *Triggered by*: Sunlight, physical activity, positive social interactions
   - *Outcome*: Improved mood, reduced anxiety, better sleep
4. **Oxytocin**
   - *Triggered by*: Physical touch, bonding activities, social interactions
   - *Outcome*: Increased trust, social bonding, feelings of security

Why this matters to leadership

As leaders, we don't just manage tasks—we influence emotions, mindsets, and environments. When we create conditions that trigger these 'happy hormones', we foster trust, motivation, resilience, and collaboration. Whether it's celebrating small wins to boost dopamine, promoting team bonding to release oxytocin, or encouraging laughter to spark endorphins, our actions can shape how people feel and perform. Leadership isn't just about driving results—it's about creating an atmosphere where people thrive.

CHAPTER 34

The Credo

Integrity is doing the right thing, even when no one is watching.
—**C.S. Lewis**

A Living Guide for Excellence

As the team returned from their coffee break, with their happy hormones flowing, Thomas stood ready, his voice filled with energy. "The word credo is Latin for 'I believe'. This is our commitment to our customers, partners, and each other. But for it to truly represent us, we need to build it together. Each of you has a voice in defining what our culture looks like and how we'll hold ourselves accountable for it. This credo will guide us as we grow, and it will be built by all of us, for us. Now comes the magic. This needs to reflect the values we've identified and show how we'll live them in every decision and action."

The team split into groups, each drafting a selection of statements that addressed:

- **Customer Commitment**: How we prioritize the customer experience.
- **Team and People**: How we support and respect each other.

- **Excellence and Integrity**: How we uphold the highest standards.
- **Innovation and Growth**: How we embrace the future.
- **Community and Sustainability**: How we give back and take responsibility for the future.

As the team reconvened after breaking into task groups, the room was abuzz with excitement. Ideas had been exchanged, strategies formed, and now it was time to bring it all together. The energy was palpable as Esther stood, addressing the group.

"Now that we're building this credo together," she began, "remember it's our promise. It's what we believe. Each of us is responsible for living these values every day. We need to hold ourselves and each other accountable. This will be our culture now. Trust, excellence, and human connection; that's how we act and serve both inside this dealership and beyond."

Thomas nodded. "I'm excited," he said. "This credo will guide every decision we make, every customer interaction, and every partnership with our OEMs. It's not about short-term success; it's about building something that will drive us toward Vision 2030."

Dashing Auto Group Credo

Our Mission

At Dashing Auto Group, we are committed to delivering a seamless, human-centered automotive experience where every interaction, from car buying to ownership, reflects trust, innovation, and personalized care. By building lasting relationships and exceeding expectations, we aim to redefine both the car-buying and car-ownership journeys, becoming the destination of choice for vehicle enthusiasts, individuals, families, corporate, and OEM partners alike. Together, we lead the transformation of the automotive industry through sustainability, innovation, and the human connection that sets us apart.

Our Commitment to Our Customers

We promise to provide each customer with an exceptional, personalized experience, whether they are buying a vehicle, maintaining it, or seeking advice. Our mission is to create meaningful relationships and offer seamless, memorable experiences that enhance their lives throughout the entire ownership journey. Every interaction is an opportunity to build trust, offer tailored solutions, and make our customers feel valued.

The Dashing Experience

Luxury meets trust at Dashing Auto Group. Every team member is empowered to make decisions that enhance the customer experience at every stage, from purchase to ownership. We go beyond transactions to deliver care, precision, and excellence in every interaction. We treat every customer like a guest in our home, ensuring they feel understood, respected, and valued, whether they're purchasing a vehicle, returning for service or seeking advice.

Our Partnership with OEMs

We are more than a dealership; we are a strategic partner to OEMs, aligned with their goals of innovation, sustainability, and electrification. Together, we provide customer-focused solutions that build loyalty, trust, and long-term relationships. By embracing cutting-edge technology and forward-thinking strategies, we support both our OEM partners and customers, offering an automotive experience that is innovative, sustainable, and human-centered, before, during, and after the sale.

Our Principles

- **Customer First**: We treat every customer as a valued guest, delivering a seamless, attentive, and personalized journey from the initial purchase through to the full ownership experience.
- **Unwavering Integrity**: Transparency, honesty, and ethical practices guide our relationships with customers, partners, and our community.

- **Excellence in All We Do**: We are committed to continuous improvement, constantly elevating our skills, knowledge, and services to offer the highest quality throughout the car-ownership journey.
- **Innovation for the Future**: We embrace the future by leading with cutting-edge technology, sustainable practices, and a deep understanding of industry trends.
- **Human Connection**: We build meaningful relationships. Our success is measured by the trust and loyalty we earn with every customer and partner, from their first interaction to the ongoing care of their vehicle.

Our Team Promise

We are each empowered to take ownership of the Dashing Auto Group mission, ensuring that every interaction reflects our commitment to excellence and innovation. We are not only colleagues; we are a family of professionals, working together to deliver exceptional results. Each of us is responsible for upholding Dashing Auto Group's values, knowing that our success depends on how well we support one another, our customers, and our partners throughout the entire car-ownership journey.

Thomas paused, allowing the words to resonate in the room. The team absorbed the credo, recognizing that it was more than a statement—it was a promise. A promise to their OEM partners, their customers, their community, and to each other.

The atmosphere in the room shifted, filled with a sense of shared purpose and clarity. Thomas knew that this moment marked the start of a new chapter for Dashing Auto Group, one defined by unity and vision. The credo would not only guide their actions and decisions but also empower every team member to strive for excellence. It was a vital step in their journey, one that would propel them from being a good company to becoming a truly great one.

Chapter 34: The Credo

TSG's Journal – Transformation

The energy in the dealership today was undeniable. After our collaborative sessions, we've shaped a **Vision 2030** that feels transformative, blending our legacy with bold innovation. Reconnecting with our *Why* has given us clarity, and I'm excited by the actionable steps we've outlined to move forward. Every part of our plan is designed to engage and involve our team and customers, creating a journey they're a part of.

But I'm mindful of something John mentioned at a recent convention: while ambition is essential, we can't overwhelm the team with unrealistic targets. Our vision is big, but our progress must be steady and sustainable. Finding that balance—driving transformation without overloading our people—will be key to our success.

CHAPTER 35

Embracing Our Journey

You are stronger than you think, braver than you believe, and smarter than you know.
—**A.A. Milne**

Several weeks later, the marketing team had prepared the support materials for the Vision 2030 launch. There were **branded brochures**, a **corporate video**, **infographics** breaking down the credo, and **digital presentations** ready for the all-hands meeting.

Thomas was immensely proud of his team, and deeply appreciative of Esther's guidance throughout this journey. The energy shift within Dashing Auto Group was undeniable. People talked with excitement about the future, and team engagement was at an all-time high.

It was time for Thomas to deliver the next step to the team, the community and their OEM partners. Today, the future would begin.

As the room quieted, Thomas hesitated. The weight of the moment pressed down on him, heavy and palpable. He could feel the eyes of his team on him—the anticipation, the hope. A knot tightened in his chest. Was he ready for this? The doubts swirled in his mind. This was more than a simple speech; it would lead Dashing Auto Group into an uncertain

Chapter 35: Embracing Our Journey

future, through changes he wasn't entirely sure he could navigate. The pressure was mounting, and not for the first time.

Esther must have sensed his unease. "Thomas, this speech is pivotal for Dashing Auto Group," she said softly.

"We've come so far, Esther, but there's still so much more ahead. The team needs to understand how critical this moment is. Do they see how we all need to move forward together in this rapidly evolving automotive landscape?" Thomas swallowed hard, his mind racing. Could he truly lead them through this storm? What if they failed? What if he wasn't enough?

Esther smiled, her voice calm but firm. "They know, Thomas. They feel the excitement, but they're looking to you for direction. Think of Simon Sinek's belief; you need to articulate the *Why* that's already in their hearts and minds. This isn't about words; it's the roadmap for where you're steering the company and the industry."

He took a deep breath. Esther's words had grounded him. She was right. It wasn't about him. It was about the team, the people who had been with him through every challenge, every victory, every setback. He had to be the one to guide them through this. The vision was there, but they needed to hear it from him.

"I want them to understand," he began, voice steadying, "that this isn't another milestone; it's a turning point. Everything we've built—our values of community, innovation, and sustainability—it's all coming together now." He could feel the words building momentum inside him. "I want them to know that we're not reacting to the changes in the auto industry; we're driving them."

Esther's eyes gleamed as Thomas' conviction returned. "Exactly," she said. "You've already laid the foundation. Now let them feel their role in this vision. They're not just part of a company; they're part of a movement that's reshaping the customer experience. It's about more than just selling cars; it's about building relationships, creating trust, and elevating the way we serve."

Thomas' hesitation began to dissolve, replaced by a growing resolve. "You're right, Esther. This is our moment. We're going beyond moving with the times, we're defining them. I need them to understand that Dashing Auto Group is stepping into a new era, where every detail matters, and every customer interaction feels personalized, thoughtful, and exceptional."

He paused, considering the weight of the words. It was bigger than him. It was about creating a legacy.

Esther stepped closer, her confidence unwavering. "And like Captain D. Michael Abrashoff says, you have a way of bringing out the best in your team, making them believe in what's possible. They're ready to follow you into this new era for Dashing Auto Group. They just need to hear it from you, the visionary."

The weight that had once felt suffocating now felt like an inherent calling. He could do this. The uncertainty that had plagued him was still there, but now it fueled his determination. He wasn't only leading a company; he was leading a movement—a new way forward for Dashing Auto Group and the automotive industry.

"It's time," he said, standing taller. "Time to show them the map. Together, we're going to ignite something incredible in the automotive industry. We're going to create something that blends the past, present, and future into an experience that can't be resisted."

With a final glance at his notes, Thomas stood with renewed confidence. As he stepped up to the podium, the room fell silent, all eyes on him. The excitement, the anticipation, and the sense of what was possible hung in the air. And then, Thomas began to speak.

Igniting Our Journey to Vision 2030: A Future Rooted in Purpose, Passion, and Excellence

Ladies and gentlemen, team members, valued partners of Dashing Auto Group,

Today marks the beginning of an extraordinary journey—a journey toward Vision 2030, a future we will shape together. This journey is filled with challenges and opportunities, but it begins with one simple question: Why are we here?

Chapter 35: Embracing Our Journey

We are here because we believe in something greater than ourselves. We believe in the power of innovation, connection, and purpose. Vision 2030 is more than a goal; it's our story. It's a story where Dashing Auto Group leads the automotive industry by creating sustainable, joyful journeys, driven by a passionate and innovative team.

But this story isn't only about us, it's about our customers. They are the heroes of their journeys, and we are their guides. Behind every vehicle sold, every service completed, there's a deeper story, whether it's a single parent purchasing a reliable car, a young adult celebrating their first vehicle, or a family gearing up for their next great adventure. At Dashing Auto Group, we are the ones who make these journeys possible.

Our path to Vision 2030 means elevating these stories every single day. Greatness doesn't come from grand gestures; it comes from consistent, everyday actions that deliver exceptional experiences. This is what will drive us forward. We must relentlessly pursue customer service excellence, ensuring that every interaction feels meaningful, and every service is delivered with care and precision.

But today is not just about setting a new course; it's about recognizing the people who have helped shape it. I want to take a moment to acknowledge each of you here today. Together, we have crafted this vision. This journey is not just mine; it's *ours*. Each of you has contributed your ideas, your energy, and your dedication, and that's why this vision will succeed. Because it belongs to all of us.

To achieve Vision 2030, we will focus on two types of goals:

- Tactical goals will ensure that we meet our customers' day-to-day needs, service levels, sales objectives, and operational efficiency. These will be managed daily, weekly, and monthly, ensuring we stay on track.
- Strategic and emotional goals will guide us toward Vision 2030. These goals align us with our deeper resolve—building

trust, delivering memorable experiences, and creating long-term relationships.

Every step we take, whether tactical or emotional, brings us closer to this vision.

At the heart of this journey is our credo. It's more than a statement; it's the guide for our culture. And the credo we've built together will remind us of who we are, how we treat each other, and how we serve our customers. Each of you has had a hand in creating this credo, and because of that, it's greater than a set of words; it's a living, breathing reflection of our shared values. It will guide us as we grow and evolve, ensuring that our culture remains strong and aligned with Vision 2030.

Success isn't built on vision alone. It's the result of small, disciplined steps taken daily. Whether it's ensuring that every customer interaction is handled with care or continuously finding new ways to deliver value, each step moves us closer to our long-term aspirations.

Change is inevitable. But it's not the change itself that's the challenge; it's how we respond to it. We must see change as an opportunity. Just like in luxury retail, where the customer journey is constantly evolving, we must do the same.

We will embrace data and use KPIs to measure our progress. These metrics will help us assess our goals, not to use as a stick, but to guide us so we know where we are versus where we need to be. These samples of measurement will show us where our opportunities are to be of greater service.

Vision 2030 is more than a destination; it's a commitment to each other, to our customers, and to our community. We will celebrate every step, knowing that every step is an investment in our future.

Like the best brands that blend tradition with innovation, we will foster a culture of excellence and creativity. We aren't just a business; we are a partner in the growth of our community. Engaging

Chapter 35: Embracing Our Journey

deeply with our local area, supporting causes that matter, and creating opportunities for everyone to thrive will be at the heart of who we are.

Our mission is clear:

- Innovate continuously to create experiences that meet our customers' evolving needs and desires.
- Stay vigilant to anticipate customer challenges and opportunities.
- Build a seamless digital presence that empowers customers to engage easily and personally.
- Empower our team to deliver exceptional service that enhances customer satisfaction.
- Communicate clearly to ensure our vision aligns with the aspirations of our customers and partners.

With each step, whether tactical or strategic, we come closer to achieving Vision 2030. The credo will guide us, ensuring that our culture grows stronger with every decision we make. Together, we will turn small steps into great strides, and in doing so, we will ignite positive journeys … together … one story at a time.

This is our moment. This is our journey. And I am honored to take it with each and every one of you.

As Thomas stepped back from the podium, the room erupted in applause, the energy elevated to new heights. Esther approached him, her smile reflecting pride and excitement. "That was exactly what we needed, Thomas. You've given them direction."

Thomas turned back to the crowd, the atmosphere buzzing with anticipation.

"Ladies and gentlemen, thank you. We've grabbed the keys, fired up the engine, and now it's time to ***embark on our journey*** toward 2030. This isn't merely any drive; it's our drive toward the future we've envisioned together. But let's remember, for us to be the best—to finish first, per se—***first we must finish***. Every mile we cover together brings us closer to making that vision real, and it's your passion and dedication that will get us there. So come on, grab the wheel, let's hit the road and make Dashing Auto Group the beacon of success that all others will follow."

CHAPTER 36

Building Energy with Cultural Transition in Mind

A strong culture is not built in a day—it's built every day.
—**Jon Gordon**

A few weeks later, TSG arrived at Dashing Auto Group later than planned, feeling the weight of a frustrating morning. As he navigated through minor setbacks like parking issues and a dentist appointment that went awry, he couldn't shake the simmering irritation. Upon finally reaching the dealership, he noticed how crowded the lot was. "Hassle factors," he muttered, echoing Esther's teachings. These small frustrations weren't simply annoyances; they were symbolic of a deeper issue—friction points that sapped the energy needed to build Dashing's luxury-driven culture.

In this moment, TSG remembered Rouhana's teachings on values and empowerment, realizing that employees need time and persistence to fully embrace cultural changes. These minor irritations, if left unaddressed, could drain the energy and focus required to build the empowered, high-performance culture they were striving for. Like Schulze's emphasis on excellence at every touchpoint, TSG knew that every detail mattered in the journey toward Vision 2030.

"John," TSG called, striding into the office with intent. "We need to address these hassle factors immediately. They're more than inconveniences; they're preventing us from building the high-energy culture we need."

He paused, gathering his thoughts. "Customers are frustrated with lengthy wait times, no parking, phones not being answered and complex processes. They struggle with confusing warranties, limited-service appointment availability, and inconsistent communication from us. Every time they hit one of these barriers, we're losing trust."

John nodded as TSG continued. "And it's not only the customers. Our staff is under constant pressure to meet high sales targets, work extended hours, and deal with outdated, complex systems that slow everything down. They're spending hours on paperwork and juggling training demands instead of focusing on the customer experience."

TSG took a deep breath, his tone firm. "If we don't tackle these head-on, we'll keep losing momentum. Let's start creating solutions for a seamless, energized environment—for customers and for the team."

John nodded in agreement. "They may seem small, but they add up fast."

"That's exactly it," TSG replied. "It's the cumulative effect. Let's gather feedback from every department and identify where these friction points are. We need to eliminate anything that drains energy or creates frustration—whether it's internal communication, customer parking, or service delays. It's more than operational fixes. It's about empowering our team to identify and resolve these issues themselves."

Bruch's framework on organizational resurfaced in TSG's mind. As well as setting ambitious goals for a team, leaders must nurture energy to sustain the effort. High positive energy wasn't a default state; it had to be built intentionally, just like a great customer experience. Horst Schulze's insights reminded him that empowerment was a choice leaders made every day: the choice to trust, to give others the authority to act, and to remove fear from decision-making.

With that thought, TSG returned to his laptop and began drafting a memo to his leadership group. If they were to reach Vision 2030, they couldn't rely on quick wins or motivational slogans. They needed a cultural foundation built on clarity, trust, and the relentless elimination of barriers. It was time to realign, to ensure that every department leader understood not just what was expected, but why their role in this journey mattered so deeply.

Once he finished typing, TSG leaned back and read the memo one last time. It wasn't just a call to action—it was a blueprint for building the culture they needed. Satisfied, he hit send.

The memo read:

INTERNAL MEMO: Organizational Energy and Our Path to Vision 2030

FROM: Thomas Steven Gregory (TSG)
TO: Leadership Team
SUBJECT: Building Momentum Through Organizational Energy

Team,

I wanted to take a moment to reflect on how far we've come and share a framework for our next steps. Over the past few months, we've done more than just measure our performance—we've defined our purpose, aligned around our Vision 2030, and established a clear picture of the culture we want to build. We've clarified our Hedgehog Concept, strengthened our ties to the community, and deepened partnerships with our OEMs. What we're creating is bigger than a strategy—it's a movement driven by connection, trust, and action.

Through this process, we've learned that success isn't just about hitting performance metrics; it's about the energy that fuels our progress and the resilience to confront what holds us back. We've all felt those moments when everything clicks—when collaboration flows, partnerships strengthen, and progress feels effortless. But we've also experienced times when momentum stalls—when friction, doubt, or fatigue slow us down. Managing this energy, individually and collectively, is essential to turning our vision into reality.

Bruch's concept of organizational energy has made one thing clear: without addressing these energy-draining factors, we risk losing the momentum needed to sustain the cultural shift we're aiming for. This isn't about quick fixes or cosmetic changes—it's about creating a culture where every team member feels empowered to take ownership, embrace challenges, and solve problems at their root.

Just as Horst Schulze emphasized the importance of enabling employees to resolve issues at the first point of contact, we must foster a sense of ownership across every level of our organization. Melkart Rouhana's teachings on sustainable greatness remind us that true transformation doesn't come from grand gestures but from cultivating habits of consistency, resilience, and disciplined action.

Key Areas of Focus

1. **Identifying and Eliminating Friction Points:**
   Every team member interacts with processes that either help or hinder them. Our responsibility is to understand what slows them down and provide the tools, autonomy, and support they need to address these hurdles effectively. This applies not only within our internal teams but also in our partnerships with OEMs—we need to remove barriers and create seamless collaboration.

2. **Building Empowerment Through Ownership:**
   Empowerment isn't just a slogan—it's the result of clear communication, mutual trust, and the freedom to act. Are we giving our teams and our OEM partners the clarity and confidence to make decisions that align with our vision and values? Do our people feel safe enough to take ownership and innovate without fear of failure? True ownership begins when people know they're trusted to make a difference.

3. **Maintaining High-Energy Consistency:**
   Achieving Vision 2030 will be a result of disciplined, sustained action. This is a marathon, not a sprint. Small, consistent

improvements—whether in customer service, technology integration, or team collaboration—compound over time and drive us toward our goals. Our leadership approach must model this consistency so that it becomes a mindset embedded in everything we do, inspiring both our internal teams and our OEM partners to stay the course.

What's Next?

We've laid a solid foundation, but there's more we need to explore. We must dig deeper to understand the real stories behind the data. What's motivating our people? What's frustrating them? What's holding back our team and OEM partners from fully engaging in this journey? What's missing from our communication? The answers to these questions will help us align our processes with our mission and ensure that Vision 2030 isn't just a vision—it's an experience we're building together.

I'm asking each of you to reflect on what "empowerment" looks like in your departments and identify specific friction points that need our attention. I also want your ideas for how we can cultivate the kind of energy that makes our culture resilient and unshakable in the face of challenges. Remember, Cipher's greatest advantage has always been our moments of doubt and disconnection. Our greatest strength will be our ability to maintain belief and momentum—together.

This isn't just my vision—it's ours. The more aligned we become, the stronger our collective impact will be. Our success isn't defined by the absence of obstacles, but by how we choose to overcome them. The automotive world is watching, and together, we're setting a new standard.

Let's keep pushing forward—step by step, with purpose, conviction, and trust in each other.

Best regards,
Thomas

Small Wins Lead to Big Change

Following the publication of the memo, TSG gathered his leadership group the next day to discuss its contents and introduced them to the *flywheel effect,* as described by Jim Collins, as the process of building momentum in a business through consistent, disciplined effort over time. TSG began, "Imagine pushing a massive flywheel—at first, it's hard work, requiring tremendous effort just to get it to budge. But with each push, the wheel turns slightly faster, and as momentum builds, it becomes easier to keep it spinning. There's no single defining moment or breakthrough; instead, success comes from small, deliberate actions that compound over time. Eventually, the flywheel moves with its own momentum, propelling the organization forward with sustained growth and success.

"The *flywheel effect* matters in creating high positive energy because it fosters a sense of progress, alignment, and shared accomplishment within an organization. As the flywheel begins to move, every small consistent action reinforces a feeling of forward momentum, which energizes the team and builds confidence in the process. Employees see tangible results from their efforts, creating a virtuous cycle where success inspires more success.

"When the team knows their actions contribute to a greater vision, aligned with clear goals, it generates positive energy by replacing doubt or stagnation with enthusiasm and a sense of collective achievement. Over time, this momentum becomes self-sustaining, driving the organization to greater heights while keeping the workforce engaged, motivated, and optimistic about the future.

"Therefore, by eliminating one hassle at a time, we create a flywheel effect of positive energy and momentum. Every small win would be a step toward creating the seamless, luxury-driven experience promised in Vision 2030."

Thomas put up on the projector screen the organizational energy matrix as portrayed by Bruch and Vogel to discuss and demonstrate with his team a key teaching from their book *Fully Charged*.

Chapter 36: Building Energy with Cultural Transition in Mind

Organizational Energy Matrix

	High Intensity	Low Intensity
Positive Energy	**High Positive Energy** *Engaged, motivated teams proactively working towards goals*	**Low Positive Energy** *Content but complacent, steady but lacking innovation or drive*
Negative Energy	**High Negative Energy** *Frenzied, unfocused activity, stress-driven actions*	**Low Negative Energy** *Apathy, cynicism, low engagement, inertia*

How to Use This Matrix

- **High Positive Energy**: Our aim is to place the team here by fostering engagement, motivation, and clear goals.
- **Low Positive Energy**: Watch for complacency; while the team is content, they lack drive and innovation.
- **High Negative Energy**: Beware of overloading the team, leading to frantic, unfocused work driven by stress.
- **Low Negative Energy**: Address apathy and disengagement to avoid stagnation and declining performance.

Driving Positive Energy and Eliminating Hassle Factors

"To build high positive energy," TSG said, "the solution will be more than fixing operational issues. It will be about creating a culture of continuous improvement and empowering employees to own their impact. This process involves three key steps:

1. **Empower Employees:** Giving ownership of eliminating daily frustrations to every team member. This will foster collaboration and encourage innovative solutions, creating a sense of pride in their work.

2. **Streamline Processes:** Aligning internal processes with Dashing Auto Group's luxury vision will ensure that every step of the customer journey feels seamless, enhancing trust and loyalty.
3. **Celebrate Small Wins:** Accumulating small changes over time will propel Dashing Auto Group closer to its Vision 2030 goals."

The Ripple Effect of Positive Energy

TSG continued. "Each improvement creates a feedback loop:

- **Employees** feel empowered, boosting engagement and morale.
- **Customers** experience faster, more personalized service, leading to increased satisfaction and loyalty.
- **Innovation** thrives, as the team now has the bandwidth to focus on creative solutions instead of getting bogged down by inefficiencies.

"By addressing these friction points head-on, Dashing Auto Group won't just be improving operational efficiency, we will be building a resilient, adaptive organization ready to thrive in the face of industry disruption."

Action Plan: Reimagining the Customer Experience Together

Now that TSG had provided the leadership group with a deeper understanding of hassle factors, organizational energy and the flywheel effect, he invited them to collaborate on reimagining the customer experience. This was more than fixing parking or communication issues; it was about embodying the core values of trust, innovation, and excellence at every level.

With the town hall approaching and the launch of the digital ideas board through Workplace by Facebook, the team felt renewed energy and purpose. Workplace was more than a communication tool—it had become a digital space where team members could engage in real time, celebrate wins, share ideas, and provide feedback in a way that felt inclusive and empowering.

Chapter 36: Building Energy with Cultural Transition in Mind

This approach directly aligned with Donald Miller's *StoryBrand* philosophy, where the leader plays the role of the guide, helping the employees—the heroes of the story—navigate their journey toward success. By fostering open communication and collaboration, the platform positioned each team member as a vital contributor to the dealership's evolution. Features like live Q&As, discussion boards, and instant feedback loops created a sense of ownership, allowing employees to see that their voices were not only heard but were shaping the dealership's future.

Through shared victories and transparent leadership, employees felt connected to something greater than their individual roles. Workplace helped reinforce the connection between their daily contributions and the larger ambition of Vision 2030, nurturing the type of engagement Miller describes—where purpose and participation intersect, fueling a culture of positivity, resilience, and shared progress.

With the leadership group now gathered, Thomas handed a note to his team that Esther had prepared earlier.

> "Cultural transitions in an organization take time and persistence because people don't immediately adapt to change. Leaders must remain steadfast as they guide the team through uncertainty and resistance. Cultural shifts require consistent reinforcement of values and empowerment. Without sustained leadership, the momentum can fade and old habits resurface. By staying persistent, leaders ensure that the desired culture is internalized, transforming daily operations and aligning everyone with the long-term vision for success."

Esther had reinforced the importance of intentional, consistent leadership. By focusing on these small yet meaningful changes, Dashing Auto Group would transform into a dealership that truly embodies its values. Along with reducing frustrations, the changes would help it become the dealership of the future—one hassle-free, customer-centered step at a time.

Thomas and the leadership group acknowledged to each other this critical fundamental truth:

It's not enough to simply introduce change—it must be nurtured, reinforced, and celebrated consistently, so the team doesn't just work in the business but feels *invested* in the vision that drives it.

In that shared understanding, they saw the real measure of success—not in quarterly reports or individual wins, but in the collective belief that every step they took together, no matter how small, was building something far greater than any one of them could achieve alone.

CHAPTER 37

How Do You Eat an Elephant?

Little by little, a little becomes a lot.
—**Tanzanian Proverb**

Dashing Auto Group's Transformation Journey

The clouds had cleared, and the scorching summer sun beat down on Thomas as he stood before the colossal elephant statue in the town square. His grandmother's words echoed in his mind: "How do you eat an elephant? One bite at a time." That advice perfectly captured the transformation he had undergone.

Esther had written Thomas a note, one he now pulled from his sports jacket as he sat on a bench in the town square.

Thomas,

I believe you've been a good manager, excelling at keeping operations smooth, meeting targets, and solving daily problems. As a manager, your focus was on doing things right—ensuring efficiency, maintaining control, and focusing on short-term objectives. You made sure everything ran as expected, guiding your team to follow plans, and hit goals. But as the automotive industry continued to face disruptive changes, you realized that managing wasn't enough. The business, and the industry, needed leadership.

You have become a good leader. You shifted from managing tasks to setting a vision for the future. Leadership meant doing the right things—aligning the team around long-term goals, inspiring innovation, and guiding them through uncertainty. You learned that a true leader empowers others, focusing beyond operational matters to motivating the team to see the bigger picture.

However, becoming a great leader—a Level 5 leader—is your ultimate challenge. Level 5 leadership requires a unique blend of humility and fierce resolve, where the success of the company is placed above personal ego. It's about leading with purpose, empowering your team to take ownership, and always keeping the long-term vision in mind. Greatness is not simply about managing or leading well, but about building something enduring, guided by ambition, empathy, and humility.

Level 5 leaders are a rare combination of humble, selfless, and fiercely driven individuals who focus on creating great companies with long-term success in mind. They avoid the spotlight, give credit to others for achievements, yet maintain an unwavering determination to do whatever it takes for the company to thrive.

Their focus is on building lasting success that extends beyond their own tenure, making them the transformative leaders capable of taking their organizations from good to great.

Keep the council close and encourage your team to read these wonderful authors' works, learn from them, and grow. The more they develop, the more Dashing Auto Group will thrive, building a legacy of lasting success.

Kind regards,
Esther

Chapter 37: How Do You Eat an Elephant?

He folded the note carefully, feeling the value of her words.

As he sat there, Thomas glanced at the elephant statue once more. He knew the journey ahead wouldn't be completed in a single leap—he would continue to tackle it, one bite at a time. But for now, with Esther's continuing guidance and the lessons of the council that she had laid out, the path to greatness felt clearer.

CHAPTER 38

Win the Day

Winners never quit, and quitters never win.
—**Vince Lombardi**

TSG stood before his team, his eyes gleaming with determination. He let the silence build, anticipation filling the room. Then, with a steady voice, he delivered his message:

"Winning the day isn't about grand gestures or monumental achievements. It's about the small victories, the incremental improvements, and the consistent effort we put in every single day. Each customer we delight, each process we improve, each team member we uplift—these are the building blocks of our success. When we focus on winning today, we're not just preparing for 2030; we're creating it."

TSG let his message sink in before continuing, his voice firm.

"As Admiral McRaven wrote, 'Life is hard and there are forces that will try to break us down, but if we stand tall and strong against the odds, then life will be what we make of it, and we have the power to make it great. No matter what happens, never, ever, ring the bell!' The future we envision doesn't come in one giant leap; it unfolds in the countless moments where we choose to persist, to never give up. So, let's win this day. And by doing so, we'll win our future."

Chapter 38: Win the Day

The room was silent for a moment, charged with unspoken agreement. Then, slowly, nods spread across the room. TSG could feel it—the shift from individual commitment to collective resolve.

"As McRaven's SEAL team knew, greatness isn't built in isolation but through an unbreakable bond—one forged by trust, shared hardship, and a commitment to never let each other fail," TSG added, his voice steady. "When we move forward together, like a SEAL team in perfect synchronicity, we become more than a team—we become unstoppable."

In that moment, they weren't just leaders of departments—they were a united force, ready to face whatever came their way and win, one day at a time.

TSG's Journal – Wisdom

As I close this journey toward becoming ambidextrous, I'm struck by the profound wisdom in this Japanese proverb:

"Vision without action is a daydream.
Action without vision is a nightmare."

This sentiment encapsulates the very essence of what we've been striving for at Dashing Auto Group. Our Vision 2030 is bold and inspiring, but it would remain nothing more than a beautiful daydream if we didn't pair it with decisive action. Every day, we're taking concrete steps—improving our customer experience, investing in our team's development, embracing new technologies—to turn this vision into reality.

Conversely, I've seen firsthand the chaos that can ensue from action without vision. In the fast-paced world of automotive retail, it's tempting to react to every market shift, every new trend, without a clear direction. But that path leads to a nightmare of wasted resources, confused employees, and dissatisfied customers.

Our journey toward ambidextrous leadership has been about finding the perfect balance between these two extremes. We're cultivating the ability to dream big while also staying grounded in practical day-to-day actions. We're learning to innovate for the future while also optimizing our current operations.

This balance isn't always easy to maintain. There are days when the vision seems too distant and the immediate challenges too pressing. But then I remind myself and our team, every action we take, no matter how small, is a step toward that vision. And every aspect of our vision informs the actions we take today.

As we move forward, I'm committed to nurturing both our visionary thinking and our capacity for decisive action. We'll continue to refine our Vision 2030, ensuring it remains a beacon guiding us toward a bright future. And we'll keep honing our ability to take meaningful, vision-aligned actions every single day.

To my team at Dashing Auto Group, to our customers, to our suppliers, and the community (now that it's incorporated into this book), let's embrace both the dreamer and the doer within us. Let's envision a future so compelling it inspires us into action. And let's take actions so aligned with our vision that they bring our dreams to life.

CHAPTER 39

A New Dawn

The heart has its reasons which reason knows nothing of.
—**Blaise Pascal**

Time had passed since that pivotal morning when Thomas had stood on the balcony of his seventh-floor apartment, peering through the early morning drizzle at the glowing neon sign of Dashing Auto Group. Now, standing in the bustling showroom of Dashing's flagship store, he marveled at the transformation—not simply of his dealership, but of the entire industry.

Cipher, once an existential threat, had been relegated to its rightful place—a cog in the wheel, not the wheel itself. Not because Cipher had disappeared, but because they had adapted and grown beyond its reach. What had begun as a defensive strategy had evolved into a bold revolution—a revolution rooted in the one thing Cipher could never replicate: human connection.

But this revolution wasn't born overnight—it was built by leaders who embraced ambidexterity, balancing the demands of today while boldly shaping tomorrow. Thomas' ability to navigate both optimization and exploration had been critical. He and his leadership team had dared to reimagine what was possible by blending present-day skills, learning, resilience, adaptability, and purpose.

The industry had taken notice and embraced Dashing Auto Group's three-step blueprint, which had since become an industry standard:

Dashing Auto Group's Blueprint for Transformation: A Model for the Industry

1. **Lead with Empathy:**
   True transformation begins with understanding people—not just customers, but employees and partners as well. Combine the precision of data with the warmth of human care to deliver personalized experiences that technology alone cannot achieve. Empathy is the bridge between customer needs and meaningful solutions.

2. **Collaborate to Innovate:**
   Break down barriers and build bridges between all stakeholders—OEMs, dealerships, and customers. Success comes from a unified effort, where ideas and expertise flow freely, creating partnerships that drive innovation and shared growth. Collaboration is more than a strategy; it's the foundation of a thriving industry fueled by mutual trust.

3. **Elevate Every Interaction:**
   Treat every customer touchpoint as an opportunity to create lasting connections. Go beyond the transaction to uncover the deeper motivations—the *Why* behind every decision. By focusing on building trust and delivering seamless, human-centered experiences, you foster relationships that endure far beyond a single sale.

Thomas scanned the showroom, a vibrant blend of innovation and human connection. A sales consultant guided a customer through a virtual reality test drive, their conversation punctuated by laughter as the customer marveled at the lifelike simulation. Nearby, a service technician used AI-powered diagnostics to explain vehicle maintenance, breaking

Chapter 39: A New Dawn

down complex details into simple, relatable terms that left the customer feeling confident and informed.

Technology was seamlessly woven into every interaction, but it was the human touch—the warmth in their voices, the attentiveness in their gestures—that brought it all to life.

This was the embodiment of ambidextrous leadership—the ability to integrate cutting-edge tools while remaining steadfast in their commitment to empathy and collaboration. Thomas knew that this journey wasn't just about implementing new processes; it was about reshaping their purpose.

Every interaction felt intentional, crafted not just to meet a need but to build a relationship. The showroom wasn't just a space to transact—it was a place where customers felt seen, understood, and valued. This wasn't simply a transformation of operations; it was a redefinition of what it meant to lead in a connected world.

The journey to this moment hadn't been without its challenges. There were moments of doubt, resistance from traditionalists, and countless obstacles. Yet, through it all, Thomas and his allies—including visionary leaders at the OEM—had stayed the course. Together, they had turned Vision 2030 from an ambitious dream into a living reality.

"Did you ever imagine we'd end up here already?" Esther asked, stepping beside Thomas with a proud smile.

"Not even in my wildest dreams," Thomas replied, his gaze lingering on the seamless harmony of people and technology. The hum of activity, the delight of a customer, and the warmth of the technician's patient explanation painted a vivid picture of what they had built.

"But this is what happens when you truly collaborate—when you see past individual limitations and focus on shared potential. This is what becoming ambidextrous means."

"And in doing so, we've created something that will last," Esther added, her voice filled with quiet pride.

Thomas nodded, his smile deepening as the weight of their shared journey washed over him.

They weren't merely saving their business—they were redefining the industry itself. What was once heralded as the Fourth Industrial Revolution had transformed into a human-centered renaissance, where technology amplified human potential, and people gave technology its soul.

As the sun set, casting a warm glow through the glass walls, the scene in the showroom felt symbolic. This wasn't the culmination of their efforts—it was a milestone on an ongoing journey. For Thomas, Dashing Auto Group, and the entire industry, the realization was clear: the path forward would be one of trust, collaboration, and connection—a journey defined not by reaching an endpoint, but by continually striving to evolve and inspire.

Thomas walked into the gathering area where his leadership team had assembled for their checkpoint meeting. This wasn't just another session; it was a chance to pause, reflect, and celebrate how far they had come. Tonight's meeting carried extra significance. Joining them was a special guest—a partner whose vision and unwavering support had been pivotal in shaping their journey. Klaus' presence underscored the importance of collaboration and alignment as the team evaluated their current position and discussed their next steps.

Taking his place at the front of the room, Thomas addressed the team with heartfelt words.

"Tonight, we celebrate not just where we've been, but where we're going. This journey wasn't walked alone. It's been a partnership—a shared commitment to pushing boundaries and building something extraordinary."

He gestured toward the podium, where Klaus stood ready to speak.

"It is my honor to introduce someone who believed in us when we needed it most. A leader whose knowledge, vision and dedication have helped shape the future we now live in. Please welcome Klaus, our OEM partner, to share his thoughts on what's next for us all."

The room erupted in applause as Klaus stepped forward, his presence a testament to the power of collaboration.

Chapter 39: A New Dawn

Driving the Future Together

Delivered by Klaus to the Dashing Auto Group leadership team.

"Good evening, Thomas, and the incredible team at Dashing Auto Group.

As I stand here today, I'm reminded of the journey we've taken together—OEM and dealership, side by side—not as 'us and them', but as a united 'we'. That mindset has been the cornerstone of our shared success. Together, we've harnessed our collective expertise to create a customer experience that sets a benchmark not just for our industry, but for the future of mobility itself.

For too long, this relationship—OEM and dealer—has been seen as transactional, a means to an end. But today, we celebrate the evolution of that dynamic into a true partnership. Together, we've crafted something remarkable. We've proven that when we align our efforts, we can achieve outcomes far greater than the sum of our parts.

In the past, our challenges were simpler. We focused on showroom design, model mix, and ensuring consistency in how our brand was represented. But today's customers demand more. They don't solely want a product; they want to belong to a story—a story that resonates with their values, aspirations, and emotions. They want to feel part of something bigger.

This is where we've succeeded together. By focusing on customer experience—not as a buzzword, but as a guiding principle—we've delivered moments that matter. And make no mistake, technology has been a critical enabler. But as you know, technology alone does not create the magic. People do. Your people.

It's your team who brings the brand to life, creating those signature moments that stay with customers forever. They are the storytellers, the caretakers of the customer's journey, and the architects of lasting impressions. That's why hiring the right people, empowering them with meaningful leadership, and cultivating a culture of excellence have been—and will continue to be—our greatest investments.

As the great Peter Drucker once said, 'Culture eats strategy for breakfast.' Strategy may provide the roadmap, but culture is what propels us forward. And Dashing Auto Group has become a shining example of what a strong, adaptive, and customer-centric culture can achieve.

Looking ahead, the future holds new complexities. As we expand into new markets and embrace new store formats, we must remain where the customer is—not just geographically, but emotionally and digitally. Flagship stores will always be vital, but we must also meet customers in new ways—through co-branded cafés, urban showrooms, and immersive digital experiences. These touchpoints are not about transactions; they're about connections. When we get that right, the transactions will follow.

And let's not underestimate the challenges of delivering seamless customer experiences. It takes more than ambition; it requires robust technology, unified data, intuitive design, and above all, unwavering collaboration. Seamless may sound simple, but it is anything but easy. It demands excellence from every corner of our organizations.

We also live in a world that's rapidly shifting from VUCA—volatility, uncertainty, complexity, and ambiguity—to BANI: brittle, anxious, non-linear, and incomprehensible. In this world, resilience is more than a competency; it's a necessity. And resilience isn't solely about bouncing back—it's about moving forward with purpose, clarity, and strength. It's about having the courage to lead, even when the path ahead is uncertain.

Thomas, what you and your team have built here is nothing short of extraordinary. Dashing Auto Group is not simply any dealership; it is a movement—a vision of what the future of automotive can and should be. You've shown us that the road to success is

Chapter 39: A New Dawn

paved with more than a strategy; it depends upon people, culture, and a relentless focus on the customer.

So tonight, I leave you with this: Let's continue to write this story together. Let's push boundaries, challenge conventions, and redefine what it means to be a leader in this industry. Because succeeding goes beyond sales or market share—it's about creating a legacy. A legacy that inspires, connects, and drives the world forward.

Thank you, Dashing Auto Group, for being our partners in this journey. Together, we are not just navigating the road ahead—we are paving the way for generations to come."

As Klaus' final words settled over the room, applause exploded into a full-blown celebration. Thomas stood at the center, clapping with pride as his leadership team—Anne, Jane, Liam, Martin, Esther, and John—rose to their feet, exchanging high fives, fist pumps, and cheers of genuine excitement. The typically reserved Anne broke into a rare smile, meeting Jane's outstretched hand with a triumphant slap, while Liam and Martin shared an enthusiastic fist bump, their joy momentarily dissolving their professional reserve. Even Klaus found himself caught up in the energy, accepting handshakes, back pats, and spontaneous fist pumps from the jubilant group.

Amid the cheers, laughter, and shouts of encouragement, Thomas raised his voice, declaring, "This is who we are now. Let's keep going—together, we can achieve our Vision 2030!" The team drew closer, expressing their gratitude for Klaus' inspiring words and a shared recognition of the hard-fought journey that was transforming Dashing Auto Group into more than a company—a family, united by purpose with a vision for the future.

EPILOGUE

Being Ambidextrous

It was 2030, and Dashing Auto Group had evolved into more than a dealership; it had become the centerpiece of innovation in auto retailing. The once fragmented relationship between OEMs and dealers had been restored, and together they were now driving the industry forward in harmony. What began as a struggle against the tide of change had turned into a blueprint for success, transforming not only Dashing Auto Group but the entire automotive landscape.

The dealership had become a shining example of what was possible when technology, human connection, and visionary leadership converged. Leaders across the industry looked to Dashing Auto Group as the model for the future, a place where luxury, sustainability, and personalized experiences merged seamlessly. Tonight, at an event that was set to inspire the next generation of auto industry leaders, Thomas Steven Gregory was preparing to share the journey that had brought them here.

As he stood at the podium, ready to address a room filled with industry pioneers, OEM partners, and members of his own team, Thomas reflected on how far they had come, and how much further they would go. This was more than a story of transformation; it was a testament to the power of collaboration and human connection in the face of disruption.

TSG stepped onto the stage, his smile filled with pride as he took in the faces of those in attendance.

> Good evening, everyone. I'm Thomas Steven Gregory, or TSG as many of you know me. Tonight, I'm not here to talk about a business. I'm here to share the story of people, a community, and a transformation that has shaped all of us.
>
> Five years ago, we stood on the edge of something uncertain. The automotive industry was evolving rapidly, and Dashing Auto Group, this business that had been in my family for generations, faced the very real possibility of becoming irrelevant. The ground beneath us was shifting, and I felt the weight of it all. At first, I thought the villain was change itself. But I've come to realize that change wasn't the enemy. It was our greatest opportunity.
>
> Looking back now, I see that the real villain wasn't the world changing; it was the fear within us, the corrosive energy that was stifling innovation and disconnecting us from each other. It wasn't just the industry that needed to evolve, it was our culture, and more than anything, it was me. I had to change.
>
> For so long, I believed I had to be The Somebody Guy. I thought I had to do it all: make every decision, solve every problem, carry the weight of every challenge on my own. But the truth is, that mindset was holding us back. I wasn't letting my team thrive. I wasn't embracing the collaboration and innovation that would take us forward.
>
> And then, with the guidance of my mentor, Esther, I realized that leadership wasn't about being the one to do everything. It was about being the one who empowers others to lead. It was about sharing the load, trusting the team, and creating an environment where everyone could bring their best selves to the table.

We began with a vision—Vision 2030. But it wasn't only my vision. It was crafted with the input of our team, our customers, our community and, critically, our OEM partners. Together we asked, Why do we exist? What impact do we want to have? We weren't content with surviving. We wanted to thrive, to become the leaders in reshaping the future of our industry.

Our transformation was more than internal. We knew that to thrive, we had to redefine our relationship with OEMs. The old barriers between dealerships and manufacturers had to come down. We needed to become true partners, combining their cutting-edge technology with our human touch to create something new, something greater. It wasn't about resistance to change; it was about embracing the possibilities that change offered.

Central to this journey was the creation of our credo. A set of guiding principles built on integrity, innovation, and a relentless focus on the customer. This credo became the heartbeat of Dashing Auto Group. It was something we lived every single day. It was about creating experiences that mattered, building relationships that lasted, and making every interaction count.

And let me tell you, we didn't always get it right. We stumbled, we made mistakes, and there were moments when the challenges seemed too great. But it was in those moments of doubt and vulnerability that I learned the most, not only about leadership, but about the strength of this incredible team, our community, and our OEM partners.

Our greatest strength wasn't found in our processes or even in the technology we deployed; it was in our ability to connect, to empathize, to understand each other and our customers on a deeper level. That's what truly transformed us. We realized that every interaction, every service call, every sale was an opportunity to build something meaningful.

Epilogue: Being Ambidextrous

I've watched as our sales staff transformed into sustainability consultants, as our mechanics became tech wizards, and as our service representatives evolved into designers of customer experiences. They weren't simply adapting to change; they were driving it. And they were doing it with pride.

And today, I can stand here and say with full confidence that Dashing Auto Group isn't just surviving; we are thriving. We've become a hub of innovation, a leader in sustainable mobility, and a place where our people grow both professionally and personally. Our customer satisfaction is up 35 percent. We've grown online sales by 40 percent. We've reduced our carbon footprint by 42 percent. Our revenue has expanded by 50 percent. But more than that, we've built a culture. Our Employee Satisfaction Program (ESP) scores are up 78 percent. We've built a family, one that believes in the future we're creating together.

The flywheel effect took over. Those small, consistent efforts, those one percent improvements day by day started to compound. Slowly at first, but then the momentum built. And now, we're unstoppable. That's the power of collaboration, of believing in something bigger than ourselves.

To everyone who has been a part of this journey, I want to say thank you. To our team, your courage, your passion, and your dedication have made this possible. To our community, you've supported us every step of the way, and we are committed to giving back in every way we can. And to our OEM partners, together we've built a partnership that is not only about business, but about a shared vision for the future.

To the leaders out there, I have this to say:
- Embrace change as your greatest ally, not your enemy.
- Recognize that the true challenge is often within.
- Collaborate and build a culture where the human spirit thrives.
- Dream big but act incrementally, trust the flywheel effect.

- Be bold in your vision but humble in your approach.
- And above all, invest in your people. They are the ones who will turn your vision into reality.

As we look ahead, we do so with excitement and dedication. We've become truly ambidextrous, honoring our past while innovating for the future. With our strong partnerships, our guiding credo, and our unwavering focus on human connection, we're not only prepared for the future of automotive retail; we are leading it.

Thank you for being part of this incredible journey.

TSG stepped back. The room resounded with applause as the sense of achievement, camaraderie, and excitement for the future filled the space. He smiled, knowing that they had redefined the industry through the power of collaboration, human connection, and innovation.

If You Can –
the Automotive Retailer's Creed

If you can blend the cold of code with warmth of human touch,
And see in each transaction a story that means so much.
If you can harness data's power, yet still look in the eye
Of every dreaming customer who's come to you to buy.

If you can build a digital world, yet not forget the feel
Of leather-wrapped emotions when hands first grip the wheel.
If you can crunch the numbers and still hear hope's refrain
In voices of the families for whom a car's not just a name.

If you can stand in showrooms gleaming with innovation's light,
Yet be the beacon of connection in a world that's digital-bright.
If you can see in every vehicle not just metal, gears, and chrome,
But vessels carrying adventures, dreams of freedom, and of home.

If you can fill your business plan with profits guarantee,
Yet never lose the vision of what transport ought to be.
If you can meet each challenge as the industry evolves,
And keep your human core intact as technology resolves.

BECOMING AMBIDEXTROUS

If you can hold tradition dear yet boldly forge ahead,
Embracing all the changes that once filled the heart with dread.
If you can be efficient, sleek, a model of success,
Yet never let your empathy or passion grow less.

If you can do all this and more, adapt and still stay true,
To values that have always been the best part of you.
Then yours is the future, bright and full of worth,
And—what is more—you'll be the best damn dealership on Earth!

In this brave new world, where silicon meets soul,
Where every feature tells a story, and every sale's a goal,
Remember: at the heart of trade, beyond all innovation's art,
Lies the simple human connection that sets great businesses apart.

For those who make it their mission, their hedgehog-focused dream,
To be the best at blending tech and touch, efficiency, and esteem,
The world is truly their oyster, success theirs to claim,
In an industry reborn, yet wonderfully the same.

Inspired by Rudyard Kipling, *If*, originally published in 1910.

Reading List

The automotive industry is undergoing a significant transformation, driven by advancements in technology, changing consumer preferences, and evolving regulatory landscapes. To provide a comprehensive overview of these developments, this book draws on a diverse array of sources, including traditional academic resources, cutting-edge artificial intelligence models, industry reports, and influential thought-leadership content.

In my journey of learning and growth, I've been fortunate to find inspiration and guidance in the works of several remarkable authors. Their insights have not only shaped my personal understanding but have also significantly influenced the ideas presented in this book.

- *The KPI Book: The Ultimate Guide to Understanding the Key Performance Indicators of Your Business* by Jeff Smith
- *Greatness is NOWHERE* by Melkart Rouhana
- Donald Miller's *Building a StoryBrand: Clarify Your Message So Customers Will Listen*
- The leadership principles from Captain D. Michael Abrashoff's *It's Your Ship: Management Techniques from the Best Damn Ship in the Navy*
- Admiral William H. McRaven's *Make Your Bed: Little Things That Can Change Your Life … And Maybe the World*

- Simon Sinek's *Start with Why: How Great Leaders Inspire Everyone to Take Action* and *Leaders Eat Last: Why Some Teams Pull Together and Others Don't*
- *Fully Charged: How Great Leaders Boost Their Organization's Energy and Ignite High Performance* by Heike Bruch and Bernd Vogel
- Jim Collins' *Good to Great: Why Some Companies Make the Leap … And Others Don't*
- Spencer Johnson's *Who Moved My Cheese? An Amazing Way to Deal with Change in Your Work and in Your Life*
- *The Taste of Luxury: Bernard Arnault and the Moet-Hennessy Louis Vuitton Story* by Nadège Forestier and Nazanine Ravai
- Horst Schulze's *Excellence Wins: A No-Nonsense Guide to Becoming the Best in a World of Compromise*

Acknowledgements

Humanity

Eight hours with the Most Reverend Desmond Tutu—London to New York.

In late 2005, I was on an early morning British Airways flight from London to New York, anticipating a quiet journey in a forward cabin. As I settled into my seat, I was surprised to see only one other passenger in the cabin, and it was none other than the Most Reverend Desmond Tutu.

The archbishop, with his trademark warm smile, introduced himself, and what followed was an extraordinary conversation that I'll never forget. We discussed everything from his experiences during the apartheid era to his work with the Truth and Reconciliation Commission.

Tutu's humility and sense of humor shone through as he shared personal anecdotes. He spoke passionately about the concept of Ubuntu: the belief in a universal bond of sharing that connects all humanity. His eyes twinkled as he explained how this philosophy could be applied even in the most mundane situations, like our shared flight.

As we enjoyed the in-flight meal, Tutu regaled me with stories of his interactions with world leaders and his unwavering commitment to social justice. He listened intently to my own experiences, offering insightful perspectives that challenged my thinking.

The hours flew by, punctuated by moments of profound discussion and light-hearted laughter.

Tutu's ability to balance gravity with joy was truly remarkable. As we began our descent into New York, I realized I had been given a rare gift. Not just a chance encounter with a living legend, but a masterclass in compassion, forgiveness, and the power of the human spirit.

As we parted ways at Newark Airport, Tutu gave me a warm handshake and his signature blessing. That flight may have been only eight hours long, but the impact of those hours with Desmond Tutu would last a lifetime.

Community

My sincere appreciation goes to Klaus Ullrich and his remarkable colleagues, Robert Fallbacher, Joseph Pariseau, Alex Webster, and Julia Döscher. Their work as visionary community builders and passionate educators has inspired me in ways that words cannot fully express. Watching them lead with integrity, expertise, and passion, particularly through the Porsche International Dealer Academy at PAG, the Porsche Academy at PCNA, and Porsche Business Excellence program at PCA, has left a lasting impression on me and countless others.

Through their leadership-focused programs and comprehensive business curriculum, they have fostered a profound shift in the automotive industry, instilling values of empathy, innovation, and excellence. These programs have not only shaped my own approach but have also guided many professionals toward people-centered leadership and meaningful, customer-focused strategies. I am deeply honored to have been inspired by the paths they have forged and to be part of their international business program, which continues to uplift and transform our industry.

Leadership

I am truly grateful to Professor Ulrich F. Zwygart, whose mentorship and humble sharing of insights, wisdom, and knowledge have profoundly impacted my journey. His exceptional background as a former attorney-at-law and retired major general, coupled with his experience as Managing

Director and Chief Learning Officer for global corporations, has provided invaluable guidance and inspiration. Professor Zwygart's contributions extend beyond his authored leadership books to his current roles as an independent consultant and leadership instructor at the University of St. Gallen's Executive School, further enriching his ability to offer transformative guidance.

Throughout our numerous one-on-one sessions, Professor Zwygart has generously shared his deep understanding of leadership, ethics, and strategic management. His willingness to engage in meaningful discussions and offer personalized advice has been instrumental in shaping my approach to these disciplines. His ability to connect theoretical concepts with practical applications has made complex ideas accessible and relevant.

I am deeply grateful for Professor Zwygart's mentorship, which has not only enriched my academic and professional life but also fostered a greater sense of purpose and integrity in my work. His dedication to nurturing the growth and development of his students is a testament to his commitment to education and excellence.

Thank you, Professor Zwygart, for your generosity in sharing your profound knowledge, and your genuine humility. Your influence has been a guiding light, and I am honored to have had the opportunity to learn from you.

Appreciation

I would like to express my deepest gratitude to Dr. Andreas Löhmer (Dr. A) for his inspirational guidance, unwavering support, and profound influence on my journey. During his tenure as Academic Director of the Porsche International Dealer Academy and Director of Corporate Programs at the Executive School of Management, Technology, and Law (ES-HSG), University of St. Gallen, he played a transformative role in my professional growth.

As a facilitator and mentor, Dr. Löhmer not only sparked new possibilities but also propelled my ambitions to new heights. His ability to empathize, provide insightful feedback, and foster a collaborative environment was instrumental in shaping my approach and refining my work. Through his encouragement and mentorship, he instilled the confidence to explore new ideas, challenge conventions, and push beyond perceived limitations.

I am especially honored that Dr. Löhmer wrote the foreword for *Becoming Ambidextrous*—a contribution that reflects not only his wisdom and generosity but also the special friendship and evergreen guidance he extends to those he mentors. Now as a leadership coach and consultant, his dedication to developing adaptive leaders continues to inspire me and many others who have had the privilege of learning from him.

Thank you, Dr. Löhmer, for your invaluable insights, your commitment to leadership excellence, and your steadfast belief in helping others reach their full potential. Your influence has been a guiding light, and I am profoundly appreciative of the lasting impact you have had on my professional journey.

Stewardship

Learning happens in many ways—through lessons, experiences, and the people who guide us. Dr. Rachel Brooks and her colleagues at the University of St. Gallen's Executive School exemplify disciplined stewardship, leading the program with both structure and intent while fostering an environment where growth is meaningful and inspiring.

Their leadership reflected rigor and accountability, ensuring high standards while creating space for engagement, reflection, and confidence-building. Yet, what made their approach truly impactful was the balance of discipline and empathy—the ability to challenge while supporting, to set expectations while understanding individual journeys.

The skills they apply are essential not only to the success of the program but also in their transferability. Their disciplined approach to leadership, coupled with a deep sense of empathy, has influenced my own leadership journey. I have benefited greatly from adopting these same principles, applying them in my own work, and seeing their impact in fostering growth, engagement, and meaningful change—insights that are also reflected in *Becoming Ambidextrous*.

I have the deepest admiration for Dr. Brooks and her colleagues' guidance and the example they set. Their disciplined leadership, grounded in empathy, has made a lasting difference, and I feel fortunate to have learned from them.

Recognition

As this journey comes to a close, I find myself reflecting not only on the lessons shared in these pages but also on the people whose quiet support has made this possible.

To my family and friends—your presence in my life has been an enduring source of strength and joy.

To Karen, Adam, Ruth, Nick, John, Dave, James, Jane, Scott, Peter, and Annette—your insights, kindness, and unwavering belief have been a constant source of inspiration. Whether through thoughtful conversations, timely encouragement, or simply being there when it mattered most, you've each left an imprint on this work.

To those who have offered their voices of support—whether by sharing feedback, lending a thoughtful ear, or reinforcing belief in this vision—your contributions, though not always visible, have been invaluable. You have helped shape this book in more ways than you may realize, reminding me that no journey worth taking is ever truly walked alone.

This book, at its heart, is a story about connection, resilience, and collaboration—and it's as much a reflection of the people in my life as it is of the ideas on these pages. Thank you for being part of that story.

Producing a book is a team effort, and *Becoming Ambidextrous* is a significantly stronger book because of the expertise and effort from my editor, Patrice Shaw from PS Editing and my book designer, Kirsty Ogden from Brisbane Self Publishing Service. I am incredibly grateful for your excellent work.

To the loyal customers and communities that welcomed our dealerships, I extend my sincere gratitude. Your trust and feedback pushed us to continually improve and exceed expectations, allowing us to contribute to local economies and become a part of each neighborhood we served.

I am deeply appreciative of the talented individuals and various teams who have been on this journey with me—many of whom I am proud to call friends. Your dedication, excellence, and drive for success propelled our achievements and earned us industry recognition. Each accolade and milestone reached is a testament to your hard work and unwavering commitment to excellence.

To the industry partners, suppliers, competitors, mentors, and friends within the automotive community who have been instrumental in fostering growth, innovation, and collaboration, thank you for your invaluable guidance and shared commitment to advancing the sector. The insights and wisdom I've gained from you have shaped my vision and values, and the lessons you've shared are woven throughout this book.

This book reflects the knowledge and experiences generously shared with me along the way. My hope is that these pages serve as a resource for today's and future leaders, inspiring them to approach their work with passion, integrity, humility, and a commitment to continuous learning.

With heartfelt thanks,
Adrian

A Final Note

In the crucible of leadership, where dreams are forged and destinies shaped, there exists a powerful force that separates the extraordinary from the ordinary. It's not mere optimism that propels us forward, nor is it the fleeting whisper of hope that sustains us in our darkest hours. No, it is something far more profound, far more resilient.

It is faith. An unwavering, unshakable belief in the journey's end. This faith is not blind optimism, ignoring the peril that surrounds us. Instead, it is a steely resolve that acknowledges the brutal facts of our reality while holding fast to the conviction that we will prevail.

As Jim Collins teaches us through the Stockdale Paradox, named after the indomitable Admiral James Stockdale, true greatness lies in our ability to confront the harshest truths of our situation while never losing faith in the ultimate triumph. It is this paradox that forms the bedrock of resilience, the foundation upon which all great achievements are built.

But faith alone is not enough. It must be coupled with belief—an active, dynamic force that propels us into action. While hope may whisper sweet nothings of a better tomorrow, belief rolls up its sleeves and gets to work. It is the architect of our future, meticulously planning each step, anticipating each challenge, and forging ahead with unwavering determination.

So, as you stand at the crossroads of your own journey, remember this: Optimism may brighten your day, but faith will light your path through the darkest night. Hope may comfort you in times of doubt, but belief will be the hammer and chisel with which you carve your destiny.

Never give up. Never surrender to despair. For in the annals of history, it is not the most talented or the most fortunate who leave their mark, but those who possess an indomitable spirit—a spirit forged in the fires of adversity and tempered by unwavering faith and belief.

As you face your challenges, big or small, remember the words of Collins and the example of leaders who have come before. Confront your reality with clear eyes, engage actively in your pursuit, and maintain a balanced perspective that acknowledges difficulties while never losing sight of the ultimate goal.

In the end, it is not about waiting for the storm to pass, but about learning to dance in the rain. It is about having the courage to say, "I believe we will succeed," even when the odds seem insurmountable. For it is in these moments, when we choose faith over doubt and belief over resignation, that we truly begin to write our own legend.

So go forth, with faith as your compass and belief as your fuel. The journey may be long, the path may be treacherous, but with these twin forces as your allies, there is no summit too high, no challenge too great. Your story of triumph awaits.

All you need to do is believe, persist, and never, ever give up.

AI Language Models

To gain insights into emerging trends and complex data analyses, I used state-of-the-art AI language models such as ChatGPT and Claude.ai. These models, developed by OpenAI and Anthropic respectively, offer advanced natural language processing capabilities that help analyze data and generate predictive models.

Disclaimer

The insights shared in this book are derived from my personal experience, interpretation and application of concepts presented in various published works on business, leadership and personal development. I strongly encourage readers to explore these valuable resources firsthand, as each individual may glean different insights based on their unique experiences and contexts.

 The books mentioned herein contain a wealth of knowledge that can be applied in diverse ways across various industries and leadership roles. It is important to note that my interpretations and applications of these concepts are my own and may differ from the original authors' intentions or other readers' understandings. I recommend that individuals read these works in their entirety, critically analyze the concepts presented, and develop their own informed perspectives on how to best apply these teachings in their personal and professional lives. The power of these books lies not only in their content, but in how each reader uniquely interprets and adapts the principles to their own circumstances.

 As with any business or leadership advice, it's advisable to consider one's specific situation and consult with appropriate professionals when implementing new strategies or making significant changes in one's approach to management or business operations.

About the Author

Adrian Brown is an award-winning automotive industry professional with over 35 years of experience spanning multiple facets of the automotive industry. His journey began in 1989 on the sales floor as a trainee where he enjoyed success as a sales consultant, F&I manager, and in sales management.

This hands-on experience laid the groundwork for his transition into various leadership roles with an OEM. In these roles, Adrian gained comprehensive insights into all aspects of dealership operations, including sales, aftersales, finance, customer relations, marketing and accounting.

This solid foundation of knowledge propelled Adrian with a thirst for retail into dealership investment, where he applied his expertise to build a successful career as Managing Director and Dealer Principal for multiple dealerships. Throughout his dealer ownership journey, Adrian represented prestigious brands such as Porsche, Mercedes-Benz, Volvo, Subaru, Mazda, Peugeot, MG, Jeep and others, guiding his teams to achieve in excess of a billion in sales and earning more than one hundred industry awards along the way. In addition to these roles, Adrian also served as President and as a Board Member for various dealer and industry associations.

Adrian holds a degree in business with a major in marketing from Southern Cross University, a certificate in Advanced Business Studies from the University of St. Gallen, and he has successfully graduated from the Porsche International Dealer Academy. Known for his forward-thinking approach and commitment to excellence, he has continually sought to embrace change, inspire his teams, and drive progress.

In *Becoming Ambidextrous*, Adrian shares the insights and strategies he has honed over decades in the industry, offering practical guidance for leaders aiming to thrive in an ever-evolving marketplace.

When not engaged in professional pursuits, he enjoys spending time with family and friends, watching Formula One, NFL, NRL, EPL, UCL (anything football), skiing, boating, and public speaking.

Contact

To contact Adrian Brown, visit the website: www.leadership-in-action.us

End Notes

1. MJ Piskorski & R Roi, *Developing ambidextrous leaders: A solution to strategic talent deficit,* IMD Business School (n.d.) Available at: https://www.imd.org/ibyimd/human-resources/developing-ambidextrous-leaders-a-solution-to-strategic-talent-deficit/

2. MJ Piskorski & R Roi, *Developing ambidextrous leaders: A solution to strategic talent deficit,* IMD Business School.

3. CB Gibson & J Birkinshaw, *The antecedents, consequences, and mediating role of organizational ambidexterity,* Academy of Management Journal, *Vol.*47, issue 2, pp. 209–226 (2004). Available at: https://www.jstor.org/stable/20159573

4. N Eva, A Newman, Q Miao, B Cooper & K Herbert, *Chief executive officer participative leadership and the performance of new venture teams,* International Small Business Journal, Vol 37, Issue 1, pp. 69–88 (2019). Available at: https://journals.sagepub.com/doi/10.1177/0266242618790321

5. G Eissa, RL Wyland & SW Lester, *When it's better to give than to receive: The role of knowledge sharing in the relationship between transformational leadership and follower innovative behavior,* Journal of Business Research, Vol 88, pp.1–10 (2018). Available at: https://www.sciencedirect.com/science/article/pii/S0148296318300990

6. CB Gibson & J Birkinshaw, *The antecedents, consequences, and mediating role of organizational ambidexterity.*

7. Eva et al., *Chief executive officer participative leadership and the performance of new venture teams.*
8. S Denning, *Storytelling Can Make or Break Your Leadership,* Harvard Business Review, (2020). https://hbr.org/2020/01/storytelling-can-make-or-break-your-leadership
9. *Exploring Types of Leadership Styles and Traits,* Medium.com
10. *Managing the Legacy of Long-Term Leaders: The Curious Evolution of Leadership Styles in the German Chancellery,* Tandfonline.com
11. National Automobile Dealers Association (NADA), *Annual Report* (2023). Available at: https://www.nada.org
12. National Automobile Dealers Association (NADA), *U.S. Auto Sales and Economic Analysis* (2022). Available at: https://www.nada.org
13. National Automobile Dealers Association (NADA), *Mid-Year Report* (2024). Available at https://www.nada.org
14. Microsoft, *State of Global Customer Service Report* (2018). Available at: https://www.microsoft.com
15. G Satell, *A Look Back At Why Blockbuster Really Failed (And Why It Didn't Have To),* Forbes (2014). Available at: https://www.forbes.com
16. *Timeline: Sears' 125 years of American retail history,* Reuters (2018). Available at: https://www.reuters.com
17. L Thomas, *Toys 'R' Us files for bankruptcy as struggles mount,* CNBC (2017). Available at: https://www.cnbc.com
18. N Patel, *What really happened to BlackBerry,* The Verge (2016). Available at: https://www.theverge.com
19. M J de la Merced, *RadioShack files for bankruptcy,* New York Times (2015). Available at: https://www.nytimes.com
20. WikiMili, *Wendelin Wiedeking – The Best Wikipedia Reader.* Available at: WikiMili.com
21. PCA, *First Generation Boxster: An Affordable Flat-Six Powered Roadster.* (2024) Available at: PCA.org

22. W Wiedeking, *VW kann Toyota die Stirn bieten* (2006) Interview with *Auto, Motor und Sport*. Heft. 23, pp. 174–175.
23. SR Covey, *The 7 Habits of Highly Effective People: Powerful Lessons in Personal Change*. Free Press (2004).
24. National Automobile Dealers Association, *Annual Report* (2023). Available at: https://www.nada.org
25. BF Skinner, *Science and Human Behavior*, Macmillan (1953) & BF Skinner, *The Behavior of Organisms: An Experimental Analysis*, Appleton-Century (1938).
26. SciTech Daily, *The Endowment Effect and Why People Overvalue Their Belongings* (2024). Available at: https://www.scitechdaily.com
27. Driveo, *Why Selling Your Car Online Isn't Always Easy: What You Should Know* (2023). Available at: https://www.driveo.com
28. McKinsey & Company, *The Future of Automotive Retail: Embracing Online and In-Person Advantages* (2024). Available at: https://www.mckinsey.com
29. D Miller, *Building a StoryBrand: Clarify Your Message So Customers Will Listen,* Nashville: HarperCollins Leadership (2017).